Coalitions in Parliamentary Government

Lawrence C. Dodd

Coalitions
in Parliamentary
Government

PRINCETON UNIVERSITY PRESS

Published by Princeton University Press, Princeton, New Jersey
In the United Kingdom: Princeton University Press, Guildford, Surrey

Library of Congress Cataloging in Publication Data
will be found on the last printed page of this book

Publication of this book has been aided by the Whitney Darrow
Publication Reserve Fund of Princeton University Press

Composed and printed in the United States of America
by Princeton University Press, Princeton, New Jersey

For Cheryl

Contents

Tables

Illustrations

Acknowledgments

This book culminates four years of graduate and postgraduate work. The first and most substantial academic debt I have incurred during its preparation is to William H. Flanigan and Edwin Fogelman. The idea for the study first emerged in a course, Contemporary Political Theory, taught jointly by them at the University of Minnesota. They provided a constant source of counsel as my initial ideas matured and, with W. Phillips Shively, they served as readers of the dissertation, with Flanigan as its long-suffering chairman. The Minnesota Political Data Archives provided me support for collection of the cabinet data. Flanigan and Fogelman are the initiators and directors of the Archives, and I am grateful to them for the support of the Archives and for releasing to me data collected under its auspices. I also owe a huge debt to Illa Miscoll (currently at the University of Heidelberg, Germany) for the initiative and precision she exhibited in collecting much of the cabinet data.

Numerous other individuals and institutions have provided significant help. George Bohrnstedt, Robert T. Holt, Don Martindale, W. Phillips Shively, L. Earl Shaw, and Frank Sorauf all provided instruction on various topics relevant to the study and advice on the study itself. A number of graduate colleagues at the University of Minnesota commented at length on various aspects of the study, particularly Terry L. Bock, Judith N. Gillespie, Steven T. Seitz, and Stuart Thorson. Since the completion of the initial dissertation, useful critiques have been provided by Norman Frolich, Joe Oppenheimer, John Pierce, Robert Putnam, Kenneth Shepsle, John Sinclair, and Oran Young. During the summer of 1972, I was fortunate to attend the European Consortium on Political Research in Cologne, Germany, receiving invaluable instruction on European politics from Stein Rokkan, Richard Rose, and other lecturers. The initial preparation of the study was aided by a Ford Foundation Fellowship (1971-1972) awarded through the Department of Political Science at the University of Minnesota. A 1974 Summer Research Grant from the University of Texas at Austin supported the completion of the book. While the responsibility for the shortcomings of this study are mine alone, I am deeply indebted to the foregoing individuals and institutions for their assistance.

Finally, if the responsibility for this study is mine alone, the blame for the book should not fall solely on my shoulders. If culprits are to be identified, my daughter, Meredith, and my wife, Cheryl, should be named unindicted co-conspirators. Through many efforts at plea-bargaining, Meredith maintained my sanity. Cheryl typed and retyped multiple drafts of the book, provided editorial assistance throughout, and worst deed of all, maintained her sense of humor. Meredith must await a future "job" for her payoff. It is to Cheryl that I dedicate this book.

LAWRENCE C. DODD

Austin, Texas
September 3, 1974

Abbreviations

The following list indicates the party name corresponding
to the party abbreviations employed throughout this book.
In the case of party names that are common to a number of
countries, the same abbreviation is employed to designate
parties in different countries. For example, Lib refers to the
Liberal parties of Canada, Denmark, Great Britain, and so
forth. In those cases where a party abbreviation is widely
employed throughout the literature (such as DC for the
Italian Christian Democrats) I have employed the common
abbreviation. In other cases where parties do not possess a
well-known abbreviation, I have attempted to construct an
unambiguous one. Because abbreviations often apply to
parties of the same name in different countries, the abbreviations are listed alphabetically with no country designation.

Abbreviation	*Party Name*
Act	Action
Act Lib	Action Liberal
Agr	Agrarian
Agr U	Agrarian Union
AP	Austrian People's
AR	Anti-Revolutionary
BP/BHE	Gesamtdeutsche Bloc
BV	Bayerische Volkspartei
BZ	Bavarian Zentrum
Cath	Catholic
Cath P	Catholic People's

Cath St	Catholic State
CCF	Co-operative Commonwealth Federation
CD	Christian Democracy
CDU/CSU	Christian Democratic Union/Christian Socialist Union
Cen	Center
CHU	Christian Historical Union
CNP	Clann na Pobachte
Comm	Communist
Cons	Conservative
CP	Christian People's
CS	Christian Socialist
CSV	Christlich-sozialer Volksdient
Ctry	Country
DB	Deutsch Bauernpartei
DC	Christian Democrat
DD	German (Deutsche) Democrat
Demo	Democrat
Demo '66	Democracy '66
Demo Soc '70	Democratic Socialist '70
DH	Deutsch Hannoversche
DNV	German (Deutsche) National People's
DP	German (Deutsche) Party
DV	German People's
FD	Free Democrat
FF	Fianna Fail
FG	Fine Gael
FN	Flemish Nationalist
Fr	Farmers
FSF	French Speaking Front
Gaul	Gaullist Union
Germ	German
GRD	Republican Democratic Left
Hmt	Heimet
HQ	Homme Quelconque
Ind	Independent
Ind Rad	Independent Radical

Ind Rep	Independent Republican
Ind Soc	Independent Socialist
ISRS	Independent Socialist and Republican Socialist
Jus	Justice
KV	Conservative People's
Lab	Labour
Lb	Landbund
Lib	Liberal
Lib-Cons	Liberal-Conservative
Lib F	Liberal Freedom
Lib Ven	Liberal Venstre
L-Lib	Laur-Liberal
L Rad	Left Radical
L Rep	Republicans of the Left
L Soc	Left Socialist
Lv	Landvolkspartei
LW Soc	Left Wing Socialist
Md'SI	Movement d'Independent Sicilien
Mon	Monarchist
MRP	Popular Republican Movement (or Christian Democrat)
MSI	Movement Social Italien
N Coal	National Coalition
N Demo	New Democrat
Nf	Neofascist
NPP	National Party for Progress
N Soc	National Socialist
Nz	Nazis
PGN	Pan German Nationalist
Pol Rad	Political Radical
Pol Ref	Political Reform
Pop Demo	Popular Democrat
Pouj	Poujadist
PP	Patriotic People's
PPF	People's Party for Freedom
PPS-T	Parti Populaire Sud-Tyrolien

Prog	Progressive
PSd'A	Parti Sarde d'Action
P Soc	Pacifist Socialist
Pst	Peasant
Rad	Radical
Rad Lib	Radical Liberal
Rad-Rad Soc	Radical and Radical Socialist
Rad Rep	Radical Republican
Rad Soc	Radical Socialist
Ref	Reform
Rep Lib	Republican Liberal
Rep Soc	Republican Socialist
Ref	Reform
Rep Lib	Republican Liberal
Rep Soc	Republican Socialist
SD	Social Democrat
S Lab	Social Labour
Soc	Socialist
Soc Comm	Social Communist
Soc Cred	Social Credit
Soc Rad	Socialist Radical
S Tax	Single Taxers
Swed P	Swedish People's
URD	Republican and Democratic Union
U Soc	United Socialist
Ven	Venstre
UDSR	Union Democratique et Socialiste de la Resistance
UF	United Farmers
URD	Republican and Democratic Union
WF	Walloon Front
Wk	Workers
W Lab	Walloon Labour
Wst	Wirtschaftspartei
Z	Zentrum

Coalitions in Parliamentary Government

1 | Introduction

Democratic politics is plagued by an overriding dilemma: how to secure responsive yet authoritative government. To produce the desired balance, most Western nations have instituted some form of parliamentary government. In a parliamentary system, executive power resides in the prime minister and his cabinet. The cabinet government is selected by a popularly elected representative legislature. The selection process entails negotiation and bargaining among various factions or parties so that the act of cabinet installation ideally serves to authorize and legitimize the direction of public policy. This direction is reflected in the factional or partisan composition of the cabinet.

The cabinet is held accountable to and can be dissolved by the parliament. In this sense, the executive is democratically selected and can be democratically deposed. While possessing the parliament's mandate, the prime minister and his cabinet have considerable power. Policy formulation and implementation are primarily at the initiation and direction of the cabinet, with the parliament legitimizing public policy by enacting it into law. In addition, the cabinet possesses all of the discretion normally given to a chief executive. Thus parliamentary government provides for strong executive authority.[1]

[1] On the nature of parliamentary democracy see Michael Ameller, *Parliaments* (London: Cassell and Co., Ltd., 1966); C.M.F. Campion and D.W.S. Liddendale, *European Parliamentary Procedure: A Comparative Handbook* (London: George Allen and Unwin, Ltd.,

The neat conceptual symmetry of parliamentary democracy makes it tempting indeed as a solution to the democrat's dilemma. It has found friends even among American political analysts, especially those disconcerted with the deadlock that often characterizes American presidential democracy.[2] Unfortunately, parliamentary government is not without its shortcomings. Because of the desire for a popularly constrained and responsive executive, cabinet governments possess no guaranteed tenure. A prime minister and his cabinet hold office only as long as they have the confidence of a parliamentary majority. This situation allows for intrigue of the highest order, as parties and factions maneuver to bring down one cabinet and replace it with a more acceptable one. Consequently, the history of Western parliamentary democracies is strewn with cabinets that fell from power only days or months after installation.

1953); Carl J. Friedrich, *Constitutional Government and Democracy* (Boston: Ginn and Co., 1950), pp. 222-237, 296-386; and Joseph LaPalombara, *Politics within Nations* (Englewood Cliffs, N.J.: Prentice-Hall, 1974), pp. 189-228.

[2] Though they reflect varying degrees of passion and commitment, the list includes Woodrow Wilson, David Lawrence, Walter Lippmann, William Y. Elliott, C. Perry Patterson, and George E. Reedy. See Woodrow Wilson, "Committee or Cabinet Government?" *Overland Monthly* 3 (January 1884), 25; the views of Lawrence and Lippmann are discussed in Don K. Price, "The Parliamentary and Presidential Systems," *Public Administration Review* 3 (Autumn 1943); William Y. Elliott, *The Need for Constitutional Reform* (New York: McGraw-Hill, 1935); C. Perry Patterson, *Presidential Government in the United States* (Chapel Hill: University of North Carolina Press, 1947); George E. Reedy, *The Twilight of the Presidency* (New York: New American Library, 1970). The persistence of this view should be evident in that its advocates range from Wilson, writing in 1884, to Reedy, a perceptive observer of Presidential government during the 1960s. For an excellent comparative analysis of legislative behavior in a parliamentary and congressional setting, see John E. Sinclair, "Legislators and Lobbyists in Canada and the United States: The Impact of Institution on Individual Behavior," unpublished Ph.D. dissertation, State University of New York at Buffalo, 1973.

The rise and fall of cabinets dictate the fate of the common man's interest. The installation of a new cabinet provides for one group's ascendancy, another's demise. With rapid and persistent alteration in cabinet government, no group's interests can be served. Transient cabinets have little time to initiate and pass legislation, much less to supervise its effective administration. Even when cabinet changes are only variations on a dominant ideological or partisan theme, the intrigue surrounding cabinet alterations can destroy the momentum and authority of executive actions.[3]

Despite these problems, parliamentary democracy cannot be dismissed out of hand as an ineffective political institution. The parliamentary world includes among its members some of the most stable regimes of modern times: such nations as Australia, Great Britain, the Netherlands, and Sweden, to list only a few. And in spite of the constant opportunity for cabinet overthrow, all Western parliamentary regimes have experienced durable cabinet government. Indeed, if there is any one behavioral characteristic of parliamentary government in general, it is the diversity of experiences that are found among parliamentary regimes. The durability of cabinets varies tremendously both between countries and within countries over time. The most dramatic example of the former is the contrast between Great Britain (1918-1940, 1945-1974), where cabinets persisted in office over forty months on the average, and the Third and Fourth French Republics (1918-1940, 1945-1958), where cabinets averaged approximately nine and one-half months' duration. The variation within countries is no less dramatic. For example from 1918 to 1932, cabinets in Wei-

---

[3] See Karl Dietrich Bracher, "Problems of Parliamentary Democracy in Europe," in Herbert Hirsch and M. Donald Hancock, eds., *Comparative Legislative Systems* (New York: The Free Press, 1971), p. 354.

mar Germany persisted for approximately ten months; by contrast, in the Federal German Republic (1949-1974), cabinets have lasted for approximately thirty-six months.[4]

Thus the paradox, the mystery of parliamentary government that baffles and fascinates the political analyst. Parliamentary government does exemplify the democrat's search for representative institutions that nevertheless allow a strong executive. Some parliamentary regimes have refined the politics of authoritative yet responsive government to a fine art. Yet the history of parliamentary government also provides eloquent testimony to human contentiousness, to the persistent struggle for power and advantage that, in its most extreme manifestation, makes the spoils of victory meaningless. Why do some cabinets endure whereas others do not? Why do some parliamentary regimes experience a high frequency of durable cabinets while others see them rarely? These are among the most interesting questions of comparative political analysis. They encapsulate a fundamental problem of democratic theory: the foundations of responsive yet authoritative government.

PARTY SYSTEMS AND CABINET DURABILITY:
THE LOWELL THESIS

Since the days of A. Lawrence Lowell, students of parliamentary democracy have argued that durable cabinets require majority party government. As Lowell writes:

> It is . . . an axiom in politics that, except under very peculiar circumstances, coalition ministries are short lived compared with homogeneous ones.

[4] Estimating the durability of cabinets depends on one's measure of durability. In these estimations, as throughout this book, a cabinet lasts as long as no change occurs in the parties holding ministerial positions.

A cabinet which depends for its existence on the votes of the Chamber can pursue a consistent policy with firmness and effect only when it can rely for support on a compact and faithful majority.

Thus, Lowell concludes, "the parliamentary system will give a country strong and efficient government only in case the majority consists of a single party."[5]

Since the publication of Lowell's argument in *Governments and Parties in Continental Europe* in 1896, virtually every generation of political scientists has echoed and reaffirmed his thesis. This can be seen in a brief review of some of the most noted political classics written in the past fifty years.[6]

Lord Bryce, *Modern Democracies*, 1921:

An administration formed by a coalition of parties is usually weak, not merely because the combination is unstable, but because men whose professed principles differ are likely to be entangled in inconsistencies or driven to unsatisfactory compromises. [In multiparty parliaments, each party] becomes a focus of intrigue. [The parties]

[5] *Governments and Parties in Continental Europe*, Vol. 1 (Cambridge: Harvard University Press, 1896), pp. 73-74. See also A. Lawrence Lowell, *The Governments of France, Italy and Germany* (Cambridge: Harvard University Press, 1914), pp. 70-74; A. Lawrence Lowell, *Greater European Governments* (Cambridge: Harvard University Press, 1918), pp. 152-155. These latter works continue Lowell's earlier perspective. In the third study, published toward the end of the Great War, he notes (p. 152) that "very peculiar circumstances" include situations "like those brought about by this war."

[6] See James Bryce, *Modern Democracies*, Vol. 1 (New York: The Macmillan Co., 1921), pp. 121-122; see also Vol. 2, pp. 347-348; Harold J. Laski, *Parliamentary Government in England* (New York: The Viking Press, 1938), pp. 56-57. Maurice Duverger, *Political Parties* (London: Methuen and Co., Ltd., 1951), pp. 407-408.

make bargains with one another and by their combination, perhaps secretly and suddenly formed, successive ministries may be overturned, with injury to the progress of legislation and to the continuity of national policy. Since there must be parties, the fewer and stronger they are, the better.

Harold Laski, in *Parliamentary Government in England*, 1938, reviews the argument that durable government requires a majority party system:

With some writers, indeed, this position has assumed the position of an axiom; and it is strongly argued that this is the best method of working representative government. I believe this to be true. . . . The multi-party system . . . either makes for coalition government, with its inherent erosion of principle; or for minority government, which is always likely to be weak.

Maurice Duverger, *Political Parties*, 1951:

Multipartism weakens the government in a parliamentary regime. . . . The absence of a majority party makes it necessary to form heterogeneous . . . cabinets based on a coalition, or else minority cabinets. . . . A programme of government action is therefore possible only for a very short period, for limited objectives, and very lukewarm measures. . . . Cabinet collapses which are exceptional and rare under the two party system become normal and frequent and are scarcely mitigated by the fact that the same men are often to be found in different ministerial combinations.

In our own generation, Lowell's thesis is reflected in the work of Jean Blondel, who writes that the "duration [of cabinet governments] is unquestionably influenced by the type of party system prevailing in the country."[7] According to Blondel:

> Two factors . . . appear to contribute to the relative duration of governments in parliamentary systems: the fact that the system is a straight clash between two parties and the fact that one-party government prevails. The two factors are quite clearly connected: one-party governments are not possible without at least one large party, except on a temporary basis. On balance, . . . it does seem that one-party government . . . is the factor contributing most decisively to the stability of governments.

In contrast to one-party governments, Blondel concludes that "coalition, whether small or large, appears directly antagonistic to stable government. . . ."[8] Blondel is joined in this perspective by Hans Daalder who hypothesizes that "coalition cabinets are bound to be unstable" and concludes that although "there is no great difference between one-party and two-party coalitions, the hypothesis seems confirmed."[9]

The empirical evidence presented in the foregoing works has been of two different types. Scholars from Bryce to Duverger supported Lowell's thesis by comparing the chaotic experience of France or Weimar Germany to the durable governments of the United Kingdom, implying that the former were typical multiparty regimes whereas the

[7] "Party Systems and Patterns of Government in Western Democracies," *Canadian Journal of Political Science* 1 (June 1968), 198.

[8] Ibid., p. 199; see also Jean Blondel, *An Introduction to Comparative Government* (New York: Praeger Publishers, 1969), p. 342.

[9] "Cabinets and Party Systems in Ten Smaller European Democracies," a report to the Round Table Conference on European Comparative Politics, Turin, Italy, September 10-14, 1969, pp. 5-6. Daalder does note that the hypothesis is less valid for individual countries, though he fails to reformulate it and examine the further implications.

latter was the typical majority party system. Blondel and Daalder have made major advancements by expanding the number of countries examined: Blondel analyzes behavior in seventeen Western parliamentary democracies from 1946 to 1966, focusing on the average differences in cabinet durability between party systems; Daalder analyzes ten smaller European democracies from 1918 to 1969.

These writers are not alone in their emphasis on the perils of multipartism and the benefits of majority partism. Similar statements can be found in many other works on party systems.[10] The result is a phenomenon that can be termed "the myth of multipartism": (1) governments in multiparty parliaments must be minority cabinets, coalition cabinets, or both; (2) by their very nature, minority cabinets and coalition cabinets are quite transient; (3) multiparty systems are consequently undesirable since they produce transient governments.

Two corollaries of this myth are *the myth of party coalitions*: coalition governments are necessarily nondurable; *the myth of majority partism*: countries seeking durable cabinets must achieve majority party government and hence a majority party system.

THE MYTH OF MULTIPARTISM REVISITED

On its face, the myth of multipartism appears supported by the evidence. It is a fact that majority party governments last longer than multiparty governments. For the countries and time periods listed in Table 1:1, majority party govern-

---

[10] As an example, consider the work of Ferdinand A. Hermens, *Democracy or Anarchy?* (Notre Dame, Ind.: University of Notre Dame Press, 1941), pp. 16-17, 68-69; see also F. A. Hermens, *Europe Between Democracy and Anarchy* (Notre Dame, Ind.: University of Notre Dame Press, 1951); F. A. Hermens, *The Representative Republic* (Notre Dame, Ind.: University of Notre Dame Press, 1958).

TABLE 1:1

The Countries and Time Periods Investigated

Country	Time Period
Australia	1919–1940, 1946–1974
Austria	1920–1932, 1945–1974
Belgium	1919–1939, 1946–1974
Canada	1921–1940, 1945–1974
Denmark	1920–1940, 1945–1974
Finland	1919–1939, 1945–1974
France	1919–1940, 1945–1958
Germany	1919–1932, 1949–1974
Great Britain	1918–1940, 1945–1974
Iceland	1927–1939, 1946–1974
Ireland	1948–1974
Italy	1946–1974
Luxembourg	1919–1940, 1945–1974
Netherlands	1918–1939, 1946–1974
New Zealand	1919–1940, 1946–1974
Norway	1918–1940, 1945–1974
Sweden	1920–1939, 1948–1974

ments have persisted for an average of fifty-five months; multiparty cabinets have lasted for an average of twenty-six months. Despite these differences, however, a degree of uneasiness should exist. Averages fail to indicate the diversity of experiences in multiparty and majority party parliaments. Can we conclude that multiparty parliaments are devoid of durable cabinets?

Table 1:2 presents life-span frequencies for all cabinets in the countries and time periods listed in Table 1:1. While it is true that cabinets in majority party systems are generally durable, it is not true that cabinets in multiparty parliaments are necessarily transient. There is wide variation in cabinet durability among multiparty parliaments, with 23 percent of all cabinets in multiparty parliaments lasting forty months or longer. Table 1:3 presents equally intriguing patterns among multiparty parliaments, providing a fre-

TABLE 1:2

A Frequency Distribution of Cabinet Durability:
Contrasts between Multiparty and Majority Party Parliaments

Months	Multiparty		Majority Party		All	
	number	percent	number	percent	number	percent
50 or more	28	(.118)	16	(.390)	44	(.158)
40 to 49	24	(.101)	7	(.171)	31	(.111)
30 to 39	22	(.092)	7	(.171)	29	(.104)
20 to 29	39	(.164)	6	(.146)	45	(.161)
10 to 19	52	(.218)	4	(.098)	56	(.201)
0 to 9	73	(.307)	1	(.024)	74	(.265)
Total	238		41		279	

Note: Percentages do not necessarily sum to 1.00 because of rounding error.

quency distribution of the durability of shortest cabinets
per parliament and coalition cabinets. As with Table 1:2,
this table indicates the dramatic differences that can obtain
when we shift our focus from averages to frequencies and
from individual cabinets to parliaments. Over the past fifty
years 33 percent of the multiparty parliaments had *no* cabi-

TABLE 1:3

A Frequency Distribution for Cabinets in Multiparty Parliaments:
Shortest Cabinets and Coalition Cabinets

Cabinet Durability (months)	Shortest Cabinet Per Parliament*		Coalition Cabinets	
	number	percent	number	percent
50 or more	26	(.184)	26	(.141)
40 to 49	21	(.149)	16	(.087)
30 to 39	17	(.121)	12	(.065)
20 to 29	18	(.128)	28	(.152)
10 to 19	18	(.128)	42	(.228)
0 to 9	41	(.291)	60	(.326)
Total	141		184	

* Includes only parliaments during which a new cabinet formed.
Note: Percentages do not necessarily sum to 1.00 because of rounding
error.

net that lasted less than forty months; the percentage would be higher if we included those parliaments in which no new cabinet formed but during which an old cabinet continued. Among all coalition cabinets in multiparty parliaments, 22 percent lasted forty months or longer. *And among all cabinets lasting fifty months or longer (including cabinets in majority party parliaments), approximately 60 percent were coalition cabinets from multiparty parliaments.*

While the average durability of cabinets may be low for all multiparty parliaments, a large number of durable cabinets have survived in multiparty regimes. The durable cabinets are concentrated in certain parliaments. In other words, multiparty parliaments do not experience some constant proportion of durable cabinets and some constant proportion of transient cabinets. Just the opposite holds: some multiparty parliaments produce durable cabinets; other multiparty parliaments produce transient cabinets. Unequivocal statements maintaining that peacetime multiparty parliaments cannot produce durable cabinets are unwarranted. Multiparty parliaments experience a wide variation in cabinet durability, including a significant number of durable governments.

DETERMINANTS OF CABINET DURABILITY: THE THESIS

The purpose of this book is to explain the variation in cabinet durability among modern parliaments, identifying parliamentary conditions that are conducive to durable government. Most parliaments during the past fifty years have been multiparty parliaments, as Tables 1:4a and 1:4b indicate. Most of the variation in cabinet durability occurs among multiparty parliaments, as Table 1:2 demonstrates. Consequently, an analysis of cabinet durability must focus most extensively on behavior that characterizes multiparty parliaments.

TABLE 1:4a

List of Parliaments Analyzed
and the Type of Parliamentary Party System:
Interwar Years, 1918-1940

Country	Majority Party System	Multiparty System
Australia	1929, 1931	1919, 1922, 1925, 1928 1934, 1937
Austria	1927	1920, 1923, 1930
Belgium		1919, 1921, 1925, 1929, 1932, 1936
Canada	1930, 1935	1921, 1925, 1926
Denmark		1920 (I, II, III) 1924, 1926, 1929, 1932, 1935
Finland		1919, 1922, 1924, 1927, 1929, 1930, 1933, 1936
France		1919, 1924, 1928, 1932, 1936
Germany		1919, 1920, 1924 (I, II), 1928, 1930
Great Britain	1922, 1924, 1931, 1935	1918, 1923, 1929
Iceland	1931	1927, 1933, 1934, 1937
Luxembourg	1919	1925, 1931, 1934, 1937
Netherlands		1918, 1922, 1925, 1929, 1933, 1937
New Zealand	1919, 1925, 1935, 1938	1922, 1928, 1931
Norway		1918, 1921, 1924, 1927, 1930, 1933, 1936
Sweden		1920, 1921, 1924, 1928, 1932, 1936
Total Number	15	78

Multiparty politics has been described quite aptly by
Maurice Duverger as a "parliamentary game." The object
of the game is to form and control the government. In the
game, a durable cabinet "must find support from a coalition
of associated parties: their alliance is always uneasy and

TABLE 1:4b

List of Parliaments Analyzed
and the Type of Parliamentary Party System:
Postwar Years, 1945-1974

Country	Majority Party System	Multiparty System
Australia	1946	1949, 1951, 1954, 1955, 1958, 1961, 1963, 1966, 1969
Austria	1945, 1966	1949, 1953, 1956, 1959, 1962, 1970
Belgium	1950	1946, 1949, 1954, 1958, 1961, 1965, 1968
Canada	1945, 1949, 1953, 1958, 1968	1957, 1962, 1963, 1965, 1972
Denmark		1945, 1947, 1950, 1953 (I, II), 1957, 1960, 1964, 1966, 1968, 1971
Finland		1945, 1948, 1951, 1954, 1958, 1962, 1966, 1970
France		1945, 1946 (I, II), 1951, 1956
West Germany	1953, 1957	1949, 1961, 1965, 1969
Great Britain	1945, 1950, 1951, 1955, 1959, 1964, 1966, 1970	
Iceland		1946, 1949, 1953, 1956, 1959 (I, II), 1963, 1967
Ireland	1957, 1965, 1969	1948, 1951, 1954, 1961
Italy	1948	1946, 1953, 1958, 1963, 1968, 1972
Luxembourg		1945, 1948, 1951, 1954 1959, 1964, 1968
Netherlands		1946, 1948, 1952, 1956, 1959, 1963, 1967, 1971, 1972
New Zealand	1946, 1949, 1951, 1954, 1957, 1960, 1963, 1966, 1969	
Norway	1945, 1949, 1953, 1957	1961, 1965, 1969
Sweden	1968	1948, 1952, 1956, 1958, 1960, 1964, 1970
Total Number	37	99

intrigues are perpetually being hatched in the lobbies of parliament to break up the early combination and replace it with a new one."[11] Some intrigues succeed and a cabinet falls; other intrigues fail and a cabinet endures. An explanation of cabinet persistency lies in understanding the parliamentary game.

This study is based on the simple premise that parliamentary government can be viewed as a game. As Middleton argued forty years ago, success in the game depends on "the nature of the coalition" that forms the cabinet.[12] The concept of game is not used for poetic expression or imagery. It is an analytic tool, a conceptual strategy that can help order the apparent chaos of multiparty politics. Through this analytic orientation, we may discover systematic patterns of cabinet formation and maintenance that were previously hidden.

The structure of my argument is as follows:

1. The object of the parliamentary game is to control the cabinet. The actors in the game are the parliamentary parties. These parties, as cohesive units, behave in a rational manner. Specifically, parties act to maximize their power within the government; thus they attempt to attain and maintain cabinet status. In their efforts, parties are constrained by the *a priori* ideological or cleavage commitments they have made to their constituents.[13]

[11] Duverger, *Political Parties*, p. 400.

[12] W. L. Middleton, *The French Political System* (London: Ernst Benn, Ltd., 1932), p. 154.

[13] The rationalist assumption is paradigmatic in the sense that—in various forms—it is evident in the writing of an entire school of political scientists. It is an analytic dimension shared by a variety of political analysts in a variety of research areas. It forms a basis for the potential unification of political analysis within a fairly well-delimited theoretical strategy. A number of these analysts are cited throughout the body of this study. See also James M. Buchanan and Gordon Tullock, *The Calculus of Consent* (Ann Arbor: The University of

2. In the parliamentary game, a cabinet is installed by parliamentary vote. If a party is to guarantee that it will be in the cabinet it must gain the support of a parliamentary majority. In a multiparty parliament this majority must be built through the combination of votes from more than one party. Under certain circumstances parties may be under such ideological or cleavage constraints that no coalition is possible; under such conditions, a minority cabinet will be installed. Under other conditions, a majority cabinet may form through the coalition of two or more parties that possess a majority of the parliamentary votes. In such a coalition each party gains a proportion of the cabinet seats in return for its votes within parliament.

3. Analytically, three different types of cabinets can form:

(a) *minimum winning cabinets*: a cabinet that contains sufficient parties to ensure a parliamentary majority, but that contains no party unnecessary to majority status.

Michigan Press, 1967); Norman Frolich, Joe A. Oppenheimer, and Oran R. Young, *Political Leadership and Collective Goods* (Princeton: Princeton University Press, 1971); Mancur Olson, Jr., *The Logic of Collective Action* (New York: Schocken Books, 1968); Thomas C. Schelling, *The Strategy of Conflict* (London: Oxford University Press, 1960); Morton A. Kaplan, *System and Process in International Politics* (New York: John Wiley, 1957). On the significance of paradigms, see Thomas S. Kuhn, *The Structure of Scientific Revolutions* (Chicago: The University of Chicago Press, 1962); Robert T. Holt and John M. Richardson, Jr., "Competing Paradigms in Comparative Politics," *The Methodology of Comparative Research*, edited by Robert T. Holt and John E. Turner (New York: The Free Press, 1970); Gabriel Almond, "Political Theory and Political Science," *The American Political Science Review* 60, No. 4 (December 1966); David B. Truman, "Disillusion and Regeneration: The Quest for a Discipline," *APSR* 59, No. 4 (December 1965). For a discussion of the rationalist perspective, see Brian Barry, *Sociologists, Economists, and Democracy* (London: Collier, Macmillan, Ltd., 1970); Oran R. Young, "Political Choice" (unpublished manuscript, University of Texas, 1974).

(b) *oversized or greater-than-minimum winning cabinets*: a cabinet that contains a party that is unnecessary to ensure the cabinet's parliamentary majority.

(c) *undersized or less-than-minimum winning cabinets*: a cabinet that does not contain sufficient parties to ensure a parliamentary majority.

Within this study I also refer to each of these types as the *coalitional status* of the cabinet.

4. The type of cabinet that forms in any parliament is determined by the bargaining conditions that exist within parliament. There are two relevant bargaining conditions: (a) information certainty and (b) the *a priori* willingness of parties to bargain. As these conditions vary within a parliament or between parliaments, the coalitional status of the cabinets will vary. The higher the *a priori* willingness of parties to bargain and the greater the certainty of bargaining information during the cabinet formation process, the larger the probability that a minimum winning cabinet will form.

5. The durability of the cabinets that form during the parliamentary game is determined by the coalitional status of the cabinets. Minimum winning cabinets will be quite durable. Oversized and undersized cabinets will be more transient. By inference, cabinet durability is determined indirectly by the parliamentary bargaining conditions, since these bargaining conditions determine cabinet coalitional status.

These propositions may seem simple—almost deceptively simple. As is the case with so many simple statements, they can carry a powerful punch. They strike directly at the heart of Lowell's statement that "except under very peculiar circumstances, coalition ministries are shortlived." Likewise, they take issue with Blondel's statement that "coalition, whether large or small, appears directly antagonistic to stable government. . . ." Rather, certain types of coalition may be a foundation of durable government. To the degree that this approach is sustained by rigorous analysis, it may clarify the nature of cabinet durability in multiparty parliaments.

The remainder of this book is devoted to an explication and analysis of these propositions. In Part I, Chapter 2 outlines the basic theory of cabinet formation and maintenance in multiparty parliaments. The propositions outlined above are developed in this theory. The theory is not a rigorously deductive, mathematically verified system. Rather, it is a "quasi-deductive" and hopefully plausible effort to start with fairly explicit assumptions and to reason verbally from these assumptions to testable generalizations that can clarify our understanding of cabinet formation and maintenance. Quite clearly, the theory is open to modification and extension by more rigorous logicians.

Chapter 3 links the propositions of the theory to parliamentary party systems by providing empirical interpretations of the two bargaining conditions.[14] The argument is that the type of party system existing within the parliament

[14] For discussions of the nature and significance of empirical interpretation see Holt and Richardson, "Competing Paradigms in Comparative Politics," in *The Methodology of Comparative Research*; Carl G. Hempel, *Aspects of Scientific Explanation* (New York: The Free Press, 1965), pp. 111-112, 130-133, 184-185; John Kemeny, *A Philosopher Looks at Science* (Princeton: Van Nostrand, 1959), pp. 134-138. For a more general discussion of the relation between empirical and theoretical analysis in comparative politics see James A. Bill and Robert Hardgrave, *Comparative Politics: The Quest for Theory* (Columbus, Ohio: Charles E. Merrill, 1973), pp. 1-41. For an excellent example of theory interpretation and testing, see Norman Frolich, Joe A. Oppenheimer, Jeffrey Smith, and Oran Young, "Rationality and Voting." A paper presented at the Annual Meeting of the Public Choice Society, Spring 1974, New Haven, Conn. (To be published in *APSR*, 1977.)

partially determines the degree of information certainty and *a priori* willingness to bargain among parties in parliament. Specifically, (1) the more fractionalized and unstable the parliamentary party system is, the more uncertain information is in the parliamentary bargaining between parties; (2) the greater the conflict between parties on the salient ideological or cleavage dimensions characterizing the parliament, the greater are the *a priori* constraints on bargaining among parties. The resulting thesis can be diagrammed in the following manner:

Parliamentary Party System ⟶ Parliamentary Bargaining Conditions ⟶ Cabinet Coalitional Status ⟶ Cabinet Durability

The clear inference of the thesis is that the parliamentary party system does effect cabinet durability. In this sense the thesis is an extension of Lowell's emphasis on the role of the parliamentary party system. The thesis departs from Lowell's position, however, in three major ways: first, cabinets within multiparty parliaments are viewed as subject to wide variation in durability; second, party coalitions are viewed as a potential source of durability as well as transiency; third, the impact of party systems on cabinet durability is a much more complex and multivariate process than Lowell and his followers indicate.

The thesis results from the convergence of two schools of analysis. The first school is composed of Lowell and his followers; it emphasizes the influence of the parliamentary party system on cabinet durability. The second school includes von Neumann and Morgenstern, Riker, Leiserson, Axelrod, Browne, Groennings, De Swaan, and others.[15] Some

[15] John von Neumann and Oskar Morgenstern, *The Theory of Games and Economic Behavior* (Princeton: Princeton University Press, 1944); William H. Riker, *The Theory of Political Coalitions*

of these scholars were instrumental in developing game-
theoretic models while others, particularly the initial works
of Michael Leiserson, have emphasized the potential utility
of game-theoretic models in the study of multiparty parliamentary settings. The thesis of my study restructures and
synthesizes the work of these two schools into a broader
theory of cabinet formation and maintenance.

RESEARCH DESIGN

There are, of course, a variety of ways to test the hypotheses
derived in Part I. The nature of the theory—its focus on
explaining the durability of cabinets in real-world parliaments—dictates that the most *powerful* test of the theory is to
demonstrate that the predictions (or postdictions) of the
theory do hold for real-world parliaments. While experimental tests in small-group settings may help generate and

---

(New Haven: Yale University Press, 1962); Michael Leiserson,
"Factions and Coalitions in One-Party Japan: An Interpretation Based
on the Theory of Games," *APSR* 62 (September 1968); Michael
Leiserson, "Coalitions in Politics: A Theoretical and Empirical Study,"
unpublished Ph.D. dissertation, Yale University, New Haven, 1966;
Robert Axelrod, *Conflict of Interest* (Chicago: Markham Publishing
Co., 1970); Eric Browne, "Testing Theories of Coalition Formation
in the European Context," *Comparative Political Studies* 3 (January,
1971); Eric Browne and Mark N. Franklin, "Aspects of Coalition
Payoffs in European Parliamentary Democracies," *APSR* 68 (June
1973); Erik Damgaard, "The Parliamentary Basis of Danish Governments: The Patterns of Coalition Formation," *Scandinavian Political Studies* 4 (1969), 30-57; see also the articles by Sven Groennings,
E. W. Kelly, Abraham De Swaan, and others in Sven Groennings,
E. W. Kelly, and Michael Leiserson, eds., *The Study of Coalition
Behavior* (New York: Holt, Rinehart and Winston, Inc., 1970). After
the completion of this study, I became aware of a recent study that
is an excellent addition to this literature, though the book itself did
not figure in the formulation of the analysis presented here. See
Abraham De Swaan, *Coalition Theories and Cabinet Formations* (San
Francisco: Jossey-Bass, Inc., 1973).

refine such a theory, only real-world tests allow us to really estimate the theory's general power and viability. As a consequence, I have chosen to interpret and test hypotheses drawn from the theory by estimating the degree to which predictions of the theory hold for real-world parliaments.

Any such test faces a number of complications. As Nadel writes, a "main difficulty . . . lies precisely in defining . . . surrounding circumstances and their bearing on the correlations we extract. . . . We cannot assume that the 'background features' are in fact irrelevant for our correlations, we can only choose our conditions so that these additional features can be disregarded."[16] In the terms of this study, innumerable surrounding circumstances may affect the applicability of the theory: cabinets may be powerless (and thus undesirable positions) owing to a powerful monarch or independent President; parties in the Western sense may not exist or may not be the basic coalitional units; extraordinary conditions such as war may alter the nature of party goals in parliament; parliaments may differ significantly in the explicit rules or implicit norms that govern the negotiation of party coalitions.

To control for these factors at least to a degree, this study is limited to parliaments for which the detrimental effect of these surrounding factors should be minimal.[17] First, parliaments have been analyzed only from 1918 to 1974; thus we omit parliaments such as those in Germany (1870-1914) in which cabinets and parties were of only tangential significance. Second, analysis focuses on Western democracies: these are the countries for which the best literature exists documenting the nature of the party system;

[16] S. F. Nadel, *The Foundations of Social Anthropology* (London: Cohen and West, Ltd., 1951), pp. 229-230.

[17] On the control of background factors by specification, see Holt and Turner, "The Methodology of Comparative Research," pp. 11-13.

and these are the nations for which we can most readily assume that parties are the autonomous and fairly cohesive units that serve as the basic actors in coalition negotiation. In addition, in focusing on Western democracies we focus on those countries most likely to share similar parliamentary procedures and norms. Third, wartime periods have been omitted,[18] as well as obvious dictatorships such as Germany and Austria during the 1930s and interwar Italy. Admittedly, these specifications do not remove the influence of all background factors that should be controlled. Nevertheless, since the most obvious contaminating factors have been removed, the resulting data bank should provide a set of parliamentary cases within which some clear pattern should emerge if the theory is to be useful in explaining specific parliamentary behavior.

Within this set of fairly similar countries (those specified in Table 1:1), the hypotheses are tested by examining the covariation of relevant variables across all countries. The basic focus is on cabinet durability. To explain variation in

[18] As noted in footnote 5, Lowell considered war one of the "very peculiar circumstances" in which coalitions might endure. The special nature of wartime politics is reflected quite well in the comments by an Australian politician of the early twentieth century: "Coalitions in the face of great national dangers are the most proper and patriotic things in the world; but coalitions at other times debase the political currency and prevent the proper working of the parliamentary machinery." These comments by George Reid reflect the widespread pejorative view of party coalitions during normal times. See Leslie F. Crisp, *Australian National Government* (Victoria: Longmans, Green, and Co., 1965), p. 325. It should be noted that I omit Israel from the analysis in this book because I consider the history of Israel over the last quarter-century, even during periods of nominal peace, as equivalent to wartime. The durable oversized cabinets in Israel are manifestations of this wartime mentality. See Marver Bernstein, *The Politics of Israel* (Princeton: Princeton University Press, 1957); Michael Brecher, *The Foreign Policy System of Israel* (New Haven: Yale University Press, 1972).

cabinet durability, I have created a data file composed of all partisan, nonprovisional cabinets formed for the specified time periods. I attempt to account for the durability of these cabinets by indicating that cabinet durability covaries with cabinet coalitional status; in turn cabinet coalitional status covaries with party system characteristics; consequently, cabinet durability covaries with party system characteristics. Throughout this analysis, "specific spatio-temporal parameters"[19] have been ignored (that is, I do not focus on individual countries); my explanation, both theoretical and statistical, is in terms of explicit variables.

This decision to analyze covariation across all specified countries—rather than pairwise, comparison, for example— is consistent with my personal view of the appropriate research strategy for a probabilistic science. In a probabilistic science, we know that our predictions are not totally determinative: we know we have not specified nor controlled all relevant background variables. Consequently, in testing our theories, we look for general tendencies rather than specific point-predictions. Any given case may vary from an ideal prediction. The comparison of two cases may yield very ambiguous results. The important finding is the existence or absence of general patterns across a wide range of carefully specified and selected cases. Thus, I feel that analysis of covariation within a specific set of relevant and similar cases is the most appropriate strategy.[20]

In the analysis of covariation, all cabinets are analyzed regardless of their position in the temporal sequence of cabinet formation and maintenance that accrues within the life of a particular parliament. While the theory outlined

[19] See Adam Przeworski and Henry Teune, *The Logic of Comparative Social Inquiry* (New York: Wiley-Interscience, 1970), p. 27.

[20] For a discussion of comparative research strategy with a different but useful perspective, see Arend Lijphart, "Comparative Politics and the Comparative Method," *APSR* 65 (September 1971), 682-693.

in Part II generates propositions concerning coalitional processes within parliament as well as broad contrasts between parliaments, the behavior within parliament is not subjected to systematic examination within this study. The strategy in this study is to determine the extent to which knowledge of party system characteristics allows us to predict the coalitional status and durability of all cabinets. Future work will examine internal parliamentary processes and the improvement in predictive power across parliaments that occurs with knowledge of a cabinet's temporal position in the coalitional sequence.

THE DATA BANK

The data employed in this study covers the countries and time periods listed in Table 1:1. Table 1:1 lists the parliaments that are examined and their multiparty or majority party status. The unit of analysis in the present study is the cabinet, not the parliament. In some cases, a cabinet will last through two or more parliaments; in other cases, several cabinets may form in one parliament. The population size I use is determined by the overall number of cabinets, not the number of parliaments. Had the latter strategy been employed, employing parliaments as the analytic unit, the number of durable minimum winning cabinets would have increased measurably, probably increasing the size of the regression coefficients presented later.

The data bank is essentially complete for the countries and time periods listed, although a few missing cases exist as a result of unavailable data. The data bank includes: a list of the cabinets that existed in the countries and periods specified as well as the parties that held ministerial positions; a list of all parties in the parliament and their parliamentary strength; a list of salient cleavages relevant to the various parliaments and party positions on these cleavage dimensions. From this data bank, five variables are created: party system conflict, fractionalization, instability, cabinet coalitional status, and cabinet durability. Part II specifies the measurement procedures whereby these variables are operationally constructed.

The data bank was prepared under the auspices of the Minnesota Political Data Archives, directed by William Flanigan and Edwin Fogelman.[21] The cabinet data was collected by Illa Miscoll and by the author. The original sources from which the cabinet data were gathered included literally hundreds of scholarly works and journals that cannot be cited in full. A genuine attempt was made to verify all cabinet data by at least two sources. Because of disagreement on the composition of many cabinets, particularly during the interwar years, verification proved a considerable task. Though it became available after the initial collection of the data in this study, a useful work for the verification process was von Beyme's masterful and comprehensive historical analysis of cabinet behavior in selected European nations.[22] For the postwar years, a basic reference was *Keesing's Archives*.

Data on the parliamentary party systems were collected by the author. In gathering the data on the parliamentary strength of parties, I relied on a series of country-specific studies as well as *Keesing's Archives, The London Times, Die Wahl der Parliamente,* and *The International Guide to Electoral Statistics.* Disagreement on the strength of parlia-

[21] For additional information in regard to the Archives, see William H. Flanigan and Edwin Fogelman, "Patterns of Political Development and Democratization," and "Patterns of Democratic Development," in John V. Gillespie and Betty A. Nesvold, eds., *Macro-Quantitative Analysis* (Beverly Hills, Calif.: Sage Publications, 1971).

[22] Klaus von Beyme, *Die Parlamentarischen Regierunssysteme in Europe* (Munich: R. Piper and Co., 1970), especially pp. 901-967.

mentary parties does exist between various references. In attempts to choose among sources, I used those figures for which agreement could be found among two or more sources; lacking such agreement, I employed that source most contemporaneous with the parliament in question. Determination of salient parliamentary cleavages and party positions on the cleavages involved subjective judgments on my part (Chapter 5 in Part II describes the procedures followed). The bibliography provides a selected list of works examined in making these judgments.

CONCLUSION

In *Theory and Processes of History*, Frederick Teggart writes that

> Every result in nature is a riddle to be solved, and the initial difficulty in investigation is the discovery of a clue which may be followed up. . . .

> What ensues . . . is sustained cogitation. . . . The imagination of the inquirer is put to test in the construction of a working model of a process or processes; his critical ability is called upon to check his ideas by the facts.[23]

Why does the durability of cabinets vary so greatly among parliamentary democracies, particularly those experiencing multiparty politics? This is the immediate riddle to be solved. It is interesting not only as a "result in nature" that is innately puzzling. With its resolution we come closer to understanding the requisites of stable democratic regimes and the impact that different types of party systems have on democratic government.

The "clue" on which I focus is Middleton's suggestion

[23] *Theory and Processes of History* (Berkeley: University of California Press, 1962), pp. 162-164.

that "the Executive is strongest when the Government is the trusted agent of a coalition of natural allies. . . ."[24] My underlying suspicion is that cabinet durability is strongly influenced by the type of coalition that forms the cabinet. Cabinet coalitional status is a product of at least three factors: the degree of cleavage conflict, fractionalization, and stability characterizing a parliamentary party system. This focus derives from a synthesis of two perspectives within comparative political analysis—perspectives I shall term the Lowell school and the Leiserson school. I focus on party systems because political parties are the basic contemporary organizations through which individuals unite in the quest for political power; party system structure and continuity thus should tell us something about the bargaining conditions that prevail as parliamentarians negotiate among themselves to invest political power in particular parliamentary leaders. A game-theoretic orientation is employed because of the coalitional nature of party negotiations. Based on these orientations, Part I of the study presents a theory of cabinet formation and maintenance. Part II indicates the operational procedures whereby the propositions derived in Part I are rendered testable.

Part III tests the theory "by the facts." Chapter 7 investigates the propositions of the study among multiparty parliaments:

1. Do minimum winning cabinets form in multiparty parliaments that are defractionalized, stable, and avoid extreme levels of party system polarization?

2. Do oversized cabinets form in nonconflictual multiparty parliaments that are fractionalized and unstable?

3. Do undersized cabinets form in highly conflictual, fractionalized and unstable multiparty systems?

[24] Middleton, *The French Political System*, p. 154.

4. Are minimum winning cabinets more durable than oversized or undersized cabinets?

5. Are we justified in arguing, therefore, that durable cabinets form in a wide range of cleavage conflict conditions so long as the parliamentary party system is not highly fractionalized and/or unstable?

Chapter 8 argues that the propositions developed in Part I should not be restricted to multiparty parliaments alone; as both minimum winning and oversized cabinets can form in majority party parliaments, the theory should likewise apply in that setting. Based on this perspective, Chapter 8 investigates cabinet behavior among majority party parliaments and then presents the findings of the study when regression analysis is conducted for all partisan cabinets in all peacetime parliaments from 1918 to 1974. Chapter 9 concludes the empirical analysis by contrasting cabinet behavior for interwar and postwar parliaments.

Part IV concludes the study. Chapter 10 emphasizes the limitations of the analysis, identifying areas for more extensive future analysis. Chapter 11 discusses the substantive significance of the findings for our perceptions of party systems and democratic government. In anticipating this conclusion, it is interesting to reflect on the comments made by British Foreign Secretary James Callaghan when asked during the winter cabinet crisis of 1974 about the possibility of coalition government in Great Britain. "A coalition is like a mule," Callaghan responded. "It has no pride of ancestry and no hope of posterity." This is the view prevailing among academics and politicians alike. It is a myth that blinds us to the broader range of political associations through which we might seek both authoritative *and* representative government.

I | Theory

2 | A Theory of Cabinet Formation and Maintenance in Multiparty Parliaments

Nowhere is the mystery of politics more evident than in multiparty parliaments. Leadership must be found amid a variety of parties, none of which possesses a legislative majority. It is these parties that essentially negotiate the formation and decline of cabinet ministries. In the most complicated situations, the negotiation process resembles a game in which parties maneuver like blind men in search of the levers with which to control their nation's highest office. In less complex circumstances, parliamentary negotiations are more clearly a game of bargaining and coalitions in which party opposes party in a calculated maneuvering for ministerial power.[1] The simplicity of Lowell's thesis re-

[1] For discussion of party behavior in various countries, see Walter Rice Sharp, *The Government of the French Republic* (New York: D. Van Nostrand Co., Inc., 1938), pp. 73-77; Sven Groennings, "Patterns, Strategies and Payoffs in Norwegian Coalition Formation," in *The Study of Coalition Behavior*, ed. Sven Groennings, E. W. Kelly, and Michael Leiserson (New York: Holt, Rinehart and Winston, Inc., 1970); Peter H. Merkl, "Coalition Politics in West Germany," in *The Study of Coalition Behavior*; Herbert P. Secher, "Coalition Government: The Case of the Second Austrian Republic," *APSR* 52 (September 1958); D. K. Rustow, *The Politics of Compromise: A Study of Parties and Cabinet Government in Sweden* (Princeton: Princeton University Press, 1955). See also the various essays in Robert A. Dahl, ed., *Political Oppositions in Western Democracies* (New Haven: Yale University Press, 1966); and the country-specific works specified in the bibliography. For more general discussions, see Maurice Duverger, *Political Parties* (London: Methuen and Co., Ltd., 1951), pp. 281-351; Joseph LaPalombara and Myron Weiner,

flects perhaps an unwillingness to decipher the parliamentary game.

This chapter presents one strategy by which to decipher the game of multiparty politics. The strategy relies on a modification of the general game-theoretic model presented by William Riker in his study of political coalitions.[2] Riker's model is expanded to include *a priori* willingness of actors to bargain. The result is a theory of cabinet formation and maintenance in multiparty parliaments. In the theory, parliamentary parties are treated as the basic actors. This convention is followed to simplify and clarify the presentation. Clearly, parliamentary parties are not homogeneous and monolithic entities but are themselves coalitions of factions held together by leaders through the use of a variety of payoffs.[3] In addition, it may be that some members of parliament do not belong to parliamentary parties, or that members of various parties belong to supraparty organizations that cut across various parties. These factors can influence cabinet formation and maintenance. They are complications that can be added after a simple framework has been constructed and tested. The thrust of the present study is to

---

eds., *Political Parties and Political Development* (Princeton: Princeton University Press, 1966); Leon D. Epstein, *Political Parties in Western Democracies* (New York: Praeger Publishers, 1967); Sven Groennings, "Notes toward Theories of Coalition Behavior in Multiparty Systems: Formation and Maintenance," in *The Study of Coalition Behavior.*

[2] *The Theory of Political Coalitions* (New Haven: Yale University Press, 1962).

[3] See Duverger, *Political Parties*, pp. 61-132; Epstein, *Political Parties in Western Democracies*, pp. 98-129; Frank J. Sorauf, *Party Politics in America* (Boston: Little, Brown and Co., 1968), pp. 82-92. At a more theoretical level, see Norman Frolich, Joe A. Oppenheimer, and Oran R. Young, *Political Leadership and Collective Goods* (Princeton: Princeton University Press, 1971).

construct a reasonably realistic framework and to examine its explanatory utility.[4]

THE BASIC FRAMEWORK

Let us assume that political parties enter parliament in a quest for governmental power. This quest originates at the electoral level as the parties seek popular support for their candidates. At the electoral stage, each party articulates a political program designed, at least in part, to attract a political following so as to maximize the party's legislative strength within parliament. The quest for power culminates as a party or set of parties forms the cabinet and suoooo fully maintains control of the cabinet for a time sufficient to enact and administer their legislative program. Consequently, the quest for power can be perceived as an attempt by each party to maximize its participation in and strategic, long-run control of the cabinet.[5]

In a parliament with no majority party, the quest by each party for secure participation in and control of the cabinet becomes a search, in Middleton's terms, for "a coalition of

[4] Though formal parliamentary procedure can have a vital influence on cabinet formation and maintenance, this study does not include in the analysis the influence of procedures specific to particular parliaments. A systematic analysis of the nature and consequences of parliamentary procedure for cabinet behavior is clearly needed, but the available data is inadequate. For some illustrations of the impact of parliamentary procedure, see Gerhard Loewenberg, *Parliament in the German Political System* (Ithaca, N.Y.: Cornell University Press, 1966).

[5] These are general assumptions shared with numerous analysts. See for example Anthony Downs, *An Economic Theory of Democracy* (New York: Harper and Row, 1957), pp. 21-35, 142-163; Gunnar Sjöblom, *Party Strategies in a Multiparty System* (Berlingska Boktryckeriet, Sweden: Lund, 1968), pp. 68-95, 250-279.

natural allies."[6] Immediately upon the conclusion of the electoral stage, "Parties . . . [begin] trying to discern the physiognomy of the assembly, and particularly to forecast the majority—or the various possible majorities—which it is capable of producing. Groups are rarely content simply to represent shades of electoral opinion. They look forward to taking an active part in government. . . . Hence the importance of the calculation of the visible and latent tendencies of the newly elected assembly."[7] In this calculation, the central motivation is each party's desire to enter the cabinet and to maximize the significant positions that it will hold within the cabinet. As representative organizations mandated by their various constituencies to enact legislative programs, each party could seek to do no less.

This motivation dictates that in immediate negotiations, each party opposes every other party. Each party seeks its own maximum ministerial advantage. Each parliamentary party behaves as an actor in a conflictual coalitional game. The resources that a party brings to the game are its legislative votes. The desired payoff is one or more ministerial positions in the cabinet. In the game, each party seeks to enter a coalition of parties that will have a reliable majority with which to install and sustain the cabinet. At the same time, each party seeks to enter a coalition through which it can maximize its own ministerial status. This involves fairly complex calculations.

Each party must estimate not only which party coalitions can win. Each party must also determine the coalitions that are possible in the sense that each coalition partner would view the coalition as desirable. In addition, each party must estimate which coalition or coalitions will be favorable to

---

[6] W. L. Middleton, *The French Political System* (London: Ernest Benn, Ltd., 1932), p. 154.

[7] Ibid., pp. 107-108.

it in terms of ministerial seat payoffs. This calculation is complicated by the fact that some ministerial positions are more desirable than others so that the value of payoffs received in each potential coalition are not calculable strictly in terms of the number of ministerial seats obtained.

Owing to the intricacy and complexity of these calculations, parliamentary parties can be overwhelmed in coalition negotiations. To avoid this result, parties employ a basic criterion in all calculations and negotiations: they seek first and foremost to enter a minimum winning coalition. That is, they seek to enter a coalition of parties that has a reliable majority yet contains no party in the coalition that is unnecessary to majority status. This minimum winning criterion provides a base line against which all possible coalitions can be compared by the parties. If a coalition is not of minimum winning status, it is either not of winning status or contains some unnecessary party within it that could be removed from the cabinet with its ministerial payoffs being distributed among the other coalition partners. The former coalition is undesirable to a party because it would not guarantee victory in the cabinet formation and maintenance process. The latter coalition is undesirable to a party because it would waste desirable payoffs unnecessarily, denying to the party the maximum ministerial status that it could receive if only the necessary parties were included in the coalition.

Seen in this perspective, the search for natural parliamentary allies is a search for partners with which to form a minimum winning coalition. In varying coalitional conditions parties may bring other considerations to bear in addition to the minimum winning criteria. For example, parties may insist on entering coalitions only with parties of similar programmatic perspectives. Nevertheless, *ceteris paribus*, parties that seek to maximize their participation in and strategic long-run control of a cabinet in a multiparty parliament are always striving at the very least to enter a minimum winning coalition of parties.

In this effort, as actors in any conflictual coalitional game, parliamentary parties are constrained by a number of parametric factors. First, events of overriding seriousness may threaten the existence of the parliamentary system. In other words, events may transpire so as to challenge the security of the coalitional game itself. In such a situation, most clearly seen in wartime, the motivation for parties to maximize their participation in the cabinet may be overridden by the desire to save the game. Each party may be willing to sacrifice its own potential advantage momentarily. In such a situation, parties cannot be perceived as conflicting actors in a coalitional game.

Second, parties are constrained by explicit and implicit rules of the parliamentary game. An explicit rule is that a majority of 50 percent plus one of legislative votes is the level at which a coalition assures itself winning status. An implicit rule of the game is that the cabinet formation process cannot last indefinitely. The longer the coalition bargaining process lasts, the greater the pressure becomes for some cabinet to be formed. Eventually, if no majority solution can be reached, then that minority cabinet will be installed that can attain the largest plurality of votes. Such a cabinet will persist only until a larger coalition arises that is willing to take over cabinet responsibility or until parliament is dissolved.

Finally, parties are constrained in their calculations and negotiations by the bargaining conditions that prevail within parliament. As noted earlier, the quest for governmental power in a multiparty parliament can be conceived as a search by each parliamentary party for partners with which to form a minimum winning coalition. The calculations and negotiations in this search are intricate and complex. First, parties must estimate which of the possible party coalitions possesses a reliable parliamentary majority and among these coalitions which ones achieve minimum winning status. These calculations require that parliamentary parties possess reliable information as to the voting strength of the various parliamentary parties. Second, as they negotiate, parties must estimate realistically which parties are available to them as potential coalition partners. This requires knowledge as to the implicit as well as explicit commitments made by parties to one another. In other words, at any given time in parliamentary negotiations each party must possess reliable information as to the prior moves made between other parliamentary parties in coalition negotiation. Third, if parties are to enter coalitions, they must be willing to negotiate with other parties, "to form coalitions and to compromise."[8] They must be willing, at least in principle, to enter into cabinets with other parliamentary parties.

[8] This point is made clearly by Bracher and Weber:

"The cabinet crises which plagued the German Republic throughout its life were the direct consequences of the nature of German political parties, their unwillingness to form coalitions and to compromise, their rigid ideological stance, their preoccupation with prestige, and their authoritarian tradition.

"This was the price paid for the partly forced, partly voluntary rejection of parliament and parties during the monarchy, a policy whose negative aspects were pinpointed very clearly by Max Weber . . . (He) insisted that the absence of a two-party system was not the obstacle: 'Far more important is another difficulty: parliamentary government is possible only if the largest parties of the parliament are in principle *on the whole ready* to take over the responsible conduct of state. . . .'"

See Karl Dietrich Bracher, *The German Dictatorship: The Origin, Structure and Effects of National Socialism* (New York: Praeger Publishers, 1970); see also Max Weber, *Parlament und Reglerung im neugeordneten Deutschland* (Munich: Berlag von Dunder and Humblot, 1918), p. 75.

These bargaining conditions can be systematically subsumed under two categories: information certainty, and the generalized *a priori* willingness of parties to bargain.

1. Following Riker,[9] information certainty entails two elements:

a) *complete information as to weights*; this exists in a parliamentary setting when all parties know precisely the weight (that is, the reliable number of legislative votes) controlled by all parliamentary parties.

b) *perfect information as to prior moves*; this exists in the bargaining arena when each party knows all of the moves (that is, offers, bargains, counteroffers, etc.) made among all of the various parties in coalition negotiations.

2. A generalized *a priori* willingness of parties to bargain exists when all parties are willing to consider entering a cabinet coalition with any other party. In other words, there are no *a priori* constraints which circumscribe or inhibit the negotiation and coalition formation between any two parties.

If we assume first that most coalition bargaining between parties occurs under conditions unconstrained by extraordinary events such as war and second that the rules of the game specified earlier are indeed operative, then the critical factors in cabinet formation are the bargaining conditions that characterize a parliament.

THE FORMATION OF CABINET COALITIONS:
SOME PREDICTIONS

The type of party coalition that forms the cabinet will depend on the bargaining conditions that prevail within par-

[9] *The Theory of Political Coalitions*, pp. 77-89.

liament. As these conditions vary, the type of cabinet coalition that forms will vary. The following sections outline this relationship. Section 1 specifies the relation between willingness to bargain and cabinet coalitional status; Section 2 specifies the relation between information certainty and cabinet coalitional status; Section 3 summarizes the more general interactive pattern.

Cabinet Coalitional Status and the Willingness of Parties to Bargain

If parties in parliament possess a fairly generalized willingness to bargain among themselves, majority or winning coalitions should always form. In other words, so long as there are no serious *a priori* constraints on parties which make them hesitant to negotiate or strike bargains, parties can reach agreement on some majority that will govern. There should be no tendency toward minority cabinets because of time constraints on party bargaining or the inherent inability of parties to strike bargains.

By contrast, if parliamentary parties are highly constrained in their willingness to bargain among themselves, there should be a tendency toward minority cabinets. The central factor is whether a set of parliamentary parties exists that is composed of parties willing to bargain with one another and constituting a parliamentary majority. In a parliament in which every party is willing to bargain with every other party, numerous majority sets exist. However, the more specific each party is in specifying the party or parties with which it will bargain, the greater the possibility becomes that there is no set of parties willing to bargain and constituting a parliamentary majority. Consequently, the less generalized the willingness of parties to bargain among themselves, the greater is the possibility of a minority cabinet forming.

Figure 2:1 depicts the resulting relationship between the generalized *a priori* willingness of parties to bargain and cabinet coalitional status. In this graph the y axis indicates

FIGURE 2:1

The Predicted Relationship between the Willingness of Parties to Bargain and Cabinet Coalitional Status

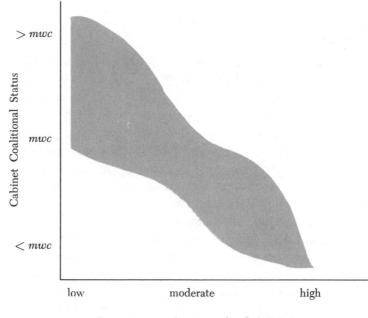

Constraints on the Generalized *A Priori*
Willingness of Parties to Bargain
Among Themselves

the coalitional status of the cabinet that forms in a parliament. This status can be of three general types.

a) *greater than minimum winning status* ($> mwc$) Cabinets in this category consist of at least one party that could be subtracted from the coalition and the cabinet's majority status sustained; the greater the number of extra parties and the greater the weight (legislative voting strength) of these parties, the more oversized a cabinet coalition is.

b) *minimum winning status* (*mwc*)

Cabinets in this category are, first, of winning or majority status and, second, do not contain any party that could be subtracted and winning (or reliable majority) status sustained.

c) *less than minimum winning status* (< *mwc*)

These cabinets do not possess a reliable parliamentary majority; the greater the number and weight of the parties required to make the coalition of minimum winning status, the greater the deviation of these cabinets from minimum winning status.

The x axis in this graph represents the generalized *a priori* willingness of parties to bargain among themselves. In conditions of extremely low constraints, every party is willing to bargain with every other party; in conditions of extremely high constraints, no party is willing to bargain with any other party.

The checkered space in Figure 2:1 specifies the relationship between cabinet coalitional status and the willingness of parties to bargain. Oversized (> *mwc*) cabinets form in conditions of low to moderate bargaining constraints. Undersized (< *mwc*) cabinets form in conditions of moderate to high bargaining constraints. Minimum winning cabinets form in a wide range of bargaining conditions; the main factor (from the standpoint of bargaining constraints) will be whether there is at least one majority set of parties that are willing to bargain. As can be seen, there is a great deal of variation in cabinet coalitional status that cannot be explained by variation in the generalized *a priori* willingness of parties to bargain. The willingness of parties to bargain determines the general range in which the coalitional status of a cabinet should fall. Within this range the coalitional status of the cabinet that forms can vary; a critical element in this variation is the degree of information certainty that exists within the parliamentary bargaining arena.

Cabinet Coalitional Status and Information Certainty

In parliaments that experience low to moderate constraints on party bargaining, variation in information certainty produces variation between minimum winning and oversized cabinet status. In other words, when conditions are conducive to the formation of majority cabinets, a critical factor determining the size of the final coalition will be the general degree of information certainty possessed by parliamentary parties. If parties can estimate precisely the strength of all other parties and the moves being made by all other parties, they will act to form minimum winning coalitions. However, if parties are unsure of the reliable votes that each possesses, or if they are unsure of one another's reliability as a coalition partner, then parties will compensate for this uncertainty by entering into oversized coalitions: a coalition of parties will form that is larger than would appear nominally necessary to the coalition's majority status.

These oversized coalitions are formed to ensure the majority status of the coalition. Oversized coalitions are possible because of the generalized willingness of the parliamentary parties to bargain. Within the coalitional status range predetermined by the generalized willingness of parties to bargain, the precise size of the coalition is determined by the degree of information certainty that exists. The more information uncertainty there is, the more the parties will seek to compensate and thus the greater the number and size (weight) of the "extra" parties that will be brought into the coalition.

By contrast, in parliaments experiencing moderate to high constraints in party bargaining, information uncertainty creates or augments a tendency toward undersized cabinets. This follows if we consider the nature of calculations and negotiations in such parliaments. On the one hand, parties want to enter minimum winning coalitions. In this way they act to maximize the security of their ministerial status. If minimum winning cabinets are not possible because of the constrained nature of party bargaining, parties will seek to be in the largest possible coalition. In this way they maximize the security of the cabinet by making it as difficult as possible for a larger coalition to arise. On the other hand, in highly constrained settings parties have *a priori* reasons to avoid serving in a cabinet with certain specific parties (say, Party A) while they may be more willing to serve with other parties (say, Party B). Party B and Party C may or may not be willing to serve in cabinets together. Faced with a situation like this, each parliamentary party must possess complete and perfect information if it is to precisely calculate its maximum advantage. Complete information as to weights (reliable legislative votes) is needed if parties are to clearly calculate the size of potential coalitions. Perfect information as to prior moves is needed by parties to guard against the possibility of being drawn into a cabinet with an undesirable partner.

In a situation in which information certainty is possessed by parties, each party will realize that it cannot secretly maneuver another party into an undesirable coalition. In addition, parties can clearly calculate which party coalitions are possible and desirable. Consequently, within the coalitional status range predetermined by the willingness of parties to bargain, minimum winning status will be approached as information certainty is approached. However, as information uncertainty increases in a parliament experiencing moderate to high constraints on party bargaining, parties will tend to form smaller cabinets than would be maximally possible within the existing constraints. In such a situation, because of lack of perfect information each party (A) will be hesitant to bargain with otherwise acceptable parties (B) out of fear that, in order to create a minimum winning coalition, these acceptable parties may attempt to maneuver party A into a coalition with an undesirable party (C). In addition, because of the lack of complete information, parties would find it difficult to reliably calculate which coalition would be of the maximally desirable size; calculations and negotiations would thus take more time and under the time constraints that exist on parliamentary bargaining, parties would be forced to settle for coalitions that might be smaller than the maximally possible one rather than enter coalitions that might be undesirable for *a priori* reasons. Consequently, the greater the uncertainty of information in a parliament experiencing high constraints in the *a priori* willingness of parties to bargain, the smaller the coalitional status should be of the cabinets that form.

The seemingly paradoxical conclusion of the foregoing argument is that an increase in information uncertainty can give rise to both oversized and undersized coalitions. Parties should be able to calculate reliably minimum winning coalitions only in conditions of low information uncertainty. As information uncertainty increases, the ability of parties to calculate reliably in coalition maneuvering decreases. Thus, the type of cabinet that forms should depart from minimum winning status with the *degree* of that departure at least partially a function of the degree of information uncertainty. The *direction* of cabinet deviation from minimum winning status is dependent on the bargaining constraints that exist. As conditions depart from information certainty we can only predict that the cabinet coalitions that form should depart from minimum winning status. We cannot predict the direction of the departure unless we know the nature of the *a priori* constraints that exist within parliament. If those constraints are fairly low, oversized coalitions should form as parties attempt to compensate for uncertainty. If those constraints are fairly high, undersized coalitions should form as parties act to avoid being in coalitions with undesirable parties.

In addition, the precise degree to which parties will depart from minimum winning status cannot be predicted solely from knowledge of information certainty. Once again, the nature of the bargaining constraints must be known: the vital factor here is the precise range of possible coalitions allowed by the *a priori* constraints. Within that range, if information certainty exists, the most desirable coalition should form. As information uncertainty increases, the coalitional status should depart from the maximally desirable status with the degree of departure depending at least in part on the range of coalitions that are possible within the *a priori* bargaining constraint.

Cabinet Coalitional Status and Parliamentary Bargaining Conditions: Summary

The theme of the foregoing argument is that cabinet coalitional status is determined by the interaction of two bargaining conditions: (1) the *a priori* willingness of parties to bargain and (2) information certainty. This interaction is fairly difficult to state or to capture in a precise manner. Figure 2:2 presents the general predicted pattern. The x axis in this figure represents the bargaining conditions that exist in parliament. The y axis indicates the coalitional status of the cabinet that forms under the specified bargaining conditions. Essentially, Figure 2:2 summarizes the argument made earlier. Oversized coalitions will form if the parties are fairly unconstrained in their willingness to bargain and are uncertain in their bargaining information. Minimum winning coalitions will form under a wide range

FIGURE 2:2

The Predicted Relationship between Cabinet Coalitional Status and the Interaction of Parliamentary Bargaining Conditions

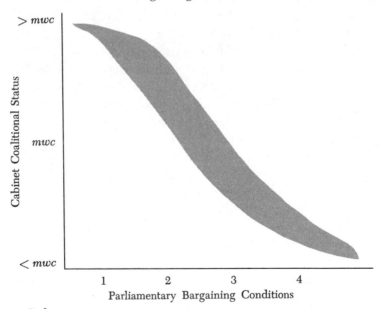

Code
1 = low constraints on bargaining and high information uncertainty
2 = low to moderate constraints and low to moderate uncertainty
3 = moderate to high constraints and low to moderate uncertainty
4 = high constraints on bargaining and high uncertainty

of *a priori* bargaining constraints as long as parties possess reasonably certain bargaining information. Undersized cabinets will form if parties are fairly constrained in their willingness to bargain and if parties are fairly uncertain as to the reliability of their bargaining information. At the extreme ends, the relationship may evidence curvilinear characteristics since coalitions cannot increase or decrease in size beyond certain absolute limits so that increases in information uncertainty beyond certain threshold limits will only reinforce (rather than augment further) the tendency toward oversized or undersized cabinets. The curvilinear characteristic of the relationship is further aggravated by the possibility that under conditions of extremely high unwillingness to bargain the constraints may be so great that only a one-party minority government is possible. Under such conditions increases in information uncertainty will only reinforce the existence of a minority cabinet rather than activate such a tendency.

THE DURABILITY OF CABINETS

The quest for governmental power does not cease with the formation of a cabinet. Parties outside of the cabinet still desire cabinet status. Parties within the cabinet may be unhappy about their ministerial payoffs. Consequently, there should be continued challenges to the composition of a cabinet both from parties outside and from parties inside the cabinet. The nature and success of these challenges will depend on the type of cabinet coalition that has formed. In particular, the minimum winning status of cabinets is vital. If a cabinet is of minimum winning status, it is in a relatively ideal position. On the one hand, it controls a majority of parliament's votes; unlike a minority cabinet it is not at the mercy of a hostile parliament that it cannot control. The cabinet should be able to meet any threat that comes solely from parties outside of the cabinet. On the other hand, there is no party in the cabinet that could be removed and the cabinet's majority status sustained; there is no unnecessary party within the cabinet possessing ministerial seats that could be redistributed to other cabinet parties. The significance of these factors can be clearly seen by contrasting minimum winning cabinets to cabinets that are not of minimum winning status.

Consider first a comparison between minimum winning and oversized coalitions. In an oversized cabinet at least one party is sharing in the ministerial payoffs that was in reality unnecessary to attaining the payoffs. There is at least one party that could be removed from the cabinet and the reliable majority of the cabinet maintained. The unnecessary status of the party(-ies) was not clear in the coalition formation stage due to information uncertainty. Once the cabinet is formed, however, it becomes obvious which parties were in on the final bargain and what the relative voting strength of these parties is. It thus becomes obvious that some party(-ies) is expendable. If this party is omitted from the cabinet, some or all of the other coalition partners will gain in the sense that they will obtain new ministerial positions formerly controlled by the expendable party(-ies). Realizing this, the various parties within the coalition act to reduce the size of the cabinet by removing at least one party. Similar action will not be taken in a minimum winning cabinet because there is no expendable party among the coalition partners. Consequently, in comparing minimum winning cabinets to greater than minimum winning cabinets, minimum winning cabinets should be more durable.

In addition, among oversized cabinets the number and relative size of the "extra" parties in the coalition are significant determinants of the precise durability of these cabinets. The more extra parties there are in a coalition and the greater the size of these parties, *ceteris paribus*, the larger the number of significant ministerial positions these "extra" parties will tend to control and the smaller the proportion of significant ministerial seats controlled by each cabinet party relative to the proportion it would control in a minimum winning cabinet. It is this relative deprivation that is important. The greater the deprivation of ministerial seats parties are suffering relative to a potential minimum winning size the more quickly parties should act to remove the deprivation: in the context of this study, the greater the oversized status of a cabinet coalition, the shorter the durability of the cabinet coalition should be.

A similar pattern occurs when we compare minimum winning cabinets with less than minimum winning cabinets. In a minority cabinet, the party or parties in the cabinet do not possess a reliable majority of legislative votes. The cabinet thus exists in a hostile environment that it cannot control. Owing to information uncertainty, the hesitancy of various parliamentary parties to bargain among themselves, and time constraints on coalition negotiations, a minority cabinet was installed. This cabinet is faced constantly with the possibility that while it attempts to govern, other parties are negotiating their differences so that they can overthrow the cabinet and attain ministerial status, or at the least force the dissolution of parliament and new elections. In fact the parties within the cabinet may themselves be negotiating with parties outside of the cabinet so as to form a larger and more secure coalition. Similar pressures do not exist for minimum winning coalitions. Consequently, minimum winning coalitions should be more durable than undersized coalitions. In addition, the more a minority cabinet departs from minimum winning status (that is, the greater the number and size of the parties that it would take to transform the cabinet to minimum winning status), the more vulnerable the cabinet is to the rise of a larger coalition or to the forced dissolution of parliament and new elections. Thus, among minority cabinets, cabinet durability should be a function of the degree to which the cabinet departs from minimum winning status.

CONCLUSION

This chapter has outlined a general theory of cabinet formation and maintenance in multiparty parliaments.[10] This theory rests on the central assumption that political parties are the basic actors in the cabinet formation process. These parties enter parliament in a quest for governmental power. In actual practice this quest involves an attempt by parties to gain secure participation in and control over the cabinet that will govern. In order to achieve this secure strategic participation in a cabinet, parties in a multiparty parliament must enter into a coalition with other parties.

Given specified rules of the parliamentary game, the coalitional status of the cabinet that forms is determined by the nature of the bargaining conditions that prevail within parliament. The first key bargaining condition is the generalized *a priori* willingness of parties to bargain among themselves. Under conditions of low *a priori* constraints, majority coalitions should form. The greater the *a priori* constraints, the greater the possibility of minority coalitions forming.

Within the range of possible coalitions that is determined by the *a priori* bargaining constraints, the vital factor influencing cabinet coalitional status is the second bargaining condition: information certainty. If bargaining information within parliament is fairly certain, then the coalition that

[10] For an interesting and stimulating set of alternative propositional formulations, see Hans Daalder, "Cabinets and Party Systems in Ten Smaller European Democracies," a report to the Round Table Conference on European Comparative Politics, Turin, Italy, September 10 through 14, 1969.

forms should approach minimum winning status. As bargaining information departs from certainty, the cabinets that form should deviate increasingly from minimum winning status. In situations of low *a priori* bargaining constraints the coalition should deviate toward oversized status; in situations of high *a priori* constraints the coalition should deviate toward undersized status.

These predictions are of more than intrinsic interest. The quest for governmental power does not cease with cabinet formation. It continues throughout the life of a parliament. Cabinets continually face challenges from dissatisfied parties within the cabinet coalition or from parties outside the cabinet coalition. The success of these challenges will be determined at least in part by the coalitional status of the cabinet. The most durable cabinets should be minimum winning cabinets. As cabinets depart from minimum winning status, cabinet durability should decrease.

It should be noted in conclusion that the theory outlined here is applicable in a more general fashion than has been indicated. This chapter has focused only on multiparty parliaments because these are the parliaments in which the significance of bargaining conditions and cabinet coalitional status can be more clearly perceived. However, the same theory is applicable to parliaments that contain a party with a secure majority. In such situations, a majority party cabinet is essentially a minimum winning cabinet. It was able to form the cabinet because of low *a priori* bargaining constraints and high information certainty. These cabinets are durable because of the strategic minimum winning status of the party.

3 | Party Systems and Coalition Processes

According to the thesis developed in Chapter 2, the coalitional status of a cabinet will be a function of the interaction between the generalized *a priori* willingness of parties to bargain and the certainty of information that exists in the bargaining process. In turn, the durability of a cabinet is a function of the cabinet's coalitional status. Minimum winning cabinets should be quite durable. Oversized and undersized cabinets should be more transient. A number of procedures can be employed to test the utility of the thesis: case analysis of an individual cabinet formation and maintenance process in a selected parliament; examination of coalition formation processes over time in one country; analysis of behavior between parliaments across countries. In the current study the strategy is to explain variation in the durability of all peacetime partisan cabinets in terms of the general differences between parliaments. As Chapter 1 indicates, parliaments do differ significantly in the durability of cabinets that form within them. Is this variation at least partially a product of observable differences between the parliamentary settings within which cabinets form? Is the theory outlined in Chapter 2 useful in identifying the relevant differences between parliaments and understanding their significance for cabinet durability?

A key to answering these questions lies in the empirical interpretations that are given to the parliamentary bargaining conditions. It may be that parliaments differ systematically in the bargaining constraints and in the degree of information certainty that characterizes each parliament as a behavioral setting. In other words, while each cabinet formation process within a given parliament may face its own peculiar bargaining conditions, all cabinet formation processes within one parliament may face a set of similar conditions that distinguish the parliament from other parliaments. If that is the case, systematic differences between parliaments should explain a considerable amount of the variation in the types and durability of cabinets that form in Western parliaments.

Among Western parliaments, the characteristics of the parliamentary party system constitute a set of variables that may well be relevant to the bargaining process. Lowell emphasized the dichotomy between majority party and multi-party parliaments; as Chapter 1 illustrated, his dichotomy vastly oversimplified matters. Perhaps Lowell was correct, however, in his emphasis on the parliamentary party system, if not in his interpretation of its precise role. As Sartori writes:

> It is usually assumed that Western-type party systems follow one of two patterns; namely, the two-party and the multi-party; and the usual implied assumption is that the whole spectrum of party pluralism can be covered with a dichotomous *Gestalt*, by using a model essentially based on paired alternatives. . . .
>
> I shall challenge both assumptions. From a descriptive point of view we are confronted in Western free Europe not with two but with three types of party systems; simple two-party pluralism, moderate pluralism, and extreme pluralism. Moreover, the important dividing line is not so much between the first and the second, but that between the second and the third, that is, between moderate

pluralism and extreme pluralism. My first point is then, that we usually misplace the essential border and that it is wrong to deal with multipartism as a single category; for there is a world of difference between the bipolar pattern of moderate pluralism and the multipolar features of extreme pluralism.[1]

Sartori's emphasis on the "world of difference" that can exist among multiparty regimes suggests that multiparty systems are not as homogeneous in their characteristics as previous scholars implied. Just as Chapter 1 indicated that considerable variation exists among multiparty parliaments in cabinet durability, considerable variation may exist also among multiparty parliaments in their party system attributes. This variation among multiparty parliaments may influence parliamentary bargaining conditions and consequently the process of cabinet formation and maintenance.

Thus the critical question becomes the identity of party system characteristics that indicate, at least to a degree, the *a priori* willingness of parties to bargain and the degree of information certainty that characterizes a parliament. The remainder of this chapter argues that such characteristics do exist. Cleavage conflict or polarization among parties influences *a priori* willingness to bargain. Party system fractionalization and instability influence information certainty.

[1] Giovanni Sartori, "European Political Parties: The Case of Polarized Pluralism," in Joseph LaPalombara and Myron Weiner, eds., *Political Parties and Political Development* (Princeton: Princeton University Press, 1966), p. 137. See also Giovanni Sartori, "The Typology of Party Systems—Proposals for Improvement," in Erik Allardt and Stein Rokkan, eds., *Mass Politics: Studies in Political Sociology* (New York: The Free Press, 1970), pp. 322-352; Douglas Rae, "A Note on the Fractionalization of Some European Party Systems," *Comparative Political Studies* 1 (October 1968), pp. 413-418.

CLEAVAGE CONFLICT AND THE A PRIORI WILLINGNESS
OF PARTIES TO BARGAIN

According to Douglas Rae and Michael Taylor, "Cleavages are the criteria which divide the members of a community or subcommunity into groups, and the relevant cleavages are those which divide members into groups with important political differences at specific times and places."[2] The existing literature on Western party systems shows that voters tend to align with parties according to the positions parties take on the salient societal cleavages. As Lipset and Rokkan write, political parties "help to crystallize and make explicit the conflicting interests, the latent strains and contrasts in the existing social structure, and they force subjects and citizens to ally themselves across structural cleavage lines and to set up priorities among their commitments to established or prospective roles in the system."[3] Within parliament, parties represent the various cleavage constituencies by which they are supported. In other words, parties "have *instrumental* and *representative* functions: they force the spokesmen for the many contrasting interests and outlooks to strike bargains, to stagger demands, and to aggregate pressures. . . ."[4]

From the theoretical perspective outlined in Chapter 2 there are two vital elements to this representative or in-

[2] Douglas W. Rae and Michael Taylor, *The Analysis of Political Cleavages* (New Haven: Yale University Press, 1970), p. 1.

[3] Seymour M. Lipset and Stein Rokkan, "Cleavage Structures, Party Systems, and Voter Alignments: An Introduction," in Lipset and Rokkan, eds., *Party Systems and Voter Alignments* (New York: The Free Press, 1967), p. 5. See also Allardt and Rokkan, eds., *Mass Politics*; Stein Rokkan, *Citizens, Elections, Parties* (New York: David McKay Co., Inc., 1970).

[4] Lipset and Rokkan, p. 5.

strumental function. First, parties must work to attain ministerial status so as to formulate, enact, and administer legislation that is favorable to their cleavage constituencies. This entails a willingness to bargain: "No party can hope to gain decisive influence on the affairs of the community without some willingness to cut across existing cleavages to establish common fronts with potential enemies and opponents."[5] Second, parties must act in a manner that advances their constituency rather than another constituency; there are limits on the bargains that they can strike in attaining power. The cleavage system is thus both a major source of the quest for power and, at the same time, a major constraint on the behavior that is possible in the quest.

Assuming, as Downs, Sartori, and others do,[6] that partisan conflict on a given cleavage issue can be depicted on a spatial continuum running from left to right, the distance between parties on a cleavage dimension indicates the political distance between them as they contemplate bargaining to form a cabinet. The greater the distance, the more parties

[5] Ibid.

[6] Anthony Downs, *An Economic Theory of Democracy* (New York: Harper and Row, 1957), pp. 114-163; Sartori, "European Political Parties," pp. 137-176; Michael A. Leiserson, "Coalitions in Politics: A Theoretical and Empirical Study" (unpublished Ph.D. dissertation, Yale University, 1966); Kenneth Janda, *Comparative Political Parties: A Cross-National Handbook* (New York: The Free Press, forthcoming, 1976); Hans Daalder, "Cabinets and Party Systems in Ten Smaller Western Democracies," a report to the Round Table Conference on European Comparative Politics, Turin, Italy, September 10-14, 1969; most of the other works cited throughout this study reflect this assumption to some degree. For a general discussion of this assumption, see Donald E. Stokes, "Spatial Models of Party Competition," *APSR* 57 (June 1963), pp. 368-377; and Brian M. Barry, *Sociologists, Economists, and Democracy* (London: Collier-Macmillan, Ltd., 1970), pp. 99-164. For an application of this assumption to questions of political stability at the regime level, see Ian Budge, *Agreement and the Stability of Democracy* (Chicago: Markham Publishing Co., 1970).

must compromise their cleavage-related policy stands if they are to coalesce in a cabinet. Some compromise can be justified if the cabinet positions gained thereby allow the party to largely fulfill the policies demanded by a cleavage constituency. The greater the compromise required to enter a coalition, however, the more difficult the compromise is to justify. Ministerial status may be achieved, but at the expense of any hope to enact or articulate forcefully most of the policies desired by the parties' cleavage constituencies. This places a clear constraint on the willingness of party leaders to bargain: they may gain cabinet status but at the high risk of electoral defeat in the next election at the hands of their disappointed cleavage constituency.

Within a given parliament therefore, the *a priori* willingness of parties to bargain depends at least in part on the nature of the cleavage conflict characterizing the parliament's party system. When all parties are concentrated in relatively close positions on a cleavage conflict continuum, *a priori* willingness to bargain should be high, *ceteris paribus*. In Figure 3:1, parties A, B, and C all fall close to the center of the continuum. In this setting cleavage conflict should not pose an overwhelming obstacle to negotiation

FIGURE 3:1

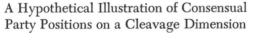

A Hypothetical Illustration of Consensual
Party Positions on a Cleavage Dimension

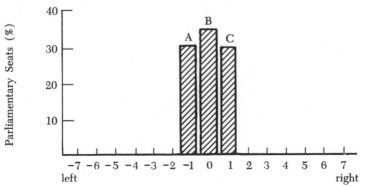

and compromise between the parties in efforts to form a cabinet. By contrast when parties are dispersed, with considerable distance separating their cleavage positions, *a priori* willingness to bargain should be quite low. In Figure 3:2 for example, parties A, B, and C are far apart from one

FIGURE 3:2

A Hypothetical Illustration of Conflictual
Party Positions on a Cleavage Dimension

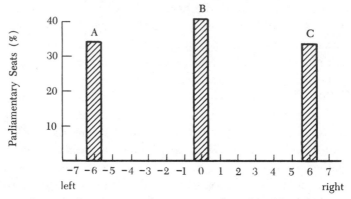

another; in this setting cleavage conflict should pose a considerable obstacle to their initial willingness to bargain.

This view of the role of cleavage conflict in cabinet formation is reflected in a number of studies. Axelrod, De Swaan, Groennings, and Leiserson all emphasize that the parties entering a cabinet are normally compatible in terms of ideological or cleavage conflict positions.[7] Robert Dahl writes that "if most people are extremists, their . . . coali-

---

[7] Robert Axelrod, *Conflict of Interest* (Chicago: Markham Publishing Co., 1970); Abraham De Swaan, "An Empirical Model of Coalition Formation as an N-Person Game of Policy Distance Minimization," in Sven Groennings, E. W. Kelly, and Michael Leiserson, eds., *The Study of Coalition Behavior* (New York: Holt, Rinehart and Winston, Inc., 1970), pp. 424-444; Groennings, "Patterns, Strategies and Payoffs in Norwegian Coalition Formation," in *The Study of Coalition Behavior*; Leiserson, "Coalitions in Politics."

tions will be . . . likely to yield to intransigent political groups implacably at odds with one another."[8] In his analysis of Weimar Germany, Karl Dietrich Bracher identifies a central factor in Germany's parliamentary deadlocks—the "unwillingness" of parties "to form coalitions and to compromise," a factor he contributes in large part to "their rigid ideological stance."[9] Finally, in an examination of Weimar Germany, the Fourth French Republic, and present-day Italy, Giovanni Sartori emphasizes the critical role of party polarization. In a highly polarized multiparty system, "the party system as a whole is hardly concerned with conflict resolution and hardly interested in performing the brokerage function. Quite the contrary, it is the very logic of party pluralization in its extreme form that impedes integration and the cohesive function."[10]

Based on this perspective, this study treats cleavage conflict or polarization as an indicator of the general *a priori* willingness to bargain that characterizes a parliamentary party system.[11] Following Sartori it is assumed that cleavage conflict or polarization is an attribute to the party system as a whole. Specifying the general *a priori* willingness of parties to bargain involves determining the general level of conflict or polarization experienced by a party system. Par-

[8] "Some Explanations," in Robert Dahl, ed., *Political Oppositions in Western Democracies* (New Haven: Yale University Press, 1966), pp. 376-377.

[9] *The German Dictatorship: The Origin, Structure and Effects of National Socialism* (New York: Praeger Publishers, 1970).

[10] Sartori, "European Political Parties."

[11] Aside from the works cited earlier, an excellent collection of essays on the relationship between social structure and party system is contained in Richard Rose, ed., *Electoral Behavior: A Comparative Handbook* (Riverside, N.J.: The Free Press, 1973); for a useful study of partisan and ideological conflict at the level of individual legislators, see Robert D. Putnam, *The Beliefs of Politicians* (New Haven: Yale University Press, 1973).

liaments evidencing a high concentration of parties along salient cleavage dimensions are experiencing high generalized willingness of parties to bargain. Parliaments that evidence high dispersion or polarization of parties along salient cleavage dimensions are experiencing low generalized *a priori* willingness to bargain.

PARTY SYSTEM FRACTIONALIZATION, PARTY SYSTEM STABILITY, AND INFORMATION CERTAINTY

As developed in Chapter 2, information certainty refers to the existence (a) of complete information in the party of various parliamentary parties (or party leaders) as to the weight (reliable voting strength) of other parties and (b) perfect information as to prior moves of parties within the parliamentary bargaining process. Two key party system characteristics that should influence each element of information certainty, that are applicable to all parliaments, and that can vary significantly between parliaments are, first, the fractionalization of the parliamentary party system and, second, the stability of the parliamentary party system. A third relevant factor is the interaction of these two variables.

Fractionalization

Party system fractionalization refers here to the number and relative strength of the parties within parliament. A highly fractionalized party system is one in which large numbers of parties have seats in parliament and these parties are of relatively equal strength. Douglas Rae has noted that parliamentary fractionalization can be important in determining the nature of the minimal majorities necessary to form a cabinet. "These differences are likely to be very important in the behavior of parliamentary party leaders who seek to build majorities in order to govern. They are also, and for the same reason, likely to relate closely to the relative stability of cabinets in various systems."[12] Focusing more precisely on the coalitional consequences of party system size, Sven Groennings argues that "the greater the number of participants in the process, the slower will be the process of coalition formation. Presumably, the greater the number of possible partners, the more complicated will be the strategies."[13]

While neither Rae nor Groennings develop the ideas further, they do point to the critical role that fractionalization may play for the certainty of information possessed by party leaders:

a) The greater the number and relative equality (in voting strength) of parties within parliament, the greater the number of relevant party relations that must be observed and considered in the coalitional bargaining process. A party leader attempting to follow the various possible bargaining moves made by other parties is faced with a difficult and, in highly fractionalized situations, a virtually impossible task. Given this situation, as the number of relevant parties increases within parliament, a decrease should occur in the ability of parties (or party leaders) to follow or to feel that they are following all moves being made by the other parties in the bargaining arena. *As party system fractionalization increases, consequently, the perfection of information as to moves should decrease.*

b) The greater the number of parties that are relevant to the bargaining process, the more difficult it should be

[12] *The Political Consequences of Electoral Laws* (New Haven: Yale University Press, 1967), p. 63.

[13] "Notes toward Theories of Coalition Behavior in Multiparty Systems: Formation and Maintenance," in *The Study of Political Coalitions*, p. 457.

to estimate with certainty the reliable strength of the various parliamentary parties. In estimating the relative strength of parties, any given party leader must observe the internal party relations of each party, or at least must feel that he would be aware of serious internal conflicts. In a parliament consisting of only three relevant parties, a party leader could well assume that he possessed reliable information as to the internal behavior of the other two parties. By contrast, in a parliament of ten relevant parties, a party leader would face a more difficult task. *As parliamentary fractionalization increases, consequently, the completeness of information as to weights should decrease.*

Based on these perspectives, the overall inference is that low fractionalization of the parliamentary party system contributes to information certainty; high fractionalization contributes to information uncertainty.

Party System Stability

The stability of the parliamentary party system refers to the continuity over time in the identity and relative strength of parties within parliament. When the identity and strength of parties is relatively constant or continuous over time the party system is highly stable. When the identity and strength of parties varies significantly over time, the parliamentary party system is unstable. Of all major attributes of Western parliamentary party system, stability is perhaps the least examined. The prevailing view among party system analysts is that the political cleavage system underlying the Western party systems has been frozen since the 1920s and that consequently the party systems have been frozen.[14] While it is true that no new cleavages have

[14] See particularly Lipset and Rokkan, "Cleavage Structures, Party Systems and Voter Alignments."

developed systematically across Western democracies and thus there are no major, institutionalized additions to the population of parties since the 1920s, it is not true that Western parliaments are devoid of short-term change and long-term alterations in the strength of parliamentary parties. Of particular importance are (1) the disappearance of parties, as in Germany between Weimar and the Federal German Republic; (2) flash parties, as in the Fourth French Republic; (3) large-scale, short-term fluctuation in the voting strength of those parties that remain from parliament to parliament.[15]

Though the literature on party systems is largely silent as to the significance of party system stability for intraparliamentary behavior,[16] it seems reasonable to assume that the greater the continuity in the identity and relative strength of parties over time the greater are, first, the opportunities for stable patterns of intraparliamentary partisan behavior to develop and, second, the greater the probable familiarity of party leaders with one another and with the probable patterns of partisan behavior. If these propositions are true, then two different consequences should follow:

a) the emergence of stable patterns of partisan behavior should improve the ability of party leaders to estimate the weight (reliable voting strength) of the various parliamentary parties. In other words, *as the stability of the parliamentary party system increases, the completeness of information as to weight should increase.*

[15] For a useful discussion of the various factors contributing to party system instability in Western parliamentary systems, see W. Phillips Shively, "Party Identification, Party Choice, and Voting Stability: The Weimar Case," *APSR* 66 (December 1972), 1203-1225.

[16] For a discussion of the general significance of party system stability or institutionalization, particularly as it relates to developing polities, see Samuel P. Huntington, *Political Order in Changing Societies* (New Haven: Yale University Press, 1968).

b) as party leaders become more familiar with one another and with the patterned behavior of parties, it should be easier for them to anticipate and follow the various moves being made in the bargaining process. In other words, *as parliamentary party system stability increases, complete information as to prior moves should increase.*

Based on these perspectives, the overall inference is that party system stability contributes to information certainty; party system instability contributes to information uncertainty.

The Interaction of Fractionalization and Instability

A third relevant determinant of information certainty may be the interaction of party system fractionalization and instability. The joint effects of fractionalization and instability may be greater than their separate additive effects:

a) Behavior among a large number of parties may not be difficult to follow if these parties have been repeatedly represented in parliaments over a significant time period and if their strength has been fairly constant so that prior behavior serves to guide current expectations.

b) Discontinuity over time in the party system may not be a serious problem in less fractionalized systems when only a few parties must be followed.

c) By contrast, the occurrence of high fractionalization and high instability together may activate or at least augment the potential effects of each. In such a situation, party leaders must follow maneuvers among a large number of parties with little past behavior to provide a reliable indication of probable parliamentary moves. In such a situation, in other words, stable partisan patterns do not exist to depress or defuse the complications created by a large number of parties.

If these projections are correct, the occurrence of high fractionalization and instability together may produce an additional degree of information uncertainty that cannot be predicted from knowledge of the effects of either variable examined separately or in an additive model.

CONCLUSION

Robert Dahl writes that although "it is exceptionally difficult to cast this proposition in operational terms, it seems clear that highly fragmented multiparty systems (Sartori's 'extreme' or 'polarized' pluralism) can lead to unstable or weak coalitions. . . ."[17] This chapter has attempted to specify the nature of the relationship between party systems and the coalitional status of cabinets. In the process, hopefully, the vague hypotheses to which Dahl refers have been clarified and propositions have been presented that are capable of operational analysis. According to the theory outlined in Chapter 2, the cabinet's coalitional status is determined by the nature of the bargaining conditions that prevail within parliament. This chapter has argued that the following characteristics of a parliament's party system constitute factors determining the nature of these bargaining conditions:

a) The lower the degree of cleavage conflict or polarization occurring among parliamentary parties, the greater the generalized *a priori* willingness of parties to bargain, *ceteris paribus*.

[17] Robert Dahl, *Polyarchy* (New Haven: Yale University Press, 1971), p. 122.

b) The more defractionalized and stable a parliamentary party system, the greater the degree of information certainty characterizing the parliamentary bargaining processes, *ceteris paribus*.

Incorporating these party system attributes, the thesis of this study can be diagramed as in Figure 3:3.

FIGURE 3:3

A Diagrammatic Representation of the Thesis

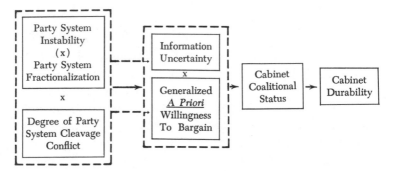

Simplifying the interaction process described in this thesis, parliaments can be divided into four broad categories:

1. Parliaments with party systems that are polarized, fractionalized, and unstable are experiencing low generalized *a priori* willingness to bargain combined with high uncertainty. In such parliaments undersized cabinets should form. As a result of attempts to resolve these cabinets toward minimum winning status (either by forming larger coalitions or dissolving parliament and holding new elections), such cabinets should be transient.

2. Parliaments with party systems that are depolarized, fractionalized and unstable are experiencing high generalized *a priori* willingness to bargain combined with high uncertainty. In such parliaments oversized cabinets should

form. Because of attempts to resolve the cabinet toward minimum winning status (by forming less oversized coalitions or dissolving parliament) these cabinets should be transient.

3. Parliaments with party systems that are polarized, defractionalized, and stable are experiencing low generalized *a priori* willingness to bargain combined with information certainty. In these parliaments, cabinets will approach minimum winning status, with the primary constraint being the degree of party system polarization. Under conditions of extremely high polarization, multiparty parliaments will experience minority cabinets as parties will not consider majority coalitions even with the existence of information certainty. These cabinets should be nondurable, falling through parliamentary dissolution. In polarized conditions that fall short of extreme cleavage conflict, minimum winning cabinets should be possible, and they should be durable.

4. Parliaments with party systems that are depolarized, defractionalized, and stable are experiencing high generalized *a priori* willingness to bargain combined with information certainty. In such parliaments, minimum winning cabinets should form. These cabinets should experience considerable durability. In Part II of this study operational definitions are offered that render these propositions testable.

Certainly the party system attributes specified in these propositions are not the only factors that influence the bargaining conditions within parliament.[18] For example, information certainty may increase the longer a parliament

---

[18] For a stimulating and provocative discussion of coalitional processes in multiparty systems, see Gunnar Sjöblom, *Party Strategies in a Multiparty System* (Berlingska Boktryckeriet, Sweden: Lund, 1968).

lasts, the more structured the interaction of party leaders, the more frequent the sessions of parliaments, or the more institutionalized the legislature. Likewise, the willingness of parties to bargain will not be a simple function of partisan cleavage conflict at the electoral stage but can be subject to shifts throughout a parliamentary session as a result of external and internal events. In addition, as Groennings has emphasized, *a priori* willingness to bargain may depend on the structure of the individual parties, the background similarity of party leaders, and the prior relationship between parties.[19] As a result of these and other reasons, among which is the fact that we expect cabinets to vary in coalitional status within certain parliaments as cabinets resolve toward minimum winning status, attempts to predict or postdict cabinets' coalitional status solely on the basis of these party system characteristics will not account for all variation.[20]

[19] Groennings, "Notes toward Theories of Coalition Behavior in Multiparty Systems," pp. 453-454.

[20] In this chapter, and throughout the book, multiparty parliament refers to any parliament with no majority party; majority party parliament refers to any parliament with a majority party.

II | Measurement

4 | Party System Fractionalization and Stability

Testing the propositions presented in Part I requires operational measures of five relevant variables. Three of the variables relate to the parliamentary party system: fractionalization, stability, and cleavage conflict. Two variables refer to cabinet characteristics: cabinet coalitional status and cabinet durability. The purpose of Part II is to specify the measures employed in rendering these variables operational. This chapter outlines the measures of fractionalization and stability. The following two chapters present measures of cleavage conflict, coalitional status, and cabinet durability. In addition these chapters provide an overview of the party system data gathered for the study.

PARTY SYSTEM FRACTIONALIZATION

Party System Fractionalization refers to the number and relative strength of parties within parliament. A highly fractionalized party system is one in which a large number of parties have seats in parliament and these parties are of relatively equal voting strength. A defractionalized party system is one in which a small number of parties have parliamentary strength. In the extreme case of defractionalization, only one parliamentary party exists. Fractionalization is significant in this study as an indicator of the number of relevant parties in the parliamentary bargaining arena. It is assumed that the more equal the voting strength of parties, the less likely any party is either to hold a pivotal position in terms of size or to be totally unimportant for coalition formation. In other words the more equal parties are in voting strength, the greater the likelihood that all parties are relevant to the bargaining process, *ceteris paribus*. The *number* of relevant parties is significant as an influence on the certainty of information: the greater their number, the lower the probability of complete and perfect information.

Comparative party analysts have employed two different measures of fractionalization. Douglas Rae introduced the first of these measures in his landmark study of electoral laws,[1] hereafter referred to as the Rae index of fractionalization; Michael Taylor and V. H. Herman have employed it in their study of government stability.[2] Its computation is as follows:

$$F_p = 1 - \left(\sum_{i=a}^{n} S_i^2 \right)$$

where S_i stands for the proportion of seats associated with the ith parliamentary party. The values of this index range between the limits of zero and one. Each party's share of parliamentary seats enters into the calculation of the coefficient though, according to Rae, in practice those below .005 are eliminated. The Rae index is particularly attractive because of its ease of calculation.

A second measure of party system fractionalization is found in the work of Kesselman and Wildgen.[3] As Wildgen

[1] Douglas W. Rae, *The Political Consequences of Electoral Laws* (New Haven: Yale University Press, 1967), pp. 47-64.

[2] "Party Systems and Governmental Stability," *APSR* 65 (March 1971), pp. 28-37.

[3] Mark Kesselman, "French Local Politics: A Statistical Examination of Grass Roots Consensus," *APSR* 60 (December 1966), pp. 963-973; John K. Wildgen, "The Measurement of Hyperfractionalization,"

is its main proponent, it will be termed the Wildgen index of fractionalization; it is also referred to as a measure of hyperfractionalization. Its computation is as follows:

$$I_t = \text{antilog} \left[- \sum_{I=1}^{m} P_I \cdot \log_e P_I \right]$$

where m equals the number of parties in Parliament t and P_I equals the proportion of parliamentary seats held by Party I in Parliament t. The lower boundary of the Wildgen index is 1.0, a score obtained when one party controls all seats in parliament; its upper boundary depends on the number of parties in parliament and their relative strength, as will be apparent momentarily. As with the Rae index, all party shares are utilized in the Wildgen index; the seat share of minor parties influences the size of the coefficient more clearly in the Wildgen index, however. Unlike the Rae index, the Wildgen measure involves fairly elaborate calculations.

Table 4:1 presents values of each fractionalization measure for different hypothetical parliamentary party systems. As the coefficients indicate, each measure is sensitive to both the number of parties in parliament and the relative share of the parliamentary seats controlled by each party: as the number of tied parties increases, the coefficient associated with each index increases. The two measures differ in a significant way, however. An increase in the number

Comparative Political Studies 4 (July 1971) 233-243. This measure is associated with information theory or, as Galtung presents it, "uncertainty." See Claude E. Shannon and Warren Weaver, *The Mathematical Theory of Communication* (Urbana: University of Illinois Press, 1959); John Galtung, *Theory and Methods of Social Research* (New York: Columbia University Press, 1967); Henri Theil, *Economics and Information Theory* (Amsterdam: North Holland Publishing Co., 1967).

TABLE 4:1

Sample Values for Fractionalization:
A Comparison of Rae and Wildgen Indices

Parliament	Rae Coefficient	Wildgen Coefficient	Party and Seat Proportion									
			1	2	3	4	5	6	7	8	9	10 20
A	.00	1.000	1.0									
B	.420	1.842	.70	.30								
C	.500	2.000	.50	.50								
D	.585	2.583	.45	.45	.10							
E	.673	3.000	.33	.33	.33							
F	.700	3.596	.40	.30	.20	.10						
G	.750	4.000	.25	.25	.25	.25						
H	.800	5.000	.20	.20	.20	.20	.20					
I	.835	6.000	.166	.166	.166	.166	.166	.166				
J	.875	8.000	.125	.125	.125	.125	.125	.125	.125	.125		
K	.900	10.000	.100	.100	.100	.100	.100	.100	.100	.100	.100	.100
L	.950	20.000	.05	.05	.05	.05	.05	.05	.05	.05	.05	.05 ... .05

of tied parties does not bring a proportional increase in the Rae coefficient, whereas it does bring a proportional increase in the Wildgen index. This difference can be critical from the standpoint of information certainty and coalition formation. A situation in which six parties have equal strength in parliament would seem to be considerably more complex than a situation in which three parties are tied. In such a contrast, the Rae index increases only from .673 to .835 whereas the Wildgen index increases from 3.000 to 6.000. This difference between the two measures holds throughout the range of possible party combinations. The Rae index increases in a curvilinear fashion, with large increases of the fractionalization coefficient in the move from one party to two tied parties; thereafter, progressively smaller increases occur in moves to three, four, five tied parties, and so forth. By contrast, as the number of tied parties increases, the Wildgen index coefficients increase in a linear fashion. In situations in which parties are not tied, the Wildgen coefficient ranges between 1.0 and the limiting score that the parliament would receive were the parties tied; in such a situation, the more equal the strength of the parties, the closer the coefficient approaches the limiting score.[4]

Because of the greater sensitivity of the Wildgen measure to increases in the number of tied parties, the Wildgen in-

[4] For other approaches, see Richard A. Pride, *Origins of Democracy*, Harry Eckstein and Ted Robert Gurr, eds., Sage Professional Papers in Comparative Politics, 1, No. 12 (1970), 708; Lawrence S. Mayer, "An Analysis of Measures of Crosscutting and Fragmentation," *Comparative Politics* 4 (April 1972); Stephen Coleman, "Measurement and the Analysis of Political Systems" (unpublished Ph.D. dissertation, University of Minnesota, 1972). An excellent discussion emphasizing the measurement problems associated with multiparty systems was published after the preparation of this study. See Davis J. Elkins, "The Measurement of Party Competition," *APSR* 68 (June 1974), 682-700.

dex is the measure of fractionalization employed throughout this study.[5] The use of this measure is particularly important because this study includes some parliaments that contain as many as fifteen parties. It must be noted, however, that the choice of the Wildgen index is arbitrary to a degree. Ideally, such a choice should be made on the basis of clear empirical knowledge (based for example on small group experimental research) as to the effect that the number and relative weight of actors has on information certainty. It is conceivable that as the number of relevant parties increases (1) information uncertainty increases, but at a progressively declining rate; (2) information uncertainty increases in a relatively linear fashion in proportion to the increase in numbers of relevant actors; (3) information uncertainty increases at an accelerating rate. Unfortunately, systematic experimental evidence does not exist to indicate the preferable property for a fractionalization measure. Thus the decision to use the Wildgen measure is a judgmental one, reflecting the author's intuitive suspicion. Appendix A presents selected coefficients that obtain when the empirical analysis of this study is replicated employing the Rae index.

Table 4:2 presents a frequency distribution of fractionalization scores for all parliaments listed in Table 1:4. In Table 4:2, as throughout the subsequent body of this study, fractionalization scores are derived from use of the Wildgen fractionalization index. In this table scores from multiparty parliaments are separated from scores for majority party parliaments. As would be expected, majority party systems

[5] For a more extensive discussion of the relative merits of the two measures, see Wildgen, "The Measurement of Hyperfractionalization" and Douglas W. Rae, "Comments on Wildgen's 'The Measurement of Hyperfractionalization,'" in *Comparative Political Studies* 4 (July 1971), 244-245.

TABLE 4:2

A Frequency Listing of Party System Fractionalization Scores:
All Western Peacetime Parliaments, 1918-1974

Fractionalization Score	Multiparty Parliaments	Majority Party Parliaments	All
1.000 to 2.499	5	27	32
2.500 to 2.999	25	12	37
3.000 to 3.499	24	8	32
3.500 to 3.999	34	3	37
4.000 to 4.499	22	2	24
4.500 to 4.999	18	0	18
5.000 to 5.999	23	0	23
6.000 to 6.999	11	0	11
7.000 to 7.999	9	0	9
8.000 to 9.999	6	0	6

experience considerably less fractionalization than multi-party systems. However, several patterns should be noted. First, a fair number of moderately fractionalized majority party systems do exist, with thirteen of the fifty-two majority party parliaments obtaining fractionalization scores greater than 3.00. As Table 4:3 indicates, majority party parliaments receiving these moderately fractionalized scores occur in Australia, Canada, Germany, Great Britain, Ireland, Italy, Luxembourg, New Zealand, Norway, and Sweden. Majority partism is not incompatible with significant parliamentary fractionalization.

Table 4:4 presents seven parliaments that illustrate the range of variation in majority party system fractionalization that is possible. In a prototypical majority party system such as New Zealand during the postwar years, as illustrated by the 1951 parliament, only two parties obtain seats in parliament; the fractionalization coefficient falls below 2.00 since the two parties are not quite tied in strength. As a third minor party is introduced into competitive majority

TABLE 4:3

High and Low Fractionalization Scores

(by country)

Country	Multiparty Parliaments		Majority Party Parliaments	
	Low (yr.)	High (yr.)	Low (yr.)	High (yr.)
Australia	2.70 (1961)	3.62 (1922)	2.59 (1946)	3.08 (1929)
Austria	2.28 (1970)	3.07 (1930)	2.20 (1945)	2.61 (1927)
Belgium	2.75 (1958)	4.94 (1936)	2.85 (1950)	—
Canada	2.79 (1925)	3.42 (1926)	1.82 (1958)	3.49 (1945)
Denmark	3.65 (1929)	5.18 (1945)	—	—
Finland	4.47 (1930)	6.19 (1970)	—	—
France	5.64 (1945)	8.78 (1956)	—	—
Germany	2.41 (1969)	9.16 (1930)	2.77 (1957)	3.44 (1953)
Great Britain	2.74 (1929)	5.16 (1918)	2.09 (1959)	3.27 (1922)
Iceland	2.90 (1933)	3.95 (1953)	2.51 (1931)	—
Ireland	3.18 (1961)	5.08 (1948)	2.72 (1969)	3.60 (1957)
Italy	4.29 (1953)	5.82 (1946)	3.33 (1948)	—
Luxembourg	3.08 (1954)	4.95 (1934)	3.40 (1919)	—
Netherlands	5.00 (1956)	8.10 (1972)	—	—
New Zealand	2.85 (1922)	3.70 (1931)	1.87 (1938)	3.10 (1919)
Norway	3.78 (1936)	6.06 (1924)	3.51 (1949)	4.22 (1945)
Sweden	3.24 (1928)	4.12 (1932)	3.46 (1968)	—

party systems, as in Great Britain (1964) or Iceland (1931), the fractionalization coefficient surpasses 2.00. In competitive majority party systems containing more than two parties, the critical factors are the number of parties and their relative strength. Thus though the parliaments in Great Britain (1964) and Iceland (1931) each contain three parties, the significantly larger size of the minor party in Iceland produces a more fractionalized party system. As the examples of Germany (1957), Norway (1953), and Sweden (1968) indicate, increases in the number of moderately significant parties in parliament (those approximating at least 10 percent of the legislative seats) result in sizable increases in the fractionalization coefficient. In typical mod-

TABLE 4:4

Examples of Majority Party Fractionalization

Country (yr.)	Parties	Seat %	Score
New Zealand (1951)			1.984
	Ref	.562	
	Lab	.438	
Great Britain (1964)			2.132
	Lab	.503	
	Cons	.483	
	Lib	.014	
Iceland (1931)			2.512
	Prog	.548	
	Ind	.357	
	SD	.095	
Germany (1957)			2.768
	CDU/CSU	.544	
	SD	.340	
	FD	.082	
	DP	.034	
Italy			3.323
	DC	.537	
	Soc & Comm	.319	
	SD	.057	
	Rep	.016	
	Lib	.033	
	Mon	.024	
	MSI	.010	
	PPS-T	.002	
	PSd'A	.002	
Sweden (1968)			3.464
	SD	.537	
	Cons	.137	
	Cen	.167	
	Lib	.146	
	Comm	.013	
Norway (1953)			4.061
	Lab	.513	
	Comm	.020	
	Ven	.100	
	CP	.093	
	Agr	.093	
	Cons	.180	

erately fractionalized majority party parliaments such as Sweden (1968) or Norway (1953), the majority party is surrounded by several smaller parties, none of which clearly dominates the minority grouping in terms of party size. In a less typical moderately fractionalized parliament such as Italy (1948), the majority party faces a moderately large second party and a series of quite small minor parties.

The foregoing examples indicate that meaningful variation in fractionalization does exist among majority party parliaments. The variation among multiparty parliaments is even more interesting. A number of multiparty parliaments have experienced low fractionalization. Forty of the 177 multiparty parliaments receive fractionalization scores falling below 3.00. The countries involved here include Australia, Austria, Belgium, Canada, Germany, Great Britain, Iceland, and New Zealand. Clearly, multipartism is not incompatible with defractionalization. Nevertheless, extremely fractionalized (in Wildgen's term, hyperfractionalized) parliaments have existed. Twenty-six of the 177 multiparty parliaments fall in the range of scores exceeding 5.99. Parliaments experiencing such hyperfractionalization have occurred in Finland, France, Weimar Germany, the Netherlands, and Norway. The existence of such parliaments, when contrasted with the existence of defractionalized multiparty parliaments, underscores Sartori's observation that multiparty systems evidence a great range in their precise characteristics. In fact, between the defractionalized multiparty parliaments and the hyperfractionalized parliaments fall a number of moderately fractionalized parliaments. Even among these there is no predominate pattern of fractionalization.

The "real-world" examples in Table 4:5 illustrate the nature of the variation in fractionalization occurring among multiparty parliaments. In the typical defractionalized

TABLE 4:5
Examples of Multiparty Fractionalization

Country (yr.)	Parties	Seat %	Score
Austria (1959)			2.345
	AP	.479	
	SD	.473	
	PGN	.048	
Australia (1963)			2.789
	Lab	.410	
	Lib	.426	
	Ctry	.164	
Luxembourg (1948)			3.513
	CS	.44	
	Soc	.28	
	Demo	.18	
	Comm	.10	
Iceland (1949)			3.696
	Comm	.173	
	SD	.135	
	Prog	.327	
	Ind	.365	
Denmark (1924)			3.851
	SD	.372	
	Rad Lib	.135	
	Cons	.189	
	Lib	.297	
	Germ	.007	
Norway (1930)			4.318
	Lab	.313	
	Wk	.007	
	Ven	.220	
	Agr	.167	
	Lib Ven	.020	
	Cons	.273	
Denmark (1968)			4.774
	SD	.354	
	Rad Lib	.154	
	Cons	.211	
	Lib Demo	.194	
	Soc	.063	
	L Soc	.023	

TABLE 4:5 (*continued*)

Examples of Multiparty Fractionalization

Country (yr.)	Parties	Seat %	Score
Finland (1927)			5.192
	S Lab	.100	
	Soc Demo	.300	
	Agr U	.260	
	NPP	.050	
	Swed P	.120	
	N Coal	.170	
Italy (1946)			5.800
	Comm	.187	
	Soc	.207	
	Act	.013	
	Rep	.041	
	DC	.372	
	Lib	.074	
	HQ	.054	
	Mon	.029	
	PSd'A	.004	
	Md'SI	.007	
	others	.012	
France (1951)			6.820
	Comm	.161	
	Soc	.171	
	MRP	.153	
	Rad	.121	
	UDSR	.030	
	Cons	.156	
	Gaul	.191	
	others	.107	
Netherlands (1967)			7.300
	AR	.100	
	CHU	.080	
	Pol Ref	.020	
	Cath P	.280	
	PPF	.113	
	Lab	.247	
	P Soc	.027	
	Comm	.033	
	Agr	.047	
	Demo '66	.047	
	others	.006	

TABLE 4:5 (*continued*)
Examples of Multiparty Fractionalization

Country (yr.)	Parties	Seat %	Score
France (1924)			8.074
	Rad-Rad Soc	.239	
	Rep Soc	.076	
	L Rad	.073	
	Soc	.179	
	Comm	.045	
	Ind	.048	
	URD	.177	
	L Rep	.065	
	GRD	.074	
	Demo	.024	
Germany (1930)			9.172
	Nz	.185	
	DNV	.072	
	KV	.007	
	CSV	.024	
	Lb	.005	
	Lv	.033	
	DB	.010	
	DV	.052	
	Wst	.040	
	DH	.005	
	BV	.033	
	Z	.118	
	DD	.035	
	S	.248	
	Comm	.133	

multiparty parliament, such as Australia (1963) or Austria (1959), two relatively large plurality parties exist in parliament, together with a minor party; such systems obtain fractionalization coefficients below 3.000. The larger the parliamentary size of the minor party, the more fractionalized is the system; thus the larger fractionalization coefficient for Australia (1963).

Seven parliaments indicate the patterns obtaining within

the moderately fractionalized range from 3.00 to 6.00. In the range from 3.00 to 4.00, the basic pattern is the existence of four parties, all of which exceed 10 percent of the parliamentary vote. Luxembourg (1948), Iceland (1949), and Denmark (1924) illustrate variations on this situation. In the least fractionalized of these parliaments, Luxembourg (1948), a major plurality party faces three significant but weaker parties. In the more fractionalized cases no dominant party exists, though the four parties do not exactly approach equality. In the fractionalized range from 4.00 to 5.00, as illustrated by Norway (1930) and Denmark (1968), four relatively strong parties exist, faced by two minor parties. Aside from the existence of the two minor parties, these parliaments are characterized by a greater equality between the four larger parties than that found in the preceding range. In the range from 5.00 to 6.00, Finland (1927) and Italy (1946) provide examples. In the Finnish parliament, five parties each attain 10 percent of the parliamentary seats; one party exists with 5 percent of the legislative seats. None of the parties exceeds 30 percent of the vote. Italy (1946) presents a different picture, approximating hyperfractionalization. One relatively large party approaches 40 percent of the seats in parliament. Facing this party are two moderate-sized parties, each approximating 20 percent of the seats. These three parties face eight party groupings, none of which attains more than 7½ percent of the seats in parliament.

The foregoing parliaments, with the possible exception of Italy (1946), contrast vividly with hyperfractionalized parliaments. Four parliaments illustrate the complexity existing among hyperfractionalized systems. The 1951 French parliament provides a remarkable real-world example of a parliament containing six relatively equal parties, each possessing more than 12 percent and less than 20 percent of the legislative seats. These six parties are joined by a seventh smaller party and a set of unattached parliamentarians so that the fractionalization coefficient falls between 6.00 and 7.00. The Netherlands (1967) provides an example of a parliament receiving a score between 7.00 and 8.00. Two parties each obtain between 24 and 28 percent of the parliamentary seats; three other parties contain between 8 and 11 percent of the parliamentary seats; and four parties control more than 2 but less than 5 percent of the seats. Overall, ten parties exist, together with a small set of factional parliamentarians (.006%). The 1924 French parliament provides a relevant contrast to the Netherlands. This parliament contains ten parties which, taken together, evidence even more fractionalization than the Netherlands; thus the fractionalization coefficient surpasses 8.00. Finally, the 1930 parliament in Weimar Germany is the extreme real-world example of hyperfractionalization. Fifteen parties obtained representation in parliament. Of these fifteen, only one surpasses 20 percent of the seats (receiving 25 percent); one party receives approximately 19 percent of the seats; two control approximately 12 percent; and eleven parties divide 30 percent of the parliamentary seats.

The foregoing examples should indicate the very significant differences in fractionalization that obtain among multiparty parliaments. Clearly, all multiparty systems are not alike in numerical composition or in the relative strength of parties. These differences in the number of parties and their relative strength suggest very real contrasts between parliaments in the situations facing party negotiations. In defractionalized settings, the parameters facing party negotiators should be fairly clear. At most, three to four relevant parties exist, with fairly clear differences obtaining between the size of the two largest parties and the smaller parties. By contrast, in hyperfractionalized settings as many as 10 to 15 parties may exist, none of which is so large as to dominate the parliamentary arena.

PARTY SYSTEM STABILITY

As employed in this study, party system stability denotes the extent of continuity over time in the identity and relative strength of parliamentary parties. A highly stable parliamentary party system exists when the identity and strength of parties remains relatively constant or continuous from parliament to parliament. A highly unstable party system exists when the identity and strength of parties varies over time. In the limiting case of instability, the parties in a parliament (t) bear no relation to the parties in the prior parliament (t-1). In the extreme case of stability, all parties in parliament t are identical to all parties in the prior parliament (t-1) with each party maintaining the precise proportional seat strength that it enjoyed in the prior parliament (t-1).

To determine the continuity (C_t) of the party system in parliament t with the party system in parliament t-1, the following measure is employed:[6]

$$C_t = \tfrac{1}{2} \sum_{I=1}^{m} \left[L_{I_{t\text{-}1}} - L_{I_t} \right]$$

where $L_{I_{t\text{-}1}} = \dfrac{\text{number of legislators for party } I \text{ at } t\text{-}1}{\text{number of legislators for parliament at } t\text{-}1}$,

$L_{I_t} = \dfrac{\text{number of legislators for party } I \text{ at } t}{\text{number of legislators in parliament } t}$, and

[6] This index is a variation on Przeworski and Sprague's measure of Party System Institutionalization. See Adam Przeworski and John Sprague, "Concepts in Search of Explicit Formulation: A Study in Measurement," *Midwest Journal of Political Science* 40 (May 1971).

$m =$ the number of parties in parliament. Any party in parliament at t-1 or t is treated as a party in parliament during both time periods.

In this measure of continuity, L_I indicates the proportion of the parliamentary seats identified with a specific party I. The proportion of seats controlled by party I in parliament t is subtracted from the proportion of seats controlled by party I in parliament t-1. The differential indicates the change from parliament t-1 to parliament t in the proportional size of party I. This procedure is followed for all parties obtaining seats in either parliament t-1 or parliament t. Parties lacking representation in one of the two parliaments receive a score (L_I) of zero for that parliament.

The proportional change differentials $(L_{I_{t-1}} - L_{I_t})$ are summed without regard to their positive or negative signs so that a score is obtained indicating the absolute change from parliament t-1 to t in the strength of parliamentary parties. This absolute score is divided by two so that the final continuity score (C_t) indicates the relative change in proportional party strength from parliament t-1 to parliament t. Table 4:6 illustrates the calculation of the continuity score. In the example, four parties obtained seats in parliament t-1; three of these parties returned in parliament t, joined by a new party unrepresented in parliament t-1. Column C indicates the change in parliamentary strength occurring for each party from parliament t-1 to t; were these percentages summed, they would cancel. Consequently, as is indicated in Column D, it is the absolute change that is summed. This sum is divided by two so that the final C_t score indicates the relative party system change that has occurred when the proportional shifts of seats from one party to another are considered.

TABLE 4:6

An Illustrative Calculation of Party System Continuity (C_t)

A		B	C	D
Parliament $t-1$ seat %		Parliament t seat %	$L_{I_{t-1}} - L_{I_t}$	$L_{I_{t-1}} - L_{I_t}$
Party 1	.40	.30	−.10	.10
Party 2	.30	.40	.10	.10
Party 3	.20	.20	.00	.00
Party 4	.00	.10	.10	.10
Party 5	.10	.00	−.10	.10
Total	1.00	1.00		.40

$$\frac{1}{2} \sum_{I=1}^{m} \left[L_{I_{t-1}} - L_{I_t} \right] = \frac{1}{2}(.40) = .20$$

Table 4:7 provides hypothetical examples of party system change, indicating the C_t score appropriate to each example. In a parliament (t) experiencing no alteration in parties or party strength from the prior parliament (t-1), C_t is .00, indicating complete continuity (example A). In a parliament experiencing complete change in the party system from the prior parliament, C_t is 1.00, indicating total discontinuity (example E). Between these limits, C_t is determined by the proportional change from parliament to parliament in seat strength of parties. It should be noted in this regard that C_t is insensitive to the type of change occurring. As the contrast between example B and C indicates, the same score represents first, a situation in which the seat changes occur as shifts among a continuing set of parties and second, a situation in which changes in seat strength occur as new parties enter parliament and/or old parties leave. The significance of this potential limitation of the measure remains unexamined throughout the remainder of the study. An important question for future work is the

TABLE 4:7

Hypothetical Examples of Party System Change

Continuity (C_t)		Party							
Score	Example	1	2	3	4	5	6	7	8
	Example A								
.00	Parliament t-1	.40	.20	.20	.20				
	Parliament t	.40	.20	.20	.20				
	Example B								
.40	Parliament t-1	.40	.20	.20	.20				
	Parliament t	.30	.00	.20	.10	.10	.10	.10	.10
	Example C								
.40	Parliament t-1	.40	.20	.20	.20				
	Parliament t	.80	.10	.05	.05				
	Example D								
.60	Parliament t-1	.40	.20	.20	.20				
	Parliament t	.00	.10	.10	.50	.30			
	Example E								
1.00	Parliament t-1	.40	.20	.20	.20	.00	.00	.00	.00
	Parliament t	.00	.00	.00	.00	.30	.30	.20	.20

significance of change in seat strength among continuing parties in contrast to changes that result from the addition of new parties and/or the departure of old parties.

Aside from the foregoing limitation, a second limitation with the C_t score is its insensitivity to party system changes that have occurred other than the changes from parliament t-1 to parliament t. As elections from one parliament may follow soon after an earlier parliamentary election, seat strength may change little from t-1 to t; by contrast, over a period to five to ten years, considerable change may have occurred in this parliamentary party system. In order to capture this type of change, the C_t scores for all new parliaments held in the five years prior to parliament t have been summed, including the C_t score for parliament t. This sum constitutes the Party System Stability (S_t) score for parliament t.

The construction of S_t does involve an arbitrary judgment. It is based on a sum of C_t scores for all new parliaments held in a country over the five years preceding parliament t. Obviously, some other procedure could have been employed; a different time span could be selected, for example. No clear rationale exists for selecting the appropriate procedure. For this reason the author has investigated all relevant propositions employing the five following operational procedures:

> PSI–A   the stability score is the C score for parliament t only.
>
> PSI–B   the stability score is the sum of the C scores for parliaments t and t-1.
>
> PSI–C   the stability score is the sum of the C scores for parliaments t, t-1, and t-2.
>
> PSI–D   the stability score is the sum of the C scores for all parliaments held in the past five years.
>
> PSI–E   the stability score is the sum of the C scores for all parliaments held in the past ten years.

Throughout the body of this study, party system stability (S_t) scores refer to PSI–D. Selected coefficients that obtain with the four other indices are reported in Appendix A.

Table 4:8 presents a frequency distribution of parliamentary party system stability (PSI–D) scores for all peacetime parliaments, 1918-1974. The table separates scores for multiparty parliaments from those for majority party parliaments. As the patterns indicate, considerable variation in party system stability exists among both majority party and multiparty parliaments. Twenty-seven percent of all peacetime majority party parliaments and 23 percent of all peacetime multiparty parliaments received party system stability scores falling below .15. This indicates that approximately 24 percent of all peacetime parliaments experience less than 15 percent cumulative change in the relative strength of parties in consecutive parliaments over the five years prior to the beginning of the parliament. By contrast, over 17 percent and 11 percent of majority party and multiparty parliaments, respectively, received party system stability scores exceeding .49. This indicates that almost 13 percent of all peacetime parliaments experienced at least

TABLE 4:8

A Frequency Listing of Party System Stability Scores:
All Western Peacetime Parliaments, 1918-1974

Stability Score	Multiparty Parliaments	Majority Party Parliaments	All
.00 to .09	15	8	23
.10 to .14	26	6	32
.15 to .19	27	7	34
.20 to .24	20	3	23
.25 to .29	27	5	32
.30 to .39	25	8	33
.40 to .49	16	6	22
.50 to .59	9	3	12
.60 to .69	7	3	10
.70 to highest	3	2	5
no data	2	1	3
Total	177	52	229

50 percent cumulative change in the relative strength of parties in consecutive parliaments over the five years preceding the sitting parliament. As Table 4:9 indicates, parliaments receiving low scores (below .15) occur in all countries except Canada and France. Countries receiving high scores (those exceeding .49) include Australia, Canada, Finland, France, Germany, Great Britain, Iceland, Italy, and New Zealand.

TABLE 4:9

High and Low Party System Stability Scores

(by country)

Country	Multiparty Parliaments		Majority Party Parliaments	
	Low (yr.)	High (yr.)	Low (yr.)	High (yr.)
Australia	.017 (1961)	.610 (1951)	.306 (1929)	.670 (1931)
Austria	.049 (1962)	.270 (1949)	.280 (1945)	.039 (1966)
Belgium	.115 (1925)	.310 (1946)	.350 (1950)	—
Canada	.268 (1972)	.711 (1962)	.160 (1968)	.700 (1958)
Denmark	.110 (1926)	.476 (1950)	—	—
Finland	.110 (1958)	.620 (1924)	—	—
France	.370 (1932)	.620 (1919)	—	—
Germany	.080 (1969)	.782 (1924II)	.350 (1957)	.461 (1953)
Great Britain	.179 (1918)	.515 (1929)	.080 (1959)	.750 (1924)
Iceland	.066 (1967)	.521 (1927)	.300 (1931)	—
Ireland	.200 (1954)	.394 (1948)	.092 (1969)	.234 (1957)
Italy	.090 (1972)	.630 (1946)	.63 (1948)	—
Luxembourg	.135 (1954)	.302 (1931)	no data	—
Netherlands	.090 (1952)	.280 (1972)	—	—
New Zealand	.355 (1922)	.720 (1928)	.010 (1963)	.430 (1935)
Norway	.060 (1961)	.472 (1921)	.120 (1957)	.247 (1949)
Sweden	.059 (1964)	.428 (1924)	.098 (1968)	—

CONCLUSION

Aside from party system fractionalization and stability as separate variables, the joint occurrence of the two variables together may have a significant independent effect on the coalitional processes within parliament. As argued in Chapter 3, the interaction of these two variables may produce an additional influence on information uncertainty that cannot be determined from knowledge of the effects of either variable examined separately or in an additive model. This relationship can be perceived as a multiplicative one. To test for its significance, the fractionalization and stability scores for each parliament have been multiplied together, creating a new variable: fractionalization (x) stability (Psf x Psi). Low interaction scores indicate a defractionalized, highly stable party system. Increase in the interactive scores indicates an increase in either fractionalization, instability, or both. High scores indicate highly fractionalized, unstable party systems in parliament.

Table 4:10 presents a frequency distribution indicating the distribution of interaction scores in multiparty and ma-

TABLE 4:10

A Frequency Listing of Party System Interaction Scores:
All Western Peacetime Parliaments, 1918-1974

Fractionalization x Stability Score	Multiparty Parliaments	Majority Party Parliaments	All
.00 to .24	7	9	16
.25 to .49	20	12	32
.50 to .74	37	5	42
.75 to .99	29	11	40
1.00 to 1.24	23	7	30
1.25 to 1.49	14	2	16
1.50 to 2.00	17	4	21
2.00 to 2.99	14	1	15
3.00 to 4.00	9	—	9
4.00 to highest	5	—	5
missing data	2	1	3
Total	177	52	229

jority party parliaments. The high interaction scores occur exclusively among multiparty parliaments. Fourteen multiparty parliaments (8 percent) receive interaction scores exceeding 2.99. As Table 4:11 indicates, such scores exist for parliaments in Finland, France, Germany, and Italy. The lowest score (below .50) occur among both multiparty (15 percent) and majority party (40 percent) parliaments. All countries have parliaments with low fractionalization (x) instability scores except Finland, France, and the Netherlands.

TABLE 4:11

High and Low Party System Interaction Scores
(by country)

| Country | Multiparty Parliaments | | Majority Party Parliaments | |
	Low (yr.)	High (yr.)	Low (yr.)	High (yr.)
Australia	.05 (1961)	1.66 (1951)	.67 (1946)	1.86 (1931)
Austria	.12 (1962)	.77 (1949)	.09 (1966)	.62 (1945)
Belgium	.33 (1958)	1.33 (1936)	1.00 (1950)	—
Canada	.87 (1972)	2.33 (1962)	.46 (1968)	1.27 (1958)
Denmark	.44 (1926)	2.26 (1950)	—	—
Finland	.58 (1954)	3.34 (1924)	—	—
France	2.37 (1946I)	4.59 (1919)	—	—
Germany	.19 (1969)	5.98 (1924II)	.97 (1957)	1.59 (1953)
Great Britain	.92 (1918)	2.38 (1929)	.17 (1959)	1.72 (1924)
Iceland	.26 (1967)	1.67 (1927)	.75 (1931)	—
Ireland	.68 (1954)	1.39 (1925)	.25 (1969)	.84 (1957)
Italy	.41 (1972)	3.67 (1946)	2.10 (1948)	—
Luxembourg	.42 (1954)	1.39 (1925)	—	—
Netherlands	.59 (1952)	2.27 (1972)	—	—
New Zealand	1.01 (1922)	2.52 (1928)	.02 (1963)	.95 (1925)
Norway	.25 (1961)	2.58 (1921)	.47 (1957)	.87 (1949)
Sweden	.27 (1964)	1.68 (1924)	.34 (1968)	—

5 | The Degree of Cleavage Conflict

Cleavage conflict entails disagreement among parties in the positions they take on the cleavage dimensions salient to a nation's electorate. In this study, the primary concern is with the degree to which parliamentary parties are concentrated in similar positions on cleavage dimensions that are salient in the elections for a given parliament. A parliament in which parties are highly concentrated is experiencing low cleavage conflict. A parliament in which parties are widely dispersed is experiencing high cleavage conflict. The inference is that the lower the degree of cleavage conflict (the more concentrated the parties are), the more generalized is the *a priori* willingness of parties to bargain. This chapter presents the procedures employed to measure the degree of cleavage conflict existing for a parliament. Three steps are involved: identifying the cleavage dimensions that are salient for a parliament; specifying party positions on the cleavage dimensions; and measuring the variance of party positions on the cleavage dimensions.

THE SALIENT CLEAVAGE DIMENSIONS

In determining the cleavages that are salient for the parliaments examined in this study, the author has conducted an extensive study of the literature on the party systems of Western Europe and the British Commonwealth. Table 5:1 provides a summary overview of the cleavages deemed salient for each country. In surveying the literature, a basic distinction emerged between the interwar and postwar years. Within each of these time periods, the identity of the salient cleavages for each country remained fairly constant. In the transition from the interwar to the postwar years, however, some major changes occurred, with several countries experiencing a reduction in the number of salient cleavages. For this reason, the interwar and postwar periods were treated separately. Within each period, the cleavages specified in Table 5:1 applied to all parliaments for the appropriate country. In identifying salient cleavages, a major consideration was whether a particular cleavage distinguished the nation's major parties. In some cases, cleavages often identified with certain countries were not employed because they failed to distinguish the nation's major parties, giving rise only to minor parties. The decision as to the salient cleavages is strictly judgmental. The bibliography specifies the works on which I relied in reaching these decisions.

The three most prevalent cleavage dimensions are economic conflict, clericalism, and support of the republic. As Table 5:1 indicates, the economic cleavage applies to all parliaments. Disagreement among parties over *economic* concerns is a factor distinguishing the major parties of all twentieth-century Western parliaments. Among the factors involved in economic conflict are disagreement over government participation in and control of economic decision-making for a country; governmental induced redistribution and equalization of wealth; the necessity and desirability of government ownership of industries; government responsibility for the social welfare of its citizens. Economic conflict in this study is treated as a general composite cleavage dimension reflecting all of these disagreements. *Clericalism* refers to conflict between parties over the proper relation-

TABLE 5:1

The Distribution of Salient Cleavages by Country

Country	Interwar Cleavage	Postwar Cleavage
Australia	economic conflict	economic conflict
Austria	economic conflict clericalism German nationalism	economic conflict clericalism
Belgium	economic conflict clericalism	economic conflict clericalism
Canada	economic conflict regionalism	economic conflict regionalism
Denmark	economic conflict	economic conflict
Great Britain	economic conflict	economic conflict
Finland	economic conflict linguistic conflict	economic conflict linguistic conflict
France	economic conflict clericalism support of the republic	economic conflict clericalism support of the republic
Germany	economic conflict clericalism support of the republic	economic conflict clericalism
Iceland	economic conflict	economic conflict
Ireland		economic conflict
Italy		economic conflict clericalism support of the republic
Luxembourg	economic conflict clericalism	economic conflict clericalism
Netherlands	economic conflict clericalism	economic conflict clericalism
New Zealand	economic conflict	economic conflict
Norway	economic conflict cultural conflict	economic conflict cultural conflict
Sweden	economic conflict foreign policy	economic conflict

ship between church and state. It involves disagreement over the desirability of a state religion, and the general attitude of government to religion. Clericalism has been a highly salient issue in the parliamentary party systems of Austria, Belgium, France, Germany, Italy, Luxembourg, and the Netherlands. Finally, *support of the republic* denotes a cleavage that is critical in those countries in which considerable conflict exists over the legitimacy of the existing form of parliamentary government. At issue are the desirability of representative government and civil liberties. The countries evidencing such conflict include France, Weimar Germany, and Italy. Aside from the foregoing cleavages, a series of conflicts exist whose critical impact on the parliamentary party system is limited to one country. These cleavages will not be detailed here.

PARTIES' CLEAVAGE POSITIONS

For each cleavage dimension, a fifteen-integer scale was employed. The scale ranges from −7 through 0 to +7 and can be conceptualized in the following manner:

The scale assumes a "left-right" dimensionality to each cleavage conflict. For each parliament in this study, the author has given each party a position on each cleavage dimension salient to that parliament. These positions correspond to one of the fifteen integers on the left-right continuum. These positions were determined by surveying the relevant literature for each country. Adjustments in party positions from parliament to parliament were made when the literature indicated that significant changes in party policies warranted such changes. Appendix B specifies the scalar positions given to the parliamentary parties of each country.

Positions on the left-right continuum were attributed to parties on the basis of the following guidelines:

1. If the cleavage dimension related to basic policy dimensions such as governmental intervention in the economy, secularization of the polity, etc., then the following meaning was imputed to the various categories of the model:

a) these are parties that are prosystem as it currently is, zero being the absolute center and —1 or +1 being parties that are center parties but that lean slightly toward the left (—) or toward the right (+).

b) these parties want moderate restructuring of the social system in order to institute some new program in regard to cleavage x.

c) these are parties that are moderate in their opposition to change toward the left and in their opposition to the present system and hark back to some aspect of prior policies in search for the desirable policy on cleavage x.

d) these parties want fundamental, radical change of the social system in regard to cleavage x.

e) these parties are reactionary in opposition to leftist change and want to return to a societal position that they maintain realizes the traditions of the past.

2. In some countries at certain times a critical salient cleavage is support of or opposition toward the political system itself. In those situations where this cleavage is salient the following interpretation is given:

a) parties that accept the political system but very hesitantly

b) parties that moderately support the present system
c) parties that moderately oppose the present system
d) parties that are extremely supportive of the present system
e) parties that extremely oppose the present system

Within the various categories (a, b, c . . .), three different numerical positions can be given, depending on whether a party falls clearly within the designated category or bears slightly toward the left or right within the given category.

The fact that these party positions are determined by the author in a judgmental decision does thrust a degree of subjectivity into the attempt at objective, replicable measurement. The availability of the judgments in Appendix B allows each reader to evaluate them and thus the general validity of the analysis. A second approach is to compare these scalar positions to analogous codings for the same parties by other political scientists. Fortunately, similar codings do exist in the work of Janda and Thomas. Janda analyzes party systems in forty-nine countries during the postwar years; Thomas analyzes party systems in twelve countries from the late 1800s to 1960. Together these two studies cover fourteen of the seventeen countries in the current study, all except Finland, Norway, and Belgium.[1]

Janda and Thomas both place parties on "left-right" issue dimensions. Parties can receive scores ranging from —5 to +5. Among the issues they consider, four concern economic conflict, one relates to clericalism, and two involve regime

[1] For additional information on the work by Janda and Thomas, see Kenneth Janda, *Comparative Political Parties: A Cross-National Handbook* (The Free Press, forthcoming, 1976); John C. Thomas, "The Decline of Ideology in the West: A Longitudinal Study of the Changing Public Policy Orientations of Political Parties in Twelve Nations," unpublished Ph.D. dissertation, Northwestern University, 1974.

support. As the three most recurrent cleavages in the current study are conflicts over economics, clericalism, and regime support, the codings developed by Janda and Thomas provide independent bases by which to evaluate the positions given parties in this study. To obtain codings comparable to the ones employed here, party positions on their four economic issues and on their two regime support dimensions have been combined, creating one economic dimension and one regime support dimension. I employ their clericalism scale unaltered. The resulting product moment coefficients are as follows:[2]

	Interwar	Postwar	Total
Economic Cleavage			
Janda	—	.856 (36)	—
Thomas	.827 (27)	.863 (30)	.825 (57)
Clerical Cleavage			
Janda	—	.800 (20)	—
Thomas	.782 (12)	.779 (15)	.776 (27)
Regime Support Cleavage			
Janda	—	.954 (4)	—
Thomas	.850 (8)	.800 (7)	.828 (15)

The parentheses indicate the number of parties on which the correlations are based. The numbers vary both because there are differences in the number of countries for which the cleavages are salient; and because data on the issue positions of some parties is incomplete. The regression coefficients for the Janda data and the Thomas postwar data are based on party positions as of 1951. The regression co-

[2] Some coefficients differ slightly from those reported in an earlier publication because (1) the Country Party and Liberal Party positions in Australia had been accidentally reversed; (2) majority party parliaments were omitted in the earlier study. See Lawrence C. Dodd, "Party Coalitions in Multiparty Parliaments," APSR 68 (September 1974).

efficients for the Thomas interwar data are based on party positions as of 1931, except for Germany and Austria, for which 1921 was used.

It must be noted that two major differences exist between the coding procedures employed in this study and those employed by Janda and Thomas. First, different spatial dimensions were employed. Janda and Thomas used an eleven-integer scale whereas this study employs a fifteen-integer scale. Because of the difference in dimensionality, correlations between the two scales will not be perfect. Second, different coding criteria were employed. The judgments of party positions for this study were based on a consideration of party orientation toward broad cleavage conflicts in an abstract manner; the codings by Janda and Thomas reflect party positions on specific issues. Considering these differences, the product moment coefficients are high. Correlations with the Janda party positions range from .800 to .954, though the latter is based only on four parties. The correlations with the Thomas party positions range from .779 to .863. The most consistent codings are those for the economic conflict dimension. The correlations for both data sets range between .825 and .863; the economic dimension is the one for which the largest number of party positions exist for comparison. The clerical dimension evidences the least consistency in coding; the coefficients range from .776 to .800 for this dimension. The least number of party positions exist for the regime support cleavage; the coefficients range from .800 to .954. In evaluating these coefficients, it should be noted that coders using the same explicit coding criteria and the same spatial dimensions will often not obtain intercoder reliability scores that are consistently as high as these. Thomas reports that his party positions were derived through double coding procedures, with intercoder reliabilities ranging from .71

to .90. In light of these various considerations, the comparisons provide a good basis for assuming the concurrent validity of the scales.

THE INDEX OF CLEAVAGE CONFLICT (DCC)

As a general indicator of the degree of cleavage conflict (DCC) characterizing a parliamentary party system, the following measure is employed:[3]

$$DCC_t = \frac{\sum_{i=1}^{N_c} \sqrt{V_{c_i}}}{N_c}$$

where N_c = the number of salient cleavages along which parties are distributed in parliament,

V_{c_i} = the variance of party positions on cleavage i in parliament t where

[3] This index is similar to one employed by Michael Taylor and V. M. Herman in their study of "Party Systems and Governmental Stability," APSR 65 (March 1971), 34. Unlike Taylor and Herman, however, more than one cleavage dimension is employed in the overall calculation of cleavage conflict. This does not resolve all of the problems associated with the index, however. Among the potentially significant factors that the index fails to consider are: (1) the relative intensity of cleavages across countries; (2) the relative salience of cleavage for each party; (3) the crosscutting nature of the cleavages. The inclusion of these factors in the cleavage conflict index would necessitate data and measurement techniques that are simply unavailable. Consequently I have employed the less complex measure, realizing that the subsequent findings require reexamination as data and measurement problems are resolved. For an excellent discussion of some of the measurement problems see Douglas W. Rae and Michael Taylor, The Analysis of Political Cleavages (New Haven: Yale University Press, 1970). See also Kenneth Shepsle's review of the book in the APSR 65 (September 1971), 740-792, and the discussion between Shepsle and the authors in the communication section of APSR 65 (December 1971).

$$V_c = \sum f_j\% (X_j - \overline{X})^2$$

given that

$X_{ji} =$ an evaluative position given by the author to party j on cleavage i in parliament t

$\overline{X} = \sum f_j\% \cdot X_j$; the mean of the X_j's (each weighted by $f_j\%$)

$f_j\% =$ the percentage of legislative seats associated with party j in parliament t.

This measure involves determining the variance (V_{c_i}) in party positions for each cleavage dimension (C_i) that is salient for a particular parliament. In determining the variance in party positions, each party's position is weighted by the proportion of seats controlled by the party in parliament. In parliaments for which more than one cleavage exists, the variance scores (more precisely, the standard deviation scores) for each cleavage dimension are summed and this sum is then divided by N_c, the number of cleavages salient for the parliament. The final DCC coefficient indicates the average variance that characterizes parliamentary parties (weighted by size) on the salient cleavages. As an interpretation of this variance, Hays writes that "the variance summarizes *how different* the various cases are from each other, just as it reflects how different each case is from the mean. Given some N cases, the more that pairs of cases tend to be unlike in their scores, the larger the variance and standard deviation."[4]

As noted above, the variance measure employed in the DCC index does weight a party's position by the number of legislators associated with the party. Party positions are weighted on the assumption that a key factor in the bargaining process is the size of the parties that are constrained

[4] William L. Hays, *Statistics* (New York: Holt, Rinehart and Winston, Inc., 1963), p. 180.

from bargaining. For example, consider the two situations present in Figure 5:1. When party positions are not weighted by party size, the two party systems are identical. Judging from party spread on the salient cleavage dimension, co-

FIGURE 5:1

Unweighted Hypothetical Example
of Party Variance on a Cleavage Dimension

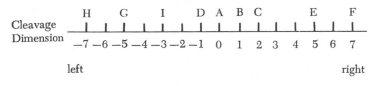

Parliament One

	H	G	I		D A B C		E	F	

Cleavage
Dimension

$-7 \ -6 \ -5 \ -4 \ -3 \ -2 \ -1 \ \ 0 \ \ 1 \ \ 2 \ \ 3 \ \ 4 \ \ 5 \ \ 6 \ \ 7$

left   right

Parliament Two

Cleavage
Dimension

$-7 \ -6 \ -5 \ -4 \ -3 \ -2 \ -1 \ \ 0 \ \ 1 \ \ 2 \ \ 3 \ \ 4 \ \ 5 \ \ 6 \ \ 7$

left   right

alition formation would appear equally difficult in the two settings. Once party strength is considered, as in Figure 5:2, a different picture emerges. In setting A, winning coalitions would not be easily constructed. They would require alliance between parties that evidence considerable differences in cleavage positions. By contrast, in setting B, a reasonably high generalized *a priori* willingness to bargain should exist. A variety of winning coalitions would appear possible as most of the legislators are in parties that are reasonably

FIGURE 5:2

Weighted Hypothetical Example of Party Variance
On a Cleavage Dimension

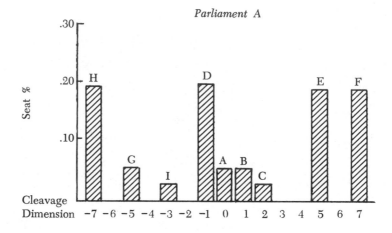

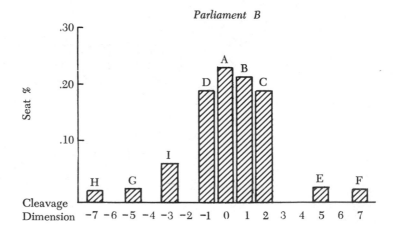

close to one another on the cleavage dimension. Table 5:2 illustrates the calculation of the V_{c_i} scores for the two parliaments presented in Figure 5:2. The standard deviation of party positions for Parliament A is 5.109 where for Parliament B it is 2.022.

An interesting "real-world" example of this situation is the contrast between the French parliament of 1928 and

TABLE 5:2

Illustrative Calculation of the Cleavage Conflict Scores

Party	Party Cleavage Position x_i	Parliament A $f_j\%$	Parliament A $f_j\% \cdot X_j$	Parliament B $f_j\%$	Parliament B $f_j\% \cdot X_j$
A	0	.050	.000	.230	.000
B	1	.050	.050	.225	.225
C	2	.025	.050	.200	.400
D	−1	.200	−.200	.200	−.200
E	5	.200	1.000	.025	.125
F	7	.200	1.400	.010	.070
G	−5	.020	−.250	.025	.125
H	−7	.200	−1.400	.010	−.070
I	−3	.025	−.075	.075	−.225
			.575		.200

Party	Parliament A $(X_j - \overline{X})^2$	Parliament A $\sum f_j\% (X_j - \overline{X})^2$	Parliament B $(X_j - \overline{X})^2$	Parliament B $\sum f_j\% (X_j - \overline{X})^2$
A	.331	.017	.040	.009
B	.276	.014	.640	.144
C	2.031	.051	3.240	.648
D	2.481	.496	1.440	.288
E	19.580	3.916	23.040	.576
F	41.280	8.256	46.240	.462
G	31.080	1.554	27.040	.676
H	57.380	11.476	51.840	.518
I	12.780	.320	10.240	.768
		$V_{c_i} = 26.10$		$V_{c_i} = 4.089$
		$\sqrt{V_{c_i}} = 5.109$		$\sqrt{V_{c_i}} = 2.022$

the German parliament of 1930. These two parliaments are similar in a number of ways. First, both possess highly fractionalized and unstable party systems. Second, at a superficial level the two party systems appear very similar in terms of cleavage conflict. They share the same three critical cleavages, as Table 5:1 indicates, and the distribution of parties on these three cleavages is very similar. As an example, Figure 5:3 presents the positions of the significant parliamentary parties on the regime support dimension.

Despite the foregoing similarities, the distribution of party strength on the cleavage dimensions differs dramatically between the two parliaments. This point is clarified in Figure 5:4. In this figure, party positions on the regime support dimension are weighted by proportional size of the parties holding the various positions. In the 1928 French parliament, by the author's subjective evaluation, the monarchists and Communists were as extreme in their opposition to the republic as the monarchist, Nazi, and Communist parties in 1930 Germany. However, the latter parties were considerably stronger in Germany than the former parties in France. Consequently, the German parliament evidences more conflict or polarization than the French parliament. The cleavage conflict score for the regime support dimension in the former is 3.457 whereas France receives a comparable score of 2.10.

Clearly, weighting party position by legislative seats incorporates a vital element into the DCC index. As constructed, the index should constitute a reasonable indicator of the average degree to which partisans in parliament share similar or different positions on the salient cleavage dimensions. If the cleavage conflict score is low, the inference is that the major parties are clustered together and that a highly generalized *a priori* willingness to bargain exists in the parliament. High cleavage conflict (DCC) scores

FIGURE 5:3

Party Positions on the Regime Support Cleavage Dimension: The French Third Republic (1928) and Weimar Germany (1930)

France (1928)

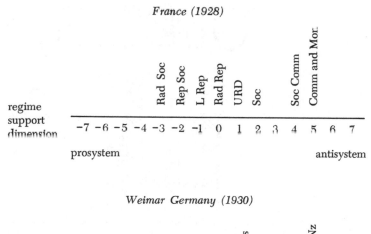

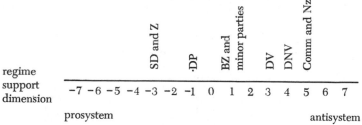

Note:

France		Germany	
Rad Soc = −3		Z and SD	= −3
Rep Soc = −2		DP	= −1
L Rep + = −1		BZ and minor parties =	1
Rad Rep = 0		DV	= 3
URD = 1		DNV	= 4
Soc = 2		Comm and NZ	= 5
Soc Comm = 4			
Comm and Mon = 5			

FIGURE 5:4

Weighted Party Positions on the Regime Support Cleavage
Dimension: The French Third Republic (1928)
and Weimar Germany (1930)

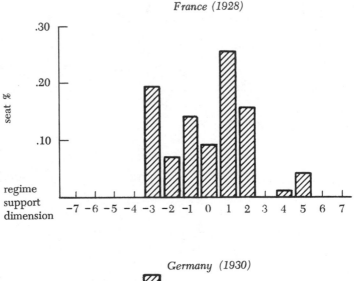

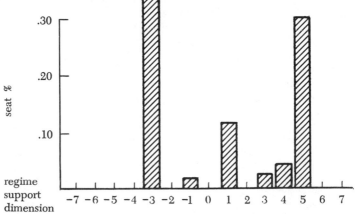

indicate that the major parties differ considerably in their positions on the salient cleavage dimensions; the generalized *a priori* willingness to bargain should be low.

As with party system fractionalization and instability, cleavage conflict varies significantly between parliaments. Table 5:3 presents the DCC scores for all peacetime par-

TABLE 5:3

A Frequency Listing of Cleavage Conflict Scores:
All Western Peacetime Parliaments, 1918-1974

Cleavage Conflict Scores	Multiparty Parliaments	Majority Party Parliaments	All
1.500 to 1.849	6	3	9
1.850 to 1.949	11	7	18
1.950 to 2.049	19	13	32
2.050 to 2.149	17	4	21
2.150 to 2.249	27	8	35
2.250 to 2.349	27	5	32
2.350 to 2.449	19	3	22
2.450 to 2.549	14	7	21
2.550 to 2.649	13		13
2.650 to 2.749	9	1	10
2.750 to 2.849	5	1	6
2.850 to highest	10		10
Total	177	52	229

liaments from 1918 to 1974. A first contrast to note between majority party and multiparty parliaments is the presence of extremely polarized parliaments among the latter but not the former. Approximately 13 percent of the multiparty parliaments have experienced cleavage conflict scores exceeding 2.649. As Table 5:4 indicates these parliaments include the 1930 Austrian parliament, the first Danish parliament of 1920, Finland (1922), France (1956), the 1930 German parliament, and the Swedish parliament in 1920. By contrast, only two (4 percent) of the majority party parliaments received extremely high cleavage conflict scores: the 1927 Austrian parliament and the New Zealand parliament in 1938.

Both multiparty and majority party systems have experienced a significant number of depolarized parliaments, though the proportion of such parliaments is much larger among the latter. Twenty percent of the multiparty parliaments received DCC scores below 2.050, including parliaments in Belgium (1925), Denmark (1971), Finland (1966), France (1928), Germany (1965), Ireland (1961), Luxembourg (1968), the Netherlands (1956), Norway (1961), and Sweden (1948). Forty-four percent of the majority party parliaments experienced depolarization, including parliaments in all countries experiencing majority partism except Belgium, Great Britain, and Iceland.

TABLE 5:4

High and Low Cleavage Conflict Scores (by country)

Country	Multiparty Parliaments		Majority Party Parliaments	
	Low (yr.)	High (yr.)	Low (yr.)	High (yr.)
Australia	2.090 (1934)	2.320 (1928)	2.030 (1931)	2.263 (1946)
Austria	2.200 (1949)	3.050 (1930)	2.030 (1945)	2.759 (1927)
Belgium	1.845 (1925)	2.460 (1946)	2.220 (1950)	—
Canada	2.190 (1921)	2.490 (1962)	1.900 (1958)	2.370 (1930)
Denmark	1.880 (1971)	2.960 (1920I)	—	—
Finland	1.945 (1966)	2.730 (1922)	—	—
France	2.043 (1928)	2.910 (1956)	—	—
Germany	1.750 (1965)	2.918 (1930)	1.857 (1957)	2.062 (1953)
Great Britain	2.330 (1918)	2.630 (1923)	2.090 (1931)	2.518 (1922)
Iceland	2.230 (1927)	2.630 (1959)	2.160 (1931)	—
Ireland	1.910 (1961)	2.310 (1951)	1.964 (1957)	2.120 (1969)
Italy	2.160 (1946)	2.530 (1953)	1.870 (1948)	—
Luxembourg	2.040 (1968)	2.560 (1948)	1.900 (1919)	—
Netherlands	2.000 (1956)	2.310 (1933)	—	—
New Zealand	2.110 (1931)	2.360 (1922)	1.936 (1949)	2.739 (1938)
Norway	1.855 (1961)	2.880 (1924)	1.800 (1949)	1.863 (1953)
Sweden	1.830 (1948)	2.980 (1920)	1.874 (1968)	—

6 | Cabinet Coalitional Status and Cabinet Durability

Of all the concepts requiring operational definition in Part II, the cabinet characteristics have received least prior consideration in the literature of comparative politics. While several studies have employed operational measures of cabinet durability, cabinet coalitional status has largely escaped systematic operational treatment in past comparative studies. The purpose of this short chapter is to specify the operational measures of these two variables employed in this study. The frequency distribution for cabinet durability is presented in Chapter 1. Chapter 7 presents the frequency distribution of coalitional status scores.

CABINET COALITIONAL STATUS

Coalitional status refers to the nature of the partisan composition characterizing a cabinet: do the ministerial party or parties constitute a minority or majority cabinet, a minimum winning or oversized cabinet, a reasonably secure or extremely vulnerable cabinet? Throughout this study it is assumed that the installation and maintenance of a cabinet requires a bare parliamentary majority: a secure cabinet must therefore control a parliamentary majority. Cabinets may be installed though the ministerial parties lack a parliamentary majority. Such cabinets are of minority status and exist only so long as some parties outside of the cabinet either abstain from voting or provide support of the cabinet by voting for it on critical questions. The parties in the cabinet do not hold a majority of the seats in parliament and thus they cannot guarantee the success of the cabinet in votes of confidence. In addition to minority cabinets, minimum winning cabinets are possible: they exist when (1) the parties in the cabinet control a parliamentary majority and (2) when no party in the cabinet could be removed and the nominal majority maintained. Finally, an oversized cabinet exists when at least one ministerial party could be removed from the cabinet and the cabinet's majority status maintained.

Coalitional status is not concerned solely with the three broad types of partisan composition. Of equal importance is the degree to which oversized or undersized cabinets deviate from minimum winning status. This deviation involves two dimensions: the number of parties involved in the deviation and the weight (size) of the parties involved in the deviation. Because of the extra bargaining costs involved, it is a greater deviation among oversized cabinets to have admitted two extra parties to ministerial status than one extra party. From the standpoint of undersized cabinets, it is a greater deviation if two additional parties rather than one would be required to provide minimum winning status. In the former situation, there are at least two parties with which to bargain and thus a greater opportunity exists to reduce at least partially the gap between a cabinet's existing minority status and minimum winning status.

Among oversized cabinets, the size of the extra parties is important as an indicator of their probable significance in the control of ministerial seats and thus the deprivation they produce for other cabinet parties. Among undersized cabinets the size of the missing parties indicates the distance of the cabinet from a secure, majority status and thus the general vulnerability of the cabinet. The greater the percentage of parliamentary votes a cabinet must obtain from legislators outside of the ministerial parties, the more difficult will be the cabinet's task in providing for a parliamentary majority during votes of confidence.

Based on these perspectives, the following index of cabinet coalitional status is employed in this study:

1. The percentage of legislative seats held by each parliamentary party is determined.

2. It is determined whether the parties in the cabinet hold a majority of the legislative seats within parliament.

3. If the parties in the cabinet do hold a majority of the seats in parliament, *but* if the subtraction of any party from the cabinet would deprive the coalition of its majority status, the cabinet is termed a *minimum winning coalition* (*mwc*).

a) All such cabinets are given a score of zero.

b) In Chapter 7, all parliaments with a majority party have been omitted from the analysis and thus all minimum winning cabinets contain at least two parties. In Chapters 8 and 9, majority party cabinets are included and thus some minimum winning cabinets possess only one party.

4. If the parties in the cabinet do not hold a majority of the seats in parliament, the cabinet is designated a less than minimum winning cabinet ($< mwc$).

a) Among less than minimum winning cabinets we are interested in determining the extent to which these cabinets deviate from minimum winning status.

b) The following formula is used to determine the extent of this deviance:

$$< mwc = -D_{mwc} = N_a \left[\sum w_a \right]$$

where w_a = the weight (percentage of legislative seats)

of those parties whose addition to the cabinet would make it a minimum winning coalition. Since more than one set of such parties can exist, choose the set whose Σw_a is smallest, given that it would still produce a minimum winning cabinet; and where $N_a =$ the number of parties whose addition to the cabinet would produce the necessary Σw_a to produce a cabinet of smallest minimum winning status. In case of ties, choose that N_a which is smallest.

5. If the parties in the cabinet hold a majority of the seats in parliament, and the subtraction of some party(-ies) will *not* deprive the coalition of its majority status, then the coalition is designated a *greater than minimum winning cabinet* ($> mwc$).

a) Among $> mwc$ cabinets, we are interested in determining the extent to which the cabinet deviates from (surpasses) minimum winning status.

b) The following formula is used to determine the extent of this deviancy:

$$ > mwc = +D_{mwc} = N_E \left[\sum w_E \right] $$

where $w_E =$ the weight (percentage of legislative seats) of those parties that could be subtracted from the cabinet and its majority status maintained. Where more than one set of such extra parties exists, choose that set with the largest Σw_E; and where $N_E =$ the number of extra parties contained in Σw_E. In cases of ties, choose that N_E which is smallest.

6. Summary. These procedures give us an indicator of the coalitional status of cabinets for nonmajority party parliaments. A score of zero indicates that a cabinet is of minimum winning status. A negative score indicates that a cabinet is of less than minimum winning status. A posi-

tive score indicates that a cabinet is of greater than minimum winning status. The larger the absolute score, the more a cabinet deviates from minimum winning status.

Table 6:1 presents hypothetical cabinets and the coalitional status scores appropriate to those cabinets. The first three examples illustrate minority cabinets. For each of the first two undersized cabinets, one party in parliament could enter the cabinet and provide minimum winning status. In the third example, two parties are necessary additions if minimum winning status is to be attained: in this example, consequently, N_a is 2. The fourth example illustrates a minimum winning cabinet. In the fifth example, an extra party is added to the minimum winning cabinet, illustrating an oversized cabinet. Examples six and seven provide alternative situations in which the cabinet contains two extra parties. Without further elaboration the reader should be able to apply the earlier rules and arrive at the appropriate coalitional status scores.

It must be acknowledged that the operational measure employed in this study is arbitrary to a degree. Other approaches consistent with the general theory could be used. As a check on the consequences of different measures, all relevant hypotheses have been examined with the following indices:

CCS1–cabinet coalitional status 1 (the index outlined above).

CCS2–cabinet coalitional status 2. The same procedures followed in CCS1 were maintained with these exceptions: (a) for $< mwc$, choose that $N_a \Sigma w_a$ that is smallest; (b) for $> mwc$, choose that $N_e \Sigma w_e$ that is largest.

CCS3–cabinet coalitional status 3. The scores are based solely on Σw_a or Σw_e without weighting by N_a or N_e. All other aspects of CCS1 are followed.

TABLE 6:1

Hypothetical Cabinets and Illustrative Coalitonal Status Scores

Example	Ministerial Parties	Missing Parties	Additional Parties	Calculus	Score
1	A + B	C	—	1 (−.06)	−.06
2	E	B	—	1 (−.20)	−.20
3	A	B + C	—	2 (−.26)	−.52
4	E + B	—	—	*mwc*	.00
5	B + C + E	—	C	1 (.06)	+.06
6	B + C + D + E	—	C + D	2 (.13)	+.26
7	A + E + B + D + F	—	E + F	2 (.42)	+.84

where:

Party seat %		Party seat %	
A = .25		D = .07	
B = .20		E = .35	
C = .06		F = .07	
		Total = 1.00	

In the body of the study, CCS1 will be reported; results based on CCS2 and CCS3 will be reported in Appendix A.[1]

CABINET DURABILITY

The final operational problem is delineating cabinet durability. Past scholars, notably Blondel, Taylor, and Herman,[2] have stated that a cabinet exists so long as no change occurs in the ministerial parties or the prime minister. For present purposes, the utility of this definition is questionable. A change in prime minister, through death for example, really does not constitute necessarily a meaningful change in cabinets if there is no other ministerial change. More importantly, the utility of operational definitions really depends on the theory within which one is working. In the present theory the key element is the coalitional behavior of parties.

---

[1] In this study I have purposely avoided including within the coalitional status index any factor reflecting the ideological compatibility or incompatibility of parties. For future consideration, however, a reasonable argument can be made that minimum winning status (or deviant status) must be considered with the ideological positions of the parties in mind. Two concepts would appear useful: minimal connected winning coalitions (i.e., cabinets composed of parties adjacent to an ideological or cleavage dimensions); minimum winning compact coalitions (in a cabinet composed of parties not only adjacent to one another but also that set of adjacent parties closest to one another on ideological or cleavage dimensions). A third variation could be employed: a minimum winning cabinet could include an "extra" party (one not nominally necessary to majority status) if the extra party held a cleavage position between two parties each of which was "necessary" to the coalition. All of these conceptual variations are useful and need investigation. For an excellent discussion introducing the concept of minimal connected winning coalitions, see Robert Axelrod, *Conflict of Interest* (Chicago: Markham, 1970).

[2] Jean Blondel, "Party Systems and Patterns of Government in Western Democracies," *Canadian Journal of Political Science* 1 (June 1968), 198-199; Michael Taylor and V. H. Herman, "Party Systems and Governmental Stability," *APSR* 65 (March 1971), 28-37.

Because of this, the most consistent approach is to define cabinet durability in terms of the maintenance of the party coalition in the cabinet. Thus the following operational definition is employed in this study: a cabinet exists so long as there is no change in the parties that compose the cabinet. This definition is consistent with the theory stated in this study since the theory centers on the conditions under which party coalitions arise and on the durability of different types of coalitions. However, several qualifications are in order.

First, this is a very limited definition of cabinet durability. Its relevance to larger questions such as regime persistence will depend on the extent to which this conception of cabinet durability is consistent with larger theories that may be developed linking cabinet durability to these other phenomena. For example, this conception of cabinet durability will be useful only partially in theories that emphasize the need for personnel continuity as a basis for effective government and regime persistence: party continuity is only one element to be discussed in personnel continuity. On the other hand, if a theory emphasizes primarily the need for party continuity in cabinets, then the conception of cabinet durability employed here would be useful.

Second, the precise operational definition of cabinet durability employed in this study is not the only conceivable one that is consistent with the theory of cabinet durability outlined in this study. A key question is this: what constitutes a breakdown or change in a party coalition within the cabinet? A variety of answers can be given. First, any alteration in the distribution of payoffs (ministerial seats) among parties could be viewed as a breakdown in the old coalition and the formation of a new one, even if the parties in the cabinet remained the same. Second, only "significant" alteration in payoff distribution is conceived to be a breakdown. Third, only changes in the parties composing the cabinet could be viewed as a change in cabinet coalitional status.

There is no easy way to choose among these approaches. Rather, my position is that the greater the number of defensible operational definitions that sustain the predictions of the theory, the more faith we have in the theory. Thus, in the long run all of the foregoing approaches should be employed. For the present, I am constrained by problems of data collection and verification. It is extremely difficult to collect and verify cabinet data for the countries and time periods covered in this study. While it proves possible to determine the identity and duration of parties in the cabinets it is more difficult to isolate all of the changes that occur in the distribution of ministerial seats among parties in a coalition. It is even more difficult to specify which ministerial seats are the most desirable ones for parties in each country's parliament. These problems have presented obstacles that have not been overcome fully for most cabinets in this study. Because of these data collection problems the third approach is employed exclusively throughout this book.

III | Analysis

7 | Party Coalitions in Multiparty Parliaments

Multiparty parliaments predominate in Western parliamentary democracies. They constitute over 75 percent of all peacetime parliaments that formed from 1918 to 1974. There is no parliamentary regime that has not experienced multiparty politics. During the first five years of the 1970s, in fact, fourteen of the sixteen nations in this study experienced at least one multiparty parliament, including Great Britain, birthplace of the two-party system.[1] Against this backdrop, it is surprising that so little systematic knowledge exists in regard to multiparty parliaments. As Chapter 1 indicates, the predominant myth is that cabinets by their very nature must be transient in multiparty regimes. Neither majority coalitions nor minority cabinets should endure. As Chapter 1 documents, this myth will not withstand close scrutiny. It simply is not true that peacetime multiparty parliaments produce only transient cabinets. Wide variation exists in cabinet durability among multiparty parliaments.

The theory outlined in Part I argues that a cabinet's coalitional status determines cabinet durability. Minimum winning cabinets should endure; as cabinets depart from minimum winning status, cabinet durability should decrease. The coalitional status of the cabinet is determined, in turn, by the nature of the bargaining conditions that exist within parliament. Oversized cabinets should form in

[1] This count excludes France, as the Fifth Republic is not included in the study.

conditions of low to moderate *a priori* bargaining constraints and low information certainty. Undersized cabinets should form in conditions of moderate to high bargaining constraints and low information certainty. Minimum winning cabinets should form under a wide range of *a priori* bargaining constraints as long as high information certainty exists. The primary exception will be in conditions of extremely high *a priori* bargaining constraints wherein no set of parties is both willing to bargain and constitutes a parliamentary majority. In such situations, information certainty will influence the degree to which the cabinet that forms departs from minimum winning status; low information certainty, however, cannot ensure a minimum winning cabinet.

The purpose of this chapter is to examine these propositions for all peacetime multiparty parliaments listed in Table 1:4. Cleavage conflict is the indicator of *a priori* willingness of parties to bargain. Party system fractionalization and instability are indicators of information uncertainty. The propositions are difficult to test because of the complex interaction hypothesized between the various parliamentary bargaining conditions. The theory does not predict simple additive relations: rather, given different degrees of *a priori* willingness to bargain (cleavage conflict), information certainty (party system fractionalization and instability) should produce exactly the opposite behavioral patterns. This is a fairly difficult process to examine. The following sections present an exploratory test of the theory that hopefully sheds new light on cabinet behavior within multiparty parliaments and suggests new directions for extensive research.[2]

[2] An earlier version of the analysis in this chapter is contained in Lawrence C. Dodd, "Party Coalitions in Multiparty Parliaments," *APSR* 68 (September 1974). Slight differences exist between the

The first test of the theory is to examine the simple relationships between party system characteristics and cabinet coalitional status. In these tests, cleavage conflict is viewed as an indicator of the generalized *a priori* willingness to bargain; the predicted relationship can be inferred from Figure 2:1. Party system fractionalization and instability are indicators of information uncertainty: in conditions of low fractionalization and low instability, minimum winning cabinets should form; as fractionalization and instability increase, cabinets should deviate from minimum winning status.

Figure 7:1 presents the pattern that obtains between party system conflict and cabinet coalitional status in multiparty parliaments, 1918-1974. This pattern indicates that there is a general relationship between party system conflict and cabinet coalitional status. Oversized cabinets form predominantly in the area of low to moderate cleavage conflict. Undersized cabinets form primarily in areas of moderate to high cleavage conflict. Minimum winning cabinets form under virtually the entire range of cleavage conflict conditions although they predominate in the area of low to moderately high cleavage conflict. Overall, the correlation between party system conflict and cabinet coalitional status is —.520. Cleavage conflict accounts for approximately 27 percent of the variance in cabinet coalitional status. A logarithmic transformation of the cleavage conflict score will not improve upon this performance—the regression coefficient actually decreases to —.509.

---

regression coefficients reported in the two studies because this chapter extends the analysis to May 1974 and consequently includes cabinets not contained in the earlier study.

FIGURE 7:1

The Covariation of Cleavage Conflict and Cabinet
Coalitional Status: All Partisan Cabinets in Peacetime
Multiparty Parliaments, 1918-1974

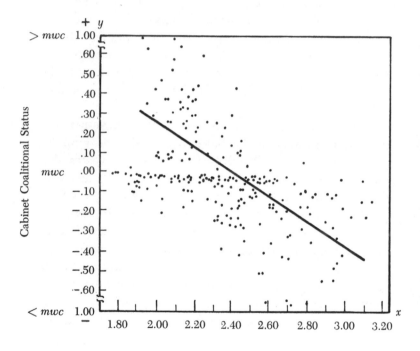

$$r = -.520 \qquad N = 238$$
$$x = 2.319 \qquad a = 0.989$$
$$y = -.017 \qquad b = -.434$$

A particularly interesting aspect of the pattern in Figure 7:1 is the fact that oversized cabinets have not formed in the most extreme range of depolarization. Below the score of 1.90, no oversized cabinet exists. The pattern could be an artifact of measurement problems associated with the cleavage conflict index. Another possibility, however, is that a slight relationship does exist in fact between cleavage conflict, fractionalization, and stability. As an empirical phenomena, in other words, some cleavage conflict may be implicit in party system fractionalization and instability. Thus fractionalization and instability (the determinants of information uncertainty and thus oversized cabinets) do not exist among the most depolarized parliaments. This suggests that the interpretive procedures followed in this study are limited in their ability to test all aspects of the analytic theory presented in Chapter 2. Nevertheless, Figure 7:1 indicates that the general pattern, if not all conceptual possibilities, does hold in the relationship between cleavage conflict and coalitional status.

Figure 7:2 presents the scatterplot relating Psf x Psi and cabinet coalitional status. The two lines in this graph indicate the average coalitional status of cabinets on either side of minimum winning status; minimum winning cabinets are entered in the determination of both lines. The patterns indicate that there is a very general relationship between cabinet coalitional status and the interaction of fractionalization with instability. To analyze the linear relation between cabinet deviation and Psf x Psi, the designation as to whether a cabinet is oversized or undersized can be dropped. Viewed in this manner a .339 regression coefficient obtains. Similar patterns hold when we examine the relation between cabinet coalitional status and fractionalization or instability taken separately. The coefficients are .293 and .308 for fractionalization and instability, respective-

FIGURE 7:2

The Covariation of Psf x Psi and Cabinet Coalitional Status:
All Partisan Cabinets in Peacetime Multiparty
Parliaments, 1918-1974

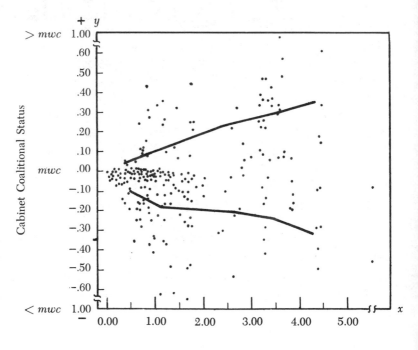

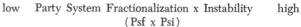

low   Party System Fractionalization x Instability   high
(Psf x Psi)

N = 238

ly, when correlated with the absolute deviation of cabinets from minimum winning status. Fractionalization, instability, and the interaction term all enter in a regression equation together at a statistically significant level. The multiple regression coefficient is .361, indicating that party system fractionalization, instability, and their interaction account for approximately 13 percent of the absolute deviation of cabinets from minimum winning status.

These findings support the hypothesis that party system fractionalization and instability influence the deviation of cabinets from minimum winning status. Minimum winning cabinets do form primarily in parliaments experiencing low party system fractionalization and instability whereas deviant cabinets predominate in the more fractionalized and unstable party systems. Nevertheless, the analysis does not constitute a full test of the theory. It indicates nothing about the *direction* of cabinet deviation from minimum winning status and little about the *degree* of cabinet deviation. According to the theory, both the direction and degree are products of the complex interaction of fractionalization and/or instability with cleavage conflict.

PARTY SYSTEMS AND CABINET COALITIONAL STATUS:
COMPLEX RELATIONSHIPS

The more complex predicted relationship between party system characteristics and cabinet coalitional status can be summarized as follows: at low levels of cleavage conflict, party system fractionalization and instability should produce a tendency toward oversized coalitions; as the degree of cleavage conflict increases, party system fractionalization and instability should create a tendency toward undersized coalitions. Low fractionalization and high stability, by contrast, should produce a tendency toward minimum winning cabinets.

In order to investigate these predictions in a simple manner, Table 7:1 divides the cleavage conflict index into four categories (ranging from low to high) and the Psf x Psi index into two categories. As Table 7:1 indicates, at every

TABLE 7:1

Coalitional Status,
Cleavage Conflict, and Fractionalization (x) Stability:
Peacetime Multiparty Parliaments

Cleavage Conflict	The Interaction of Party System Fractionalization and Instability (Psf x Psi)	
	low (.00 to .99)	high (1.00 to highest)
high		
4	−.200 (8)	−.268 (26)
3	−.077 (33)	−.157 (40)
2	−.003 (24)	+.156 (57)
1	+.0145 (36)	+.280 (14)
low		

Code:	Cleavage Conflict	Fractionalization (x) Stability
	1 = lowest to 2.049	1 = .00 to .99 (low)
	2 = 2.050 to 2.349	2 = 1.00 to highest (high)
	3 = 2.350 to 2.649	
	4 = 2.650 to highest	

Note: All entries indicate the average coalitional status scores; the parentheses indicate the number of cabinets involved.

level of cleavage conflict, parliaments experiencing low fractionalization and instability contain cabinets that approach minimum winning status more closely, as an average, than similar parliaments experiencing high fractionalization and high instability. Among parliaments experiencing low cleavage conflict, conditions of high Psf x Psi produce cabinets that, as an average, are significantly oversized. Among parliaments experiencing high cleavage conflict, conditions of high Psf x Psi produce cabinets that, as an average, are significantly undersized.

Table 7:1 demonstrates the relationship fairly well, but gives no real grasp of the significance of the relationship. In order to determine the power of the relationship using regression analysis, a complex interaction term has been created from the three party system variables. First, the party system cleavage conflict scores have been standardized. This procedure does not alter the strength of the relationship with cabinet coalitional status. It does, however, change the numerical nature of the cleavage conflict scores: low scores are now negative and high conflict scores are positive. These standardized scores have been multiplied with the unstandardized scores for party system fractionalization, party system stability, and Psf x Psi. The resulting indices will be referred to as Complex Party System Indices (CPSI): index 1(CPSI1) represents the interaction scores between party system conflict (DCC) and party system fractionalization; CPSI2 represents the interaction score between party system cleavage conflict and party system instability; CPSI3 represents the interaction score between cleavage conflict and Psf x Psi.

Large negative CPSI scores indicate parliamentary party systems that experience moderate to low cleavage conflict (thus the negative scores) and are highly fractionalized, unstable, or both, depending on the index under consideration. Employing a variation on Sartori's terminology in order to characterize such parliaments, these parliaments can be referred to as experiencing unstable and *depolarized* hyperpluralism: the party system is unstable, basically moderate in terms of interparty conflict (i.e., major parties not widely dispersed), and highly fractionalized in terms of the number and strength of parties. In such a parliament, oversized cabinets are expected. France throughout much of the Third and Fourth Republic illustrates unstable, depolarized hyperpluralism.

Large positive CPSI scores indicate parliaments that experience moderate to high cleavage conflict between parliamentary parties (thus the positive scores) and are highly fractionalized, unstable, or both. For simplicity, this condition can be referred to as unstable, *polarized* hyperpluralism: the parliamentary party system is unstable, highly fractionalized, and polarized with the major parties dispersed toward extreme positions on the salient cleavage dimensions. In such systems, undersized cabinets are expected. A number of parliaments illustrate this situation in varying degrees, including Fourth Republic France from 1956 to 1958, Weimar Germany throughout most of its existence, and interwar Norway.

The intermediate CPSI scores indicate parliaments that experience lower degrees of party system fractionalization or instability: parliaments that obtain low but positive scores possess more polarized systems. Such parliaments can be referred to as experiencing stable, polarized pluralism. In such conditions, minimum winning cabinets are expected except under extremely polarized conditions wherein parties will not consider bargaining even with information certainty; in the latter situation, minority cabinets will form. Interwar Sweden and the later years of the First Austrian Republic approach stable, extremely polarized pluralism. Luxembourg illustrates stable, moderately polarized pluralism. In contrast to these countries are those that receive low but negative CPSI scores: this experience is stable, depolarized pluralism. In such situations, minimum winning cabinets are expected. Recent experience in Australia and West Germany illustrates this condition.

The appropriate interaction (CPSI) terms have been calculated for all multiparty parliaments, 1918-1974. As an example of the resulting relationship, Figure 7:3 presents the covariation of cabinet coalitional status and CPSI3. In terms of its general form as predicted in Part 1, the relationship is curvilinear though the curvilinear characteristic obtains only in conditions of high cleavage conflict. To capture this curvilinear form employing linear statistics, the CPSI3 scores have been logarithmically transformed; the resulting product moment coefficient is —.637. Similar patterns obtain for the covariation between cabinet coalitional status and both CPSI1 and CPSI2; the product moment coefficient associated with each of these independent variables is —.547 and —.601, respectively. The multiple regression coefficient obtaining when these two variables are entered in an additive model is .618. The inclusion of CPSI3 (logged) raises the coefficient to .645 with all three variables entering the equation at a statistically significant level (.01). Cleavage conflict (DCC) also will enter the regression equation at the .01 level, but produces no interesting increase in variance explained.

These results suggest three conclusions:

1. As we move from the simple relationship between cleavage conflict and coalitional status to the more complex interactive patterns, we observe an increase in variance explained of approximately 14 percent; overall, the three CPSI variables (logged) account for over 41 percent of the variance in cabinet coalitional status.

2. It is the interactive occurrence of fractionalization and instability together, and their joint interaction with cleavage conflict, that seems most influential in deter-

FIGURE 7:3

The Covariation of CPSI3 and Cabinet Coalitional Status:
All Partisan Cabinets in Peacetime Multiparty
Parliaments, 1918-1974

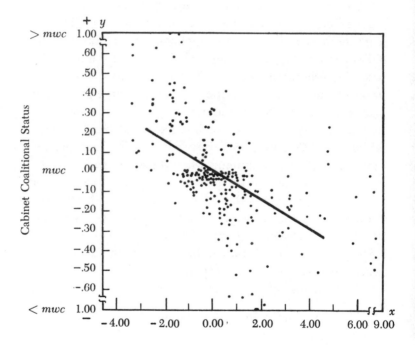

CPSI3

$r = -.573$ $N = 238$
$x = .247$ $a = -.00067$
$y = -.017$ $b = -.06695$

mining cabinet coalitional status, with CPSI3 (logged) accounting for over 40 percent of the variance in cabinet coalitional status.

3. Once its complex interaction with party system fractionalization and instability is considered, cleavage conflict has only a slight independent effect on cabinet coalitional status.

These findings support the proposition that the complex interaction between party system fractionalization, instability, and cleavage conflict determines cabinet coalitional status. This interactive process can be captured in a very parsimonious yet powerful fashion through the use of one variable (CPSI3-logged). The substantive relationship can be summarized in the following simplified manner: oversized cabinets form primarily in unstable, depolarized hyperfractionalized parliaments; undersized cabinets form in unstable, polarized, hyperfractionalized parliaments; minimum winning cabinets form under conditions of stable, polarized pluralism and stable depolarized pluralism. Of course, a good deal of variance does remain unexplained within these general patterns. Given the nature of the theory unexplained variance is to be expected: party system characteristics influence only the general range of parliamentary conditions that will prevail; within that range an ongoing process of bargaining, maneuvering, and cabinet transformations will take place. Nevertheless, these findings are strong, parsimonious, and theoretically coherent. The critical question therefore is whether they matter: is cabinet coalitional status related to cabinet durability?

CABINET COALITIONAL STATUS AND CABINET DURABILITY

According to our theory, cabinet durability is a function of cabinet coalitional status. Minimum winning coalitions should be the most durable cabinets; as cabinets deviate from minimum winning status, cabinet durability should decrease. In oversized cabinets, coalition partners will attempt to decrease the size of the cabinet toward minimum winning status so as to maximize their ministerial status. Undersized coalitions will face a tendency for larger coalitions to arise and replace them, or for parliament to be dissolved and new elections held. In either case, the further a cabinet deviates from minimum winning status, the more rapidly these maneuvers should occur.

Figure 7:4 presents the relationship that obtains between cabinet coalitional status and cabinet durability for the seventeen parliaments during peacetime years, 1918-1974. As can be seen, the general aggregate predictions derived from the theory are supported by the data. Minimum winning cabinets are more durable than oversized or minority cabinets. In addition, the durability of cabinets is a function of the degree to which cabinets deviate from minimum winning status. This relationship is curvilinear in nature. Employing w^2 (an analysis of variance statistic that indicates the percentage of variance accounted for in curvilinear relationships),[3] cabinet coalitional status explains approximately 27 percent of the variance in cabinet durability.

In order to examine the relationship employing linear statistics the absolute deviation of cabinets from minimum winning status is employed as the independent variable. In addition cabinet durability has been logged. Using these procedures, cabinet coalitional status statistically explains over 21 percent of the variance in cabinet durability (logged). A second procedure which can be employed to estimate the significance of this relationship with linear statistics is to transform the independent variable according

[3] William L. Hays, *Statistics* (New York: Holt, Rinehart and Winston, 1963), p. 544.

FIGURE 7:4

The Covariation of Cabinet Durability and Coalitional
Status: All Partisan Cabinets in Peacetime Multiparty
Parliaments, 1918-1974

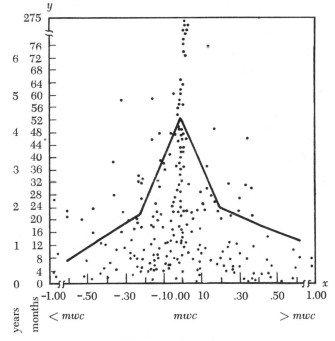

Cabinet Coalitional Status

N = 238

to the following procedure: $X' = 1/(1 + x)$. If this transformation is conducted, the resulting correlation coefficient is .493; using this procedure, cabinet coalitional status accounts for approximately 24 percent of the variance in cabinet durability (logged). Judging from these various statistical procedures, we can conclude that cabinet coalitional status does account for a sizable proportion of the variance in cabinet durability. These findings support the hypothesis that cabinet durability is at least partially a function of cabinet coalitional status.

Aside from indicating the strength of the relationship between cabinet durability and cabinet coalitional status, Figure 7:4 also indicates a second interesting pattern. Oversized cabinets are less durable generally than undersized cabinets. Taken as homogeneous groups, oversized cabinets last for approximately fifteen months on the average whereas undersized cabinets last for approximately twenty months. Among extremely deviant cabinets (those receiving an absolute score of at least .20), oversized cabinets last for eleven months whereas undersized cabinets last for fifteen months. Apparently, it is more difficult to resolve an undersized cabinet toward minimum winning status than it is to resolve an oversized cabinet toward minimum winning status. In the former, party leaders must contend not only with the possibility of information uncertainty but also with considerable *a priori* conflict between parties. In the latter the party systems are so depolarized that information certainty is the primary influence on the durability of the coalition.

PARTY SYSTEMS AND CABINET DURABILITY

Thus far we have seen that the coalitional status of cabinets is at least partially a function of the parliamentary party system whereas cabinet durability is a function of cabinet coalitional status. It should follow, therefore, that cabinet durability is an indirect function of the parliamentary party system. Figure 7:5 presents the pattern that obtains between CPSI3 and cabinet durability. Employing curvilinear (w^2) analysis, the complex interaction of party system fractionalization, instability, and cleavage conflict explains approximately 20 percent of the variance in cabinet durability among peacetime multiparty parliaments, 1918-1974. Utilizing the CPSI3 scores (logged) and collapsing them around the model point in Figure 7:5, the product moment coefficient between cabinet durability and CPSI3 (logged) is —.409. The similar product moment coefficients for CPSI1 (logged) and CPSI2 (logged) are —.307 and —.180, respectively. The multiple regression coefficient for these two independent variables in an additive model is .310. Adding CPSI3 (logged) to the regression equation raises the coefficient to .427.

These findings indicate that cabinet durability is at least partially a function of the nature of the parliamentary party system. Employing multiple regression analysis to estimate very roughly the strength of the overall relationship, the complex interaction of the party system characteristics account for approximately 18 percent of the variance in cabinet durability (logged). More importantly, one variable alone (CPSI3-logged) accounts for approximately 16 percent of the variance in cabinet durability. The substantive relationship can be summarized as follows: durable cabinets form under conditions of stable, depolarized pluralism and stable, polarized pluralism; transient cabinets form under conditions of unstable *depolarized* hyperpluralism and unstable *polarized* hyperpluralism. As parliaments experiencing unstable polarized hyperpluralism are far more numerous and extreme in their scores, the pattern has a peculiar asymmetrical form.

Clearly, the theory developed in Part I and Part II has

FIGURE 7:5

The Covariation of CPSI3 and Cabinet Durability: All
Partisan Cabinets in Peacetime Multiparty
Parliaments, 1918-1974

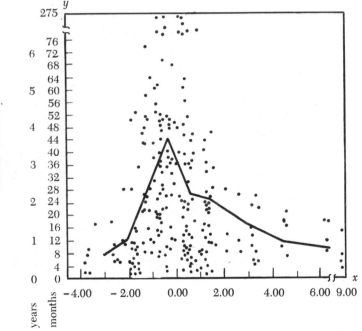

CPSI3

N = 238

yielded a parsimonious yet reasonably powerful statistical explanation of the relationship between cabinet durability and parliamentary party systems. This conclusion is particularly significant in light of three considerations: first, the analysis here applies only to multiparty parliaments, a set of parliaments for which cabinet durability has been largely unexamined heretofore; second, cabinet durability has not been averaged by parliament and thus a good deal of unexplained variance occurs as a result of within-parliament variation in cabinet durability; this within-parliament variance cannot be captured by the party system variables employed here; third, the timespan covered is quite wide, covering a wide range of environmental conditions and including some deviant cases that possibly could be omitted in the context of the theory but which have been included so that the general power of the theory can be estimated for all cabinets in peacetime multiparty parliaments.

CONCLUSION

In Chapter 3 and again in this chapter, four basic types of parliamentary party systems have been employed to simplify and summarize the complex relationship described in the theory: unstable, depolarized hyperpluralism; stable, depolarized pluralism; stable polarized pluralism; unstable, polarized hyperpluralism. These four parliamentary conditions are by no means presented as a definitive typology. They are basic tendencies representing broad conceptual contrasts between parliaments. Parliamentary life is too complex to be captured by these four contrasts; even within the fairly narrow context of the theory presented in this study, these four parliamentary situations do not capture the numerous possibilities that can and do exist in the interaction between cleavage conflict, fractionalization, and party system instability.

Realizing that these four types of parliamentary situations are employed for purposes of illustration and clarification, it is useful to conclude this chapter with some concrete examples of the behavior that is evident in these broad contrasting situations. For this purpose, ten parliaments have been selected that are fair representations of general patterns occurring among Western peacetime multiparty parliaments. Figure 7:6 presents a series of graphs indicating the weighted distribution of parties on a representative cleavage dimension for each parliament. Fractionalization, stability, and cleavage conflict scores for each parliament are presented to the right of the graph, as are relevant cabinet data. Throughout Figure 7:6 the identity of parties comprising the parliaments are ignored; the appendices provide the information from which the identities can be determined. In addition, it must be emphasized that some parliamentary party systems contained more than one salient cleavage dimension so that the situation represented in Figure 7:6 can only approximate the polarization or depolarization evident within a specific parliament.

The first situation to be examined is unstable, depolarized hyperpluralism. France (1919) and Italy (1946) provide the relevant illustrations. Both parliaments experienced considerable fractionalization combined with high party system instability. The Italian case represents the first freely elected parliament for that country in over two decades, so the instability of the party system is actually greater than the numerical score can indicate. Despite the fractionalized and unstable nature of the two parliaments, both evidence considerable depolarization. In addition, both evidence a general tendency for initial oversized cabinets to be resolved toward minimum winning status.

FIGURE 7:6

Party Polarization and Parliamentary Behavior:
Ten "Real World" Illustrations

A. *France (1919)*
clericalism 2.10

1. fractionalization: 7.40
2. stability: .62
3. cleavage conflict: 2.18
4a. First cabinet (a) + .61
          (b) 12
4b. Second cabinet (a) + .35
          (b) 12
4c. subsequent cabinet average
    (a) + .13, (b) 20(1)
5. CPSI3: −2.13

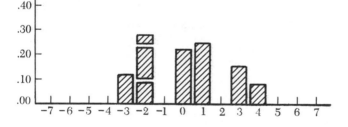

FIGURE 7:6 (continued)

B. Italy (1946)
economic 2.20

1. fractionalization: 5.82
2. stability: .62
3. cleavage conflict: 2.16
4a. First cabinet (a) + .37
(b) 2
4b. Second cabinet (a) + 46
(b) 3
4c. Third cabinet (a) + .21
(b) 10
4d. Fourth cabinet (a) + .25
(b) 5
5. CPSI3: −1.95

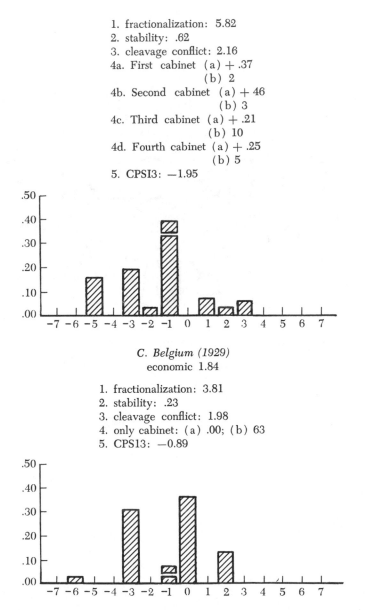

C. Belgium (1929)
economic 1.84

1. fractionalization: 3.81
2. stability: .23
3. cleavage conflict: 1.98
4. only cabinet: (a) .00; (b) 63
5. CPS13: −0.89

D. Norway (1965)
economic 2.41

1. fractionalization: —4.36
2. stability: .09
3. cleavage conflict: 1.85
4. only cabinet: (a) .00; (b) 65
5. CPSI3: —.62

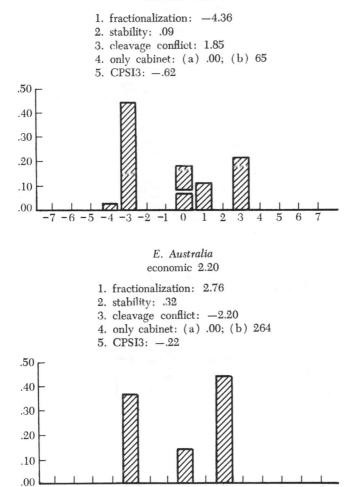

E. Australia
economic 2.20

1. fractionalization: 2.76
2. stability: .32
3. cleavage conflict: —2.20
4. only cabinet: (a) .00; (b) 264
5. CPSI3: —.22

FIGURE 7:6 (continued)

F. *Luxembourg (1951)*
economic 2.26

1. fractionalization: −3.38
2. stability: .22
3. cleavage conflict: 2.46
4. only cabinet: (a) .00; (b) 89
5. CPSI3: 0.22

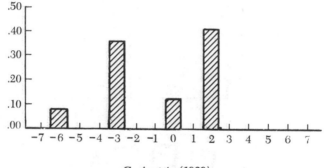

G. *Austria (1930)*
economic 3.38

1. fractionalization: 3.074
2. stability: 0.15
3. cleavage conflict: 3.05
4a. First cabinet: (a) −.12
    (b) 4
4b. Second cabinet: (a) .00
    (b) 17
5. CPSI3: 1.15

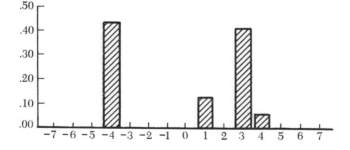

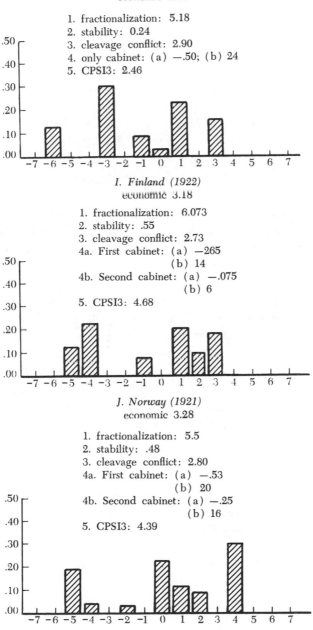

H. *Denmark (1945)*
economic 2.91

1. fractionalization: 5.18
2. stability: 0.24
3. cleavage conflict: 2.90
4. only cabinet: (a) —.50; (b) 24
5. CPSI3: 2.46

I. *Finland (1922)*
economic 3.18

1. fractionalization: 6.073
2. stability: .55
3. cleavage conflict: 2.73
4a. First cabinet: (a) —265
                   (b) 14
4b. Second cabinet: (a) —.075
                    (b) 6
5. CPSI3: 4.68

J. *Norway (1921)*
economic 3.28

1. fractionalization: 5.5
2. stability: .48
3. cleavage conflict: 2.80
4a. First cabinet: (a) —.53
                   (b) 20
4b. Second cabinet: (a) —.25
                    (b) 16
5. CPSI3: 4.39

In France (1919) the major parties are concentrated together at the center of the cleavage dimension in that parliament so that the overall DCC score is 2.18. The CPSI3 score is −2.13, indicating that this French parliament falls toward the extreme negative end of the patterns represented in Figures 7:3 and 7:5. In the 1919 French parliament, the first cabinet (headed initially by Millerand and then by Leygue) included six parties controlling over 80 percent of the legislative seats; this cabinet lasted twelve months and received a coalitional status score of .61. In the second cabinet, Briand served as prime minister, leading a twelve month cabinet composed of five parties and receiving a coalitional status score of .35. The third cabinet was headed by Poincaré; this cabinet received a coalitional status score of .13 and lasted twenty-nine months. In the 1919 French parliament, the trend was clearly toward resolving an extremely oversized initial cabinet toward minimum winning status.

The 1946 Italian parliament offers a less clear-cut but informative example of unstable, depolarized hyperpluralism. The parliament is less fractionalized than the French parliament, only approximating the range of hyperfractionalization. Nevertheless, it is an unstable party system and it is relatively depolarized, with the major parties falling to the left on the economic conflict dimension and concentrated relatively closely. In this parliament, de Gasperi was prime minister for all four cabinets. The first two were quite oversized, with the second cabinet more deviant than the first; the third and fourth cabinets are less oversized, indicating a general tendency toward the resolution of the cabinet size (with the resolution occurring *before* the Communist party ceased to support the ministerial government and withdrew from the cabinet). It should be noted that the Italian parliament represents a situation that is not uncommon in the data: a general pattern that is consistent with cabinet resolution toward minimum winning status but uneven in its precise form.

Belgium (1929), Norway (1965), and Australia (1949) represent stable, depolarized pluralism, though variations between these parliaments indicate the range of possibilities encompassed in this broad category. The parliaments in Belgium (1929) and Norway (1965) each contain six parties. The former system is less fractionalized than the latter while the latter system is more stable than the former. Both parliaments are relatively depolarized. In Belgium, a minimum winning cabinet forms composed of two parties that together control 53 percent of the parliamentary seats; the cabinet lasts sixty-three months (headed consecutively by Jasper, Renkin, Broqueville, and Theunis). In Norway, a minimum winning cabinet forms composed of four parties and lasts sixty-five months (the Borten ministry).

The 1949 parliament in Australia contrasts with the two previous parliaments in that only three parties exist. The party system is relatively depolarized, though slightly unstable. The pattern presented here is strikingly similar to the situations in modern Austria and Germany. In such de-fractionalized situations, barring party system instability and polarization (as with Britain during the interwar years) minimum winning cabinets are virtually assured. In the Australian case, the Liberal and Country parties coalesced and formed a partnership lasting two hundred sixty-four months, dissolved only by Labour's capture of a parliamentary majority in 1972. Throughout this time the Liberal and Country parties maintained distinct organizations and campaigned as distinct electoral entities. The Liberal-Country cabinet is the longest uninterrupted party coalition occurring among peacetime multiparty parliaments, 1918-1974.

The 1951 parliament in Luxembourg presents a variation on the situation in Australia. The scores of the party system in Luxembourg are similar to Australia, a primary exception being the presence of a Communist party so that the parliament is more polarized. In Luxembourg (1951) a minimum winning cabinet does form and lasts eighty-nine months. Among stable, moderately fractionalized parliaments Austria (1930) provides the extreme example of polarization; despite the relative stability of that party system and its defractionalized nature, the first cabinet was a minority cabinet. It lasted four months, followed by a seventeen-month minimum winning cabinet and the fall of the republic. For those who would often forget, the Austrian case reminds us that extreme fractionalization or instability are not necessary requisites for regime decay: extreme polarization over a period of years does nicely by itself.

The three final examples illustrate parliaments approaching unstable, polarized hyperpluralism. While each of these parliaments contains center parties, as did France in 1919, parliamentary strength is not concentrated in these center parties, nor in a dominant ideological grouping as in Italy (1946). Rather, in all three parliaments legislative strength is dispersed across the cleavage dimension with the extremist parties on each end of each cleavage dimension receiving at least 10 percent of the parliamentary seats. Combined with this polarization, the three parliaments experienced party system instability and fractionalization, though in different combinations. The Danish parliament provides an example of a phenomenon mentioned earlier in this study: extreme polarization combined with moderate fractionalization and instability. In a less polarized setting, a minimum winning cabinet might be possible under such a situation, at least following an initial, deviant cabinet. The cleavage conflict was so extreme, however, that only one party entered the cabinet; within twenty-four months parliament dissolved and new elections were held. In both the Norwegian and Finnish parliaments, judging from the overall DCC scores, the party systems were less polarized. In each, however, the party systems were more unstable and fractionalized than the Danish example. As a consequence, in each parliament an initial highly undersized cabinet formed, followed by a less deviant cabinet and, finally, by early dissolution of parliament.

Without belaboring the foregoing examples further, they should provide the reader with a reasonable sense of the fundamental patterns captured in the earlier quantitative analysis. As a further exercise, the reader should visually contrast the cleavage conditions evident in France (1919) and Italy (1946) with the patterns in Denmark (1945), Norway (1921), and Finland (1922). In addition, it might prove useful for the reader to locate each parliament on the appropriate graph presented earlier (Figures 7:3 and 7:5). In such a procedure, it is apparent that a good deal of variation exists in the graphs around the scores of the ten examples given here. Nevertheless, the ten parliaments illustrate the basic tendencies evident in the figures. They also indicate that a fair degree of variation in the earlier figures occurs as a result of variation within parliaments that is nevertheless reasonably consistent with the theory.

8 | Party Government and Cabinet Durability: All Peacetime Parliaments

In his early study of governments and parties, Lowell stressed the consequence of a cabinet's composition for cabinet durability. He argued that "a cabinet which depends for its existence on the votes of the Chamber can pursue a consistent policy with firmness and effect only when it can rely for support on a compact and faithful majority." Lowell's conclusion is that "the parliamentary system will give the country strong and efficient government only in case the majority consists of a single party." His central indicator of strong and efficient government was cabinet durability.[1]

In making these arguments and investigating their consequences, Lowell was not working within a broad set of assumptions about partisan motivations within parliament. He did not attempt to explicate systematically the meaning of "compact and faithful majority." He failed to clearly specify why one *type* of cabinet composition might have a more faithful majority and the relationship of this faithfulness to the compact nature of the cabinet. He did not consider systematically whether the conditions which would underlie the explanation of cabinet durability in single

[1] A. Lawrence Lowell, *Governments and Parties in Continental Europe*, 1 (Cambridge: Harvard University Press, 1896), 73-74; Lowell, *The Governments of France, Italy and Germany* (Cambridge: Harvard University Press, 1914), pp. 70-74.

party majority cabinets might have an analogous form in a multiparty setting.

From the perspective of the theory outlined in Part I, there is a linkage between the partisan behavior in multiparty and majority party parliaments. The linkage centers on the role of a cabinet's minimum winning status. In a multiparty setting, a minimum winning coalition of parties can form under certain conditions; if one does form, it probably will be quite durable. Analogously, a minimum winning cabinet can form in a majority party system. It will not be a *coalition* of parties. It will be a cabinet composed of one party. Nevertheless, it is of *minimum winning status* in the sense that (1) there is no unnecessary party in the cabinet and (2) the cabinet does control a majority of the seats in parliament. Seen in this perspective, majority party systems can be integrated directly into the theory developed in Part I and into the empirical analysis of the study. Chapter 7 focused on multiparty parliaments in order to demonstrate the power of the theory when limited to a multiparty setting. Yet it is equally important to gauge the power of the theory as it relates to all peacetime parliaments when majority party systems are included. That is the purpose of this chapter.

CABINET COALITIONAL STATUS AND CABINET DURABILITY

A first myth to dispel is the assumption that cabinets in majority party parliaments are all of minimum winning status. Table 8:1 presents a frequency distribution of cabinet coalitional status scores for multiparty parliaments, majority party parliaments, and the two sets combined. While it is true that most cabinets in majority party parliaments are of minimum winning status (in other words, they are single party, majority governments) a fair number of oversized cabinets have formed among majority party parliaments. Of the forty-one cabinets that have formed in majority party parliaments over the past fifty years, twelve were deviant cabinets; all of these, it should be noted, were oversized ($> mwc$). While the percentage of deviant cabinets among majority party parliaments is far less than among multiparty parliaments, the number is still sizable

TABLE 8:1

A Frequency Distribution of Cabinet Coalitional Status:
Majority Party–Multiparty Contrasts

Cabinet Coalitional Status	Cabinets in Multiparty Parliaments	Cabinets in Majority Party Parliaments	All Cabinets
$>mwc$			
+.400 to highest	13	3	16
.200 to .399	28	3	31
.100 to .199	10	3	13
.001 to .009	19	3	22
.000 (mwc)	57	29	86
−.001 to −.099	35	—	35
−.100 to −.199	34	—	34
−.200 to −.399	28	—	28
−.400 to lowest	14	—	14
$<mwc$			

and should dispel the notion that majority party systems lead automatically to government by a single majority party. Majority party parliaments containing oversized cabinets include Austria (1927 and 1945), Germany (1953 and 1957), Great Britain (1931 and 1935), and Italy (1948).

The significance of Table 8:1 is reinforced by the findings of Table 8:2. Table 8:2 indicates the average durability of cabinets that obtain cabinet coalitional status scores in the range indicated to the left. The first pattern to be noted is the general relationship between coalitional status and cabinet durability. Among both majority party systems and multiparty systems, minimum winning cabinets are durable; as cabinets depart from minimum winning status, cabinet durability decreases. In fact, whereas coalitional status accounted for 27 percent of the variance among multiparty parliaments utilizing curvilinear (w^2) analysis, coalitional status accounts for thirty-one percent of the variance in cabinet durability among all peacetime parliaments, 1918-1974. The regression coefficient between cabinet durability (logged) and the absolute deviation of cabinets from mini-

TABLE 8:2

Average Cabinet Durability at
Selected Ranges of Coalitional Status

Cabinet Coalitional Status	Cabinets in Multiparty Parliaments	Cabinets in Majority Party Parliaments	All Cabinets
.400 to highest	7 months	19 months	9 months
.200 to .399	13	35	15
.100 to .199	25	22	25
.001 to .099	18	30	20
.000 (mwc)	53	67	58
−.001 to −.099	29	—	29
−.100 to −.199	17	—	17
−.200 to −.399	16	—	16
−.400 to lowest	13	—	13

Note: All entries indicate average durability (in months) of cabinets obtaining cabinet coalitional status scores indicated to the left; durability scores have been rounded.

mum winning status is .507 (see Figure 8:1). These patterns indicate that cabinet durability is a function of cabinet coalitional status not only for multiparty parliaments but for all parliaments including majority party parliaments. Indeed when the latter are entered into the analysis, the strength of the relationship increases.

A second pattern in Table 8:2 is equally interesting. At every level of cabinet coalitional status, cabinets in majority

FIGURE 8:1

Covariation of Cabinet Durability (Logged) and Absolute
Deviation of Cabinets from Minimum Winning Status:
All Partisan Cabinets in Seventeen Western Peace-
time Parliaments, 1918-1974

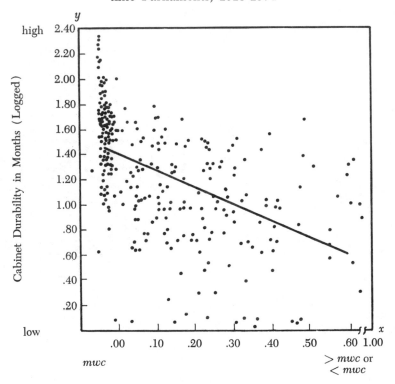

Absolute Deviation of Cabinets
from Minimum Winning Status

$r = -.507$ $N = 279$
$x = 1.256$ $a = 1.457$
$y = .157$ $b = -1.284$

party parliaments are more durable on the average than cabinets in multiparty parliaments. To a degree, it appears that Lowell was right. Single party minimum winning cabinets are more durable than minimum winning cabinets composed of party coalitions. A single party majority cabinet is more "faithful," apparently, than a multiparty coalition of analogous winning status. A number of factors surely enter into this relationship, not least of which must be the fact that a one-party government is more "compact" than a multiparty government in the sense that it is concerned only with intraparty negotiations whereas the latter must contend with intraparty and interparty bargaining. Likewise, oversized coalitions that include majority parties are more durable than oversized coalitions whose winning status is constructed on a coalition.

Thus a general ordering of the relationship between cabinet durability and coalitional status emerges. Minimum winning cabinets are more durable than those cabinets that deviate from minimum winning status. Among minimum winning cabinets, single party governments are more durable on the average than coalition cabinets. It must be emphasized, however, that both are quite durable and that the latter cabinets are considerably more durable than the literature on parliamentary government would suggest. Among deviant cabinets, oversized cabinets in majority party systems are the most durable, followed by undersized cabinets in multiparty parliaments and oversized multiparty governments.

PARTY SYSTEMS, CABINET COALITIONAL STATUS, AND
CABINET DURABILITY: ALL CABINETS

The foregoing analysis indicates that majority party systems evidence the same general relationship between cabinet coalitional status and cabinet durability as the pattern found among multiparty parliaments. It remains to be established, however, whether majority party system fractionalization, instability, and cleavage conflict have an influence on cabinet coalitional status and cabinet durability similar to the relationship among multiparty parliaments. Table 5:3 in Chapter 5 indicates that majority party systems have occurred in a much smaller range of cleavage conflict conditions than multiparty systems, with virtually all majority party parliaments occurring in systems that evidence low to moderate cleavage conflict. Cleavage conflict does not act as a great restraint against oversized cabinets. Are the resulting oversized cabinets a consequence of party system fractionalization (x) instability?

Table 8:3 specifies the average coalitional status of cabinets in majority party systems experiencing a range of fractionalization (x) instability conditions. At the lowest range, the average cabinet approximates minimum winning status. The countries with parliaments in this range include Austria, Canada, Great Britain, Ireland, New Zealand, and Sweden. Eleven cabinets formed in the eleven parliaments, averaging over seventy-five months' duration. In this calculation, as in all similar ones throughout this study, a party ministry that lasted into a second, third, fourth parliament, and so forth, is treated as the same cabinet. The two longest ministries in this range were the Conservative government in Great Britain that started in 1951 (156 months) and the National (Reform) ministry in New Zealand that started in 1957 and lasted 180 months. The shortest cabinet was the Social Democratic government in Sweden (1968); it lasted until new parliamentary elections in 1970.

Countries with parliaments in the moderate range (.50 to 1.49) include Australia, Austria, Belgium, Canada, Germany, Great Britain, Iceland, Ireland, New Zealand, and

Norway. At this intermediate range, the average cabinet is slightly oversized. Twenty-two cabinets formed in these seventeen parliaments; their average coalitional status is .085. The longest cabinet was the Labour government formed in Norway in 1945; it lasted sixteen years and was

TABLE 8:3
Average Coalitional Status and Psf x Psi:
Majority Party Systems

Psf x Psi	Parliaments	Average Coalitional Status	Number of Cabinets	Average Duration in Months
.00 to .49	Austria (1927, 1966) Canada (1968) Great Britain (1951, 1964, 1970) Ireland (1965) New Zealand (1946, 1954, 1957) Sweden (1968)	.005	11	76.5
.50 to 1.49	Australia (1929, 1946) Austria (1945) Belgium (1950) Canada (1930, 1935, 1945, 1958) Germany (1957) Great Britain (1922, 1935, 1945) Iceland (1931) Ireland (1957) New Zealand (1919, 1925, 1935) Norway (1945)	.085	20	53.8
1.50 to highest	Australia (1931) Germany (1953) Great Britain (1924, 1931) Italy (1948)	.163	9	27.8
Insufficient data	Luxembourg (1919)	.000	1	72

a single party majority government. The shortest cabinet was the first ministry formed in Austria (1945); it was extremely oversized (.968) and ended in two months with the cessation of Communist participation. The average duration of cabinets in the moderate range is 53.8 months.

In conditions of relatively high fractionalization (x) instability, cabinets approach a highly oversized status. Countries with parliaments in this range include Australia, Germany, Great Britain, and Italy. The five parliaments include nine cabinets; their average coalitional status was .163. Three of the parliaments—Germany (1953), Great Britain (1931), and Italy (1948)—experienced oversized ministries. The longest cabinet was the fifty-five month Conservative ministry in Great Britain (1951). The shortest cabinet was the initial grand coalition formed in Britain (1931). It lasted ten months, was composed of the Conservatives, Liberal Nationalists, National Labour, and Liberals; it fell with the resignation of the Liberals and was replaced by a ministry composed of the three former ministerial parties.[2] The average duration of cabinets in this range was twenty-eight months.

Table 8:4 provides the CPSI3 scores that result from the complex interaction of Psf x Psi with cleavage conflict. It likewise indicates the similarity between the party system

[2] In this study the following parties have been treated as ministerial participants in British cabinets throughout the 1930s: October 1931 to August 1932 (Conservatives, Liberal Nationals, National Labour, and Liberals); August 1932 to November 1935 (Conservatives, Liberal Nationals, National Labour); November 1935 to 1937 (Conservatives and National Liberals); 1937 (Conservatives). See William McElevee, *Britain's Locust Years 1918-1940* (London: Faber and Faber, Ltd., 1962); Dean E. McHenry, *The Labour Party in Transition* (London: George Routledge and Sons, Ltd., 1938); Emmanuel Shinwell, *The Labour Story* (London: Macdonald, 1963). Trevor Wilson, *The Downfall of the Liberal Party* (Ithaca, N.Y.: Cornell University Press, 1966).

characteristics and cabinet coalitional status among majority party and multiparty parliaments. When all cabinets are analyzed, the regression coefficient between coalitional status and CPSI3 is —.632 (logged). CPSI1, CPSI2, and DCC all enter a regression equation at a statistically significant level, raising the coefficient to .643. The overall rela-

TABLE 8:4

Average Coalitional Status Scores
in Selected Ranges on CPS13 Index

CPS13	Cabinets in Multiparty Parliaments	Cabinets in Majority Party Parliaments
4.50 to highest	—.222 (11)	—
3.00 to 4.49	—.190 (13)	—
1.50 to 2.99	—.252 (17)	—
.50 to 1.49	—.172 (35)	.000 (2)
.01 to .49	—.077 (40)	.009 (6)
.00 to —.49	.016 (34)	.000 (12)
—.50 to —1.49	.054 (51)	.175 (14)
—1.50 to —2.99	.276 (30)	.073 (3)
—3.00 to lowest	.363 (7)	.161 (3)
Missing data		1

Note: Cell entries indicate average coalitional status.

tionship between cabinet coalitional status and the interaction of the party system characteristics is roughly the same for all parliaments as it is for multiparty parliaments taken separately; in each set, the party system characteristics account for approximately 41 percent of the variance in cabinet coalitional status.

Table 8:5 indicates the general relationship that obtains between CPS13 and cabinet durability. In majority party systems, as in multiparty systems, the average durability of the cabinets at the extreme end of the CPSI3 scores is lower than the average durability of cabinets in the intermediate range. In majority party systems as for multiparty systems, parliaments experiencing unstable, depolarized hyperpluralism contain less durable cabinets than those with more stable and less fractionalized party systems. CPSI3 accounts for 23 percent of the variance in the durability of all peacetime partisan cabinets, 1918-1974; this conclusion is based on the use of curvilinear (w^2) analysis.

TABLE 8:5

Average Cabinet Durability
for Selected Ranges on CPSI3 Index

CPSI3	Cabinets in Multiparty Parliaments	Cabinets in Majority Party Parliaments
4.50 to highest	10.0 (11)	—
3.00 to 4.49	13.2 (13)	—
1.50 to 2.99	18.5 (17)	—
.50 to 1.49	25.5 (35)	37.0 (2)
.01 to .49	28.6 (40)	74.0 (6)
.00 to −.49	45.4 (34)	69.0 (12)
−.50 to −1.49	34.4 (51)	44.7 (14)
−1.50 to −2.99	11.0 (30)	44.7 (3)
−3.00 to lowest	6.0 (7)	20.7 (3)
Missing data		1

Note: Cell entries indicate the average durability (in months) of cabinets obtaining the indicated CPSI3 scores; durability scores have been rounded.

Utilizing the CPSI3 (logged) scores and collapsing them around the modal point, the product moment coefficient between cabinet durability and CPSI3 (logged) is −.431. The similar regression coefficients for CPSI1 (logged) and CPSI2 (logged) are −.237 and −.276, respectively. The multiple regression coefficient for these two independent variables in an additive model is .304. Entering CPSI3 (logged) into the regression equation raises the coefficient to .449. Cleavage conflict will enter the regression equation, but it does not produce a meaningful increase in variance explained.

These findings indicate that party system characteristics account for more variance in cabinet durability among all parliaments than among multiparty parliaments taken separately. Among multiparty parliaments, the CPSI variables accounted for approximately 18 percent of the variance utilizing a linear regression model. Among all parliaments the complex interaction of cleavage conflict with fractionalization and instability account for approximately 20 percent of the variance in cabinet durability.

CABINET FORMATION AND MAINTENANCE:
COUNTRY PATTERNS

In Chapter 7 and again in this chapter, the study has provided examples of cabinet behavior for specific countries, thereby illustrating the relationships. Future work will focus more specifically on party system changes and consequent variation in cabinet behavior by country. Nevertheless, it is useful here to provide some indication of the broad country-specific patterns that exist, indicating that the patterns found in this study are not the artifacts of behavior peculiar to one or two countries. For this purpose, Table 8:6 presents the distribution of cabinets by country for the entire time period from 1918 to 1974 (peacetime parliaments only).

In Table 8:6, cabinets are divided into six types. Two categories are given for minimum winning cabinets: single party majority cabinets (*mwcI*) and minimum winning party coalitions (*mwcII*). Oversized cabinets are divided into extremely oversized cabinets ($> mwcII$) and moderately oversized cabinets ($> mwcI$). Likewise, undersized

TABLE 8:6

The Frequency and Durability of Cabinet Types (by country)

Country	> mwcII	> mwcI	mwcI	mwcII	< mwcI	< mwcII
Australia			3 (34)	3 (133)	1 (38)	1 (11)
Austria	2 (24)	1 (40)	1 (48)	3 (105)	2 (12)	
Belgium	2 (25)	2 (20)	1 (46)	11 (35)	2 (16)	1 (1)
Canada			5 (74)		7 (30)	
Denmark				3 (77)	6 (40)	4 (30)
Finland	9 (14)	5 (16)		5 (22)	4 (12)	13 (10)
France	20 (7)	10 (15)		1 (17)	4 (12)	5 (7)
Germany	4 (24)	3 (8)		6 (34)	7 (12)	2 (10)
Great Britain	1 (10)	2 (31)	7 (59)	1 (47)	1 (26)	1 (9)
Iceland	1 (33)		1 (21)	6 (56)	2 (26)	1 (11)
Ireland			2 (75)	1 (33)	3 (38)	
Italy	5 (8)	6 (12)		1 (12)	11 (12)	1 (3)
Luxembourg	1 (8)		1 (72)	8 (65)		
Netherlands	2 (40)	6 (33)		4 (57)	2 (29)	1 (5)
New Zealand			6 (76)	1 (50)		2 (33)
Norway			1 (192)	1 (65)	9 (27)	6 (23)
Sweden			1 (24)	2 (56)	8 (39)	4 (17)

cabinets are divided into extremely undersized (< *mwcII*) and moderately undersized (< *mwcI*). Among oversized and undersized cabinets the absolute score of .20 is employed as an arbitrary threshold indicating extreme deviancy. Each cell in the table indicates the number of specified cabinet types occurring in each country. The parenthesis indicates the average durability of these cabinets.

Table 8:6 demonstrates simple but interesting patterns. Minimum winning cabinets have formed in all countries. Ten countries have experienced both single party majority cabinets and multiparty minimum winning cabinets: Australia, Austria, Belgium, Great Britain, Iceland, Ireland, Luxembourg, New Zealand, Norway, and Sweden. In one country, Canada, minimum winning cabinets have been exclusively of the single majority party variety. In six countries, minimum winning cabinets have always been party coalitions: Denmark, Finland, France, Germany, Italy, and the Netherlands. Table 8:7 specifies each parliament in which a *new* minimum winning cabinet formed, indicating a wide spread of such cabinets throughout the period from 1918 to 1974. As more than one minimum winning coalition may form in a parliament (as in the 1965 German parliament) the number of parliaments does not sum to the number of minimum winning coalitions.

As with minimum winning cabinets, all countries have experienced deviant cabinets. Oversized cabinets have formed in ten countries: Austria, Belgium, Finland, France, Germany, Great Britain, Iceland, Italy, Luxembourg, and the Netherlands. All of these countries experienced extremely oversized cabinets (> *mwcII*). In addition, every country except Luxembourg has experienced minority government. Thirteen countries have experienced extremely undersized cabinets: Australia, Belgium, Denmark, Finland,

France, Germany, Great Britain, Iceland, Italy, Netherlands, New Zealand, Norway, and Sweden.

Finally, the relationship between coalitional status and cabinet durability is a fairly constant one across all countries. Minimum winning cabinets tend to be more durable than deviant cabinets within each country. In only two

TABLE 8:7

Parliaments during which New Minimum Winning Cabinets Formed

Country	mwcI	mwcII
Australia	1929, 1931, 1946	1922, 1934, 1949
Austria	1966	1920, 1930, 1949
Belgium	1950	1921, 1925, 1929, 1946, 1949, 1954, 1958, 1961, 1965, 1968
Canada	1930, 1935, 1945, 1958, 1968	
Denmark		1929, 1957, 1968
Finland		1919, 1933, 1954, 1962
France		1932
Germany		1919, 1949, 1961, 1965, 1969
Great Britain	1922, 1924, 1935, 1945, 1951, 1964, 1970	1918
Iceland	1931	1933, 1934, 1949, 1963
Ireland	1957, 1965	1954
Italy		1972
Luxembourg	1919	1925, 1934, 1945, 1948, 1951, 1954, 1964, 1968
Netherlands		1922, 1937, 1946, 1967
New Zealand	1919, 1925, 1935, 1946, 1954, 1957	1931
Norway	1945	1931, 1965
Sweden	1968	1936, 1948

cases is the pattern unclear: Italy and France; both of these countries experienced only one minimum winning cabinet, an insufficient number to provide a reasonable test. It should be noted further that the relationship between cabinet type and cabinet durability holds well by country even when minimum winning coalitions are examined independently of single party majority cabinets. In addition, in those countries experiencing both minimum winning types, coalitions have provided more durable governments, on the average, in four countries: Australia, Austria, Iceland, and Sweden. *In the ten countries that have witnessed both types, the average durability is sixty-one months for minimum winning coalitions and sixty-three months for single party majority cabinets, indicating that the former are comparable in durability to the latter in reasonably similar country-conditions.*

A "NONOBVIOUS" CONCLUSION

This chapter has established that majority party parliaments fit nicely into the theoretical framework and empirical analysis presented in earlier chapters. In both multiparty and majority party parliaments, minimum winning cabinets are the most durable government. In the former, minimum winning cabinets are composed of party coalitions; in the latter, minimum winning cabinets are single party majority governments. Additionally, as with multiparty parliaments, oversized cabinets in majority party systems form under conditions of low cleavage conflict together with high fractionalization and high instability. Consequently, the conclusions reached in Chapter 7 hold for all parliaments as well as for multiparty parliaments. Durable cabinets form under conditions of stable, depolarized pluralism and stable, polarized pluralism, the primary exception being conditions of extreme polarization wherein no set of parties exists willing to bargain with one another and numerically capable of forming a majority cabinet. Transient cabinets form under conditions of unstable *polarized* hyperpluralism and unstable *depolarized* hyperpluralism.

This conclusion poses an interesting consequence. One of the most "obvious" generalizations in political science is the argument that ideological or cleavage conflict is a (possibly the) major source of political instability. As Eckstein writes:

> The most stable democracy is one in which men disagree, without intensity and within a narrow range, on specific issues, widely share basic orientations, and have politically weak segmented identifications. The least stable case has the opposite characteristics: extensive and intense disagreements, flowing from highly divergent orientations and strong segmental cleavages.[3]

In defining stable democracies, Eckstein maintains that they are polities "marked by what might be called intra-system stability, especially the stability of governments."[4] His illustrative index of governmental stability is the durability of cabinets. It would seem that Eckstein is suggesting, at least in part, that variation in cabinet durability is a product of the degree of cleavage conflict or polarization that characterized a parliamentary party system. As such, Eckstein's argument is the primary supplement in the literature to Lowell's explanation of cabinet durability.[5]

Despite its plausibility, the "polarization" thesis does not withstand cross-national quantitative analysis. Figure 8:2 presents the scatterplot between cleavage conflict and cabi-

[3] Harry Eckstein, *Division and Cohesion in Democracy* (Princeton: Princeton University Press, 1966), p. 38.
[4] Ibid., p. 17.   [5] Ibid., p. 18.

FIGURE 8:2

Covariation of Cabinet Durability and Cleavage Conflict:
All Partisan Cabinets in Seventeen Western Peacetime
Parliaments, 1918-1974

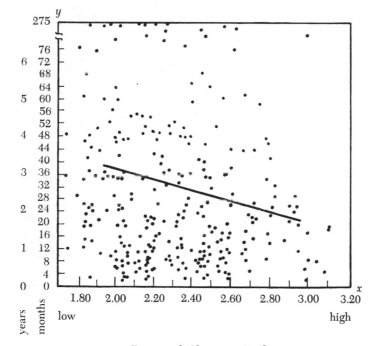

Degree of Cleavage Conflict

$N = 279$	$r = -.143$
$x = 2.307$	$a = 69.04$
$y = 30.198$	$b = 16.884$

net durability for all cabinets examined in this study: while a slight relationship obtains between the two variables, it is not of great magnitude and results primarily from the preponderance of transient cabinets under conditions of extremely high cleavage conflict. Even under extremely high conflict conditions (DCC approximates 3.0), however, the 1920 Austrian parliament gave rise to an eighty-month minimum winning cabinet. The relationship does not improve, furthermore, when cleavage conflict is logged ($r = -.141$), when cabinet durability is logged ($r = -.127$), or when both variables are logged ($r = -.128$). In addition, the coefficient between cleavage conflict and cabinet durability is $-.124$ for multiparty parliaments alone, indicating that the relationship is slightly weaker when majority party cabinets are excluded. In a similar analysis for the postwar years, Taylor and Herman constructed a measure of ideological differences between parliamentary parties for nineteen countries. They concluded that it "is immediately apparent that ideology does not play a very important role in our explanation of governmental stability."[6]

The failure of the polarization thesis, I believe, owes to the nature of cabinet formation and maintenance outlined in Part I and illustrated in the foregoing two chapters. A critical element of cabinet durability is the coalitional status of the cabinet. The more a cabinet deviates from minimum winning status, the less durable it will be. The formation of deviant cabinets is not a simple function of the degree of cleavage conflict or polarization that exists between parties. Rather, the formation of deviant (and thus nondurable)

---

[6] Michael Taylor and V. H. Herman, "Party Systems and Governmental Stability," *APSR* 65 (March 1971), 32-35. Taylor and Herman did find a stronger relationship than the one found in this study. No definitive reasons can be given for this, but it must be noted that they included only economic conflict in their determination of ideological conflict.

cabinets depends on the complex interaction of cleavage conflict, fractionalization, and instability. If cleavage conflict is low, cabinets in a fractionalized and unstable party system will deviate toward an oversized coalitional status. If cleavage conflict is high, cabinets in a fractionalized and unstable party system will deviate toward an undersized coalitional status. The former situation constitutes unstable depolarized hyperpluralism; the latter constitutes unstable polarized hyperpluralism. In both situations, cabinets are transient.

A number of parliaments illustrate the difference between unstable *depolarized* hyperpluralism and unstable *polarized* hyperpluralism. At the end of Chapter 7, France (1919) and Italy (1946) illustrate the former situation whereas Finland and Norway illustrate the latter. In Chapter 5 cleavage conflict occurring in the French (1928) and German (1930) parliaments was illustrated by party positions on the regime support dimension. Those two parliaments illustrate vividly the contrast. In both parliaments, cabinets were transient yet the transiency occurred for quite different reasons, at least from the perspective of our theory. In the French parliament (1928) the party system was depolarized (receiving a DCC score of 2.04) fractionalized (6.72), and unstable (.47). Its CPSI3 score was -3.37. As a consequence of the low bargaining constraints combined with information uncertainty, the French parliament experienced oversized cabinets: the average coalitional status of those cabinets that formed during the first half of the parliament was .40; they lasted an average of five months. The average coalitional status of the cabinets in the last half of the parliament was .28, averaging nine months' duration. The last cabinet, with a minimum winning status of approximately .07, was the most durable cabinet, lasting seventeen months. By contrast, the German parliament was highly polarized, receiving a DCC score of 2.92. In addition, it experienced a high degree of fractionalization (9.16) and instability (.35), receiving a CPSI3 score of 6.53. Its two cabinets were both undersized with an average coalitional status score of —.276. Their average durability was thirteen months. These minority cabinets resulted in the early dissolution of parliament and played a key role in the fall of Weimar Germany.

The French Fourth Republic offers a concluding example of the contrast. The Fourth Republic opened with a reasonable degree of agreement among major parties in their positions on the salient political cleavages. At the beginning of the parliament that lasted from 1946 to 1951, the primary cleavage acting as a constraint on party bargaining was clericalism; on both the economic dimension and regime support dimension, the major parties were reasonably close to one another. By 1956, the parliamentary environment had altered significantly. With the decline of the MRP, clericalism became a less conflictual cleavage; this change was more than offset, however, by increased polarization on the other two cleavages. Between 1946 and 1956, the Communists became more extreme in their economic policies and in their opposition to the regime. Simultaneously, the Conservatives and Poujadists emerged in 1956 as sizable supporters of economic traditionalism and opponents of the existing parliamentary regime. As a result of these changes, the DCC score increased from 2.14 in 1946 to 2.91 in 1956. Figure 8:3 indicates the pattern obtaining for the economic conflict dimension in each parliament, indicating a change from 1.93 to 3.13 from 1946 to 1956.

While a marked increase in polarization occurred over the ten-year period, the other party system characteristics remained fairly similar. The primary change was an increase in parliamentary fractionalization from 6.09 (1946) to 8.78

FIGURE 8:3

Polarization in the French Fourth Republic:
Two Examples

France, 1946 II

1. fractionalization: 6:09
2. stability: .50
3. cleavage conflict: 2.14
4. Cabinets:
   a. + .408; 4 months
   b. + .08; 14 months
   c. + .26; 6 months
      (average for six cabinets)

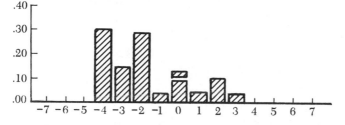

France, 1956

1. fractionalization: 8.78
2. stability: .50
3. cleavage conflict: 2.71
4. Cabinets:
   a. −.32; 16 months
   b. −.44; 6 months
   c. −.09; 5 months
   d. −.51; 1 month

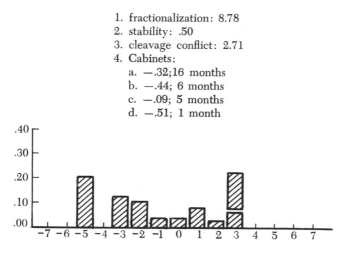

(1956); during both parliaments, nevertheless, the parliament experienced hyperfractionalization. In regard to party system stability, both parliaments received a score of .50. Assuming the fractionalization and instability are useful indicators of information uncertainty, both French parliaments experienced considerable information uncertainty. The 1946 parliament illustrates unstable *depolarized* hyperpluralism whereas the 1956 French parliament illustrates unstable *polarized* hyperpluralism. The CPSI3 scores for the former is −1.93; by contrast, the CPSI3 score for 1956 is 8.83, the most extreme CPSI3 score obtained in this study. The resulting cabinet behavior roughly resembles that which is expected in the two parliaments. In the 1946 parliament, the first cabinet was oversized (.408) and lasted for four months, followed by a less deviant cabinet (.08) which lasted for fourteen months; thereafter the pattern is less clearcut, as the cabinets fluctuate in size (with all but one being oversized), unable to attain a "coalition of natural allies." By contrast, the 1956 parliament begins with two highly undersized cabinets, resolves toward a less deviant minority cabinet, and ends with an extremely undersized cabinet. As with the 1930 German parliament, the unstable, extremely polarized, hyperfractionalized French parliament brought the Fourth French Republic to a close.

TWO CAVEATS

The foregoing discussion indicates that the polarization thesis fails because it envisions cabinet transiency only among undersized or minority cabinets. Oversized cabinets, which form in depolarized conditions, are overlooked. Interestingly, Eckstein formulated his thesis in a case study of Norway, focusing particularly on the interwar years. During that time, the Norwegian party system was highly polarized, experiencing a large number of transient minority cabinets. When we broaden our comparative focus, however, it becomes clear that oversized majority cabinets are just as transient (in fact, more transient) than undersized cabinets. Cabinet transiency can afflict depolarized parliaments just as surely as polarized parliaments. The critical factor in each case is the extent of party system fractionalization and instability.

Once the relationship is perceived in this manner, there is a sense in which Eckstein's general theory may be more plausible. It may be that the same interpretation or systemic consequence should not be attached to transient oversized cabinets as to transient minority cabinets. The detrimental consequences described by Eckstein that obtain from transient minority cabinets may not accrue (at least not as often or as immediately) from transient oversized cabinets. For example, with respect to partisan or policy continuity, the avoidance of disruptive elections, or the maintance of widespread popular attachment to the cabinet ministry, transient oversized cabinets may be preferable to transient minority cabinets. This is not to suggest, of course, that transient oversized cabinets have no detrimental regime effects. Many scholars would argue that the transiency of oversized cabinets during the years from 1946 to 1956 led to the electoral disenchantment that produced the polarization evident in the 1956 French parliament. However, those who wish to use cabinet durability as an index to regime stability should at least consider the possibility that transient minority cabinets be given more weight than transient oversized cabinets. If such a procedure is followed, Eckstein's theory assumes a more defensible stance since minority cabinets form primarily in the more conflictual or polarized cleavage systems.

In addition, it is important to realize that the relationship between cleavage systems and cabinet durability is not just a question of the relationship of cleavage polarization to cabinet durability. Any cleavage system has at least three separate characteristics: the complexity of the cleavage system structure; the institutionalization of cleavage structure attachments; the degree of cleavage dimension conflict. The complexity of a cleavage system's structure refers to the number of cleavage dimensions that are salient in a polity and the degree to which these dimensions cross-cut one another. The degree of cleavage dimension conflict refers to the intensity and extremity of electoral polarization on the salient cleavage dimensions. Cleavage structure institutionalization refers to the degree to which first, the cleavage dimensions salient to an electorate are continuous over time; second, cleavage positions of the electorate on each cleavage dimension have solidified; and third, these cleavage positions have been formalized through stable electoral attachments to specific political parties.

If we accept the proposition that a parliamentary party system is partially a product of a polity's cleavage system,[7] then the three cleavage characteristics specified above are factors that give rise to the party system characteristics analyzed in this study. Cleavage system complexity influences party system fractionalization. The extremity of electoral polarization on cleavage dimensions influences the degree of cleavage conflict that will characterize a parliamentary party system. Cleavage system institutionalization influences the stability of the parliamentary party system.

---

[7] See Erik Allardt and Stein Rokkan, eds., *Mass Politics* (New York: The Free Press, 1970); Seymour M. Lipset and Stein Rokkan, eds., *Party Systems and Voter Alignments: Cross-National Perspectives* (New York: The Free Press, 1967); Stein Rokkan, *Citizens, Elections, Parties* (New York: David McKay Company, 1970); Robert A. Dahl, ed., *Political Oppositions in Western Democracies* (New Haven: Yale University Press, 1966).

Interpreted in this manner, the findings presented in this study do suggest a relationship between cleavage systems and cabinet durability. Nondurable cabinets will exist in polities possessing a highly complex and uninstitutionalized cleavage system. If the cleavage system is highly conflictual or polarized the nondurable nature of cabinets will be due to a tendency toward minority cabinets. If the cleavage system is not highly conflictual, the nondurable nature of cabinets will be due to a tendency toward oversized cabinets.

9 | Interwar–Postwar Contrasts

In the foregoing chapters, this study has examined propositions without regard to historical era. Yet evaluating the theory and its utility requires differentiating between eras. First, predictions of the theory may hold well for one era but not for another; if so, contrasts between time periods will force confrontation with this fact and hopefully lead to refinement and improvement in the theory. Second, historical eras may differ in the nature of the bargaining conditions that characterize parliaments and consequently in the patterns of cabinet formation and maintenance relevant to the different time periods. By taking each period separately, therefore, parts of the theory can be examined more closely while simultaneously illuminating behavioral patterns within a historical era. Third, it is important to examine and contrast behavior of different time periods because political analysts think in terms of historical eras, often explaining behavior in sweeping generalizations that emphasize the uniqueness of an age and deemphasize analytic continuities. To the extent that unique patterns do characterize each era, the theory must be broadened to include processes that are specific to a particular era. Likewise, to the extent that the theory outlined earlier can account for behavioral patterns in several distinct time periods, political historians are forced to confront the underlying analytic continuities and incorporate systematic theory into historical explanation. With these considerations in mind, I shall in this chapter contrast the patterns of the interwar years between 1918 and 1940 with the patterns for the postwar years from 1945 to 1974.

INTERWAR–POSTWAR CONTRAST: GENERAL CHARACTERISTICS

World War II is a clear watershed for the parliaments examined in this study. The period between World War I and World War II was an experimental age in parliamentary government. Countries such as Austria, Germany, Finland, and Iceland experienced genuine parliamentary government for the first time. In others such as Australia, Belgium, and Canada, party systems underwent vast change, introducing multipartism to systems that previously enjoyed majority party government. And in all countries, interwar parliaments witnessed recurrent economic crisis and worldwide depression.

The years following World War II provide a very different picture. Most of the countries entered the postwar period with considerable experience in parliamentary government. The party systems that were young in the early twenties had matured and solidified by the late forties. Even those countries such as Germany and Austria for whom parliamentary government was a distant memory of the twenties and early thirties experienced significant continuity with the interwar years in the major parties that emerged after World War II. Finally, the postwar years saw economic prosperity to a degree unparalleled in the prior history of the twentieth century.

Differences between the interwar and postwar years are reflected clearly in the party systems that characterized the two periods (see Tables 9:1, 9:2, and 9:3). Interwar parliaments experienced party system fractionalization, instability, and cleavage conflict. Almost 20 percent of the inter-

TABLE 9:1

A Frequency Distribution of Cleavage Conflict Scores
For All Peacetime Parliaments, 1918-1974,
Interwar–Postwar Contrasts

Cleavage Conflict	Multiparty Parliaments		All Parliaments	
	Interwar	Postwar	Interwar	Postwar
1.500 to 1.849	1 (.013)	5 (.051)	1 (.011)	8 (.059)
1.850 to 1.949	0	11 (.111)	1 (.011)	17 (.125)
1.950 to 2.049	5 (.064)	14 (.141)	8 (.086)	24 (.177)
2.050 to 2.149	6 (.077)	11 (.111)	7 (.075)	14 (.103)
2.150 to 2.249	9 (.115)	18 (.182)	13 (.140)	22 (.162)
2.250 to 2.349	15 (.192)	12 (.121)	16 (.172)	16 (.118)
2.350 to 2.449	8 (.103)	11 (.111)	9 (.097)	13 (.096)
2.450 to 2.549	5 (.064)	9 (.091)	7 (.075)	14 (.103)
2.550 to 2.649	7 (.090)	6 (.061)	7 (.075)	6 (.044)
2.650 to 2.749	9 (.115)	0	10 (.108)	0
2.750 to 2.849	5 (.064)	0	6 (.065)	0
2.850 to 2.949	3 (.038)	2 (.020)	3 (.032)	2 (.015)
2.950 to highest	5 (.064)	0	5 (.054)	0
Total	78	99	93	136

Note: Percentages do not necessarily sum to 1.00 because of rounding error.

war parliaments obtained fractionalization scores exceeding 5.99; 33 percent obtained instability scores exceeding .39; and over 25 percent obtained cleavage conflict scores exceeding 2.649. Comparable figures for the postwar years were 5.8, 13.2, and 1.5 percent, respectively. By contrast, the postwar period reflects party system defractionalization, stability, and depolarization. Over 19 percent of the postwar parliaments received fractionalization scores falling below 2.50; 33.8 percent obtained stability scores falling below .15; and 36 percent obtained cleavage conflict scores falling below 2.05. Comparable figures for the interwar years were 6.4, 9.9, and 10.8 percent, respectively. These patterns are equally striking, as the tables indicate, when multiparty parliaments are examined separately.

TABLE 9:2

A Frequency Distribution of Fractionalization Scores
For All Peacetime Parliaments, 1918-1974,
Interwar–Postwar Contrasts

| Fractionalization | Multiparty Parliaments | | All Parliaments | |
	Interwar	Postwar	Interwar	Postwar
1.00 to 2.49	0	5 (.051)	6 (.065)	26 (.191)
2.50 to 2.99	11 (.141)	14 (.141)	16 (.172)	21 (.154)
3.00 to 3.49	9 (.115)	15 (.152)	13 (.140)	19 (.140)
3.50 to 3.99	14 (.179)	20 (.202)	14 (.151)	23 (.169)
4.00 to 4.49	13 (.167)	9 (.091)	13 (.140)	11 (.081)
4.50 to 4.99	6 (.077)	12 (.121)	6 (.065)	12 (.088)
5.00 to 5.49	7 (.090)	9 (.091)	7 (.075)	9 (.066)
5.50 to 5.99	0	7 (.071)	0	7 (.051)
6.00 to 6.49	5 (.064)	2 (.021)	5 (.054)	2 (.015)
6.50 to 6.99	2 (.026)	2 (.021)	2 (.022)	2 (.015)
7.00 to 7.49	4 (.051)	2 (.021)	4 (.043)	2 (.015)
7.50 to 7.99	3 (.038)	0	3 (.032)	0
8.00 to 8.49	2 (.026)	1 (.010)	2 (.022)	1 (.007)
8.50 to highest	2 (.026)	1 (.010)	2 (.072)	1 (.007)
Total	78	99	93	136

Note: Percentages do not necessarily sum to 1.00 because of rounding error.

Despite these differences between eras, cabinet durability varies significantly within both periods. As Table 9:4 indicates, both eras contain a significant number of durable cabinets as well as a significant number of transient cabinets. During the interwar years, over 13 percent of the cabinets lasted at least fifty months and 25 percent lasted less than ten months. During the postwar years, 17 percent lasted at least fifty months and almost 28 percent lasted less than ten months. In regard to shortest cabinets per parliament (see Table 9:5), significant variation within eras continues to exist. In 20 percent of the interwar parliaments, the shortest cabinet lasted at least fifty months whereas 23 percent lasted no more than nine months. During the post-

TABLE 9:3

A Frequency Distribution of Stability (PSI-D) Scores
For All Peacetime Parliaments, 1918-1974,
Interwar–Postwar Contrasts

	Multiparty Parliaments		All Parliaments	
PSI-D	Interwar	Postwar	Interwar	Postwar
.00 to .09	1 (.013)	14 (.141)	1 (.011)	22 (.162)
.10 to .14	7 (.090)	19 (.192)	8 (.086)	24 (.176)
.15 to .19	7 (.090)	20 (.202)	8 (.086)	26 (.191)
.20 to .24	5 (.064)	15 (.152)	5 (.054)	18 (.132)
.25 to .29	16 (.205)	11 (.111)	17 (.183)	15 (.110)
.30 to .34	8 (.103)	3 (.030)	11 (.118)	5 (.037)
.35 to .39	9 (.115)	5 (.051)	10 (.108)	7 (.051)
.40 to .44	6 (.077)	2 (.020)	9 (.097)	2 (.015)
.45 to .49	5 (.064)	3 (.030)	6 (.065)	5 (.037)
.50 to .54	3 (.038)	3 (.030)	4 (.043)	5 (.037)
.55 to .59	3 (.038)	0	3 (.032)	0
.60 to .64	3 (.038)	3 (.030)	3 (.032)	4 (.029)
.65 to .69	1 (.013)	0	3 (.032)	0
.70 to highest	2 (.026)	1 (.010)	3 (.032)	2 (.015)
missing data	2 (.026)		2 (.022)	1 (.007)
Total	78	99	93	136

Note: Percentages do not necessarily sum to 1.00 because of rounding error.

war years, 25 percent lasted fifty months whereas 24 percent of the shortest cabinets lasted no more than nine
months. While slight variations exist between eras, with the
interwar years tilted slightly toward less durable cabinets,
the differences are not overwhelming. Perhaps the most interesting contrast is the lower durability of interwar majority
party parliaments.

These contrasts between the interwar and postwar years
provide some interesting puzzles. The less institutionalized
nature of parliaments during the interwar years and the
greater crisis environment of those years engenders doubt
as to the applicability of the theory during that time period:
does the theory operate well even in a period of institutional

TABLE 9:4

Cabinet Durability in Peacetime Parliaments: Interwar–Postwar Contrasts

Cabinet Durability (months)	Multiparty Parliaments		Majority Party Parliaments		All	
	Interwar	Postwar	Interwar	Postwar	Interwar	Postwar
50 or more	12 (.112)	16 (.122)	5 (.313)	11 (.440)	17 (.138)	27 (.173)
40 to 49	9 (.084)	15 (.115)	2 (.125)	5 (.200)	11 (.089)	20 (.128)
30 to 39	9 (.084)	13 (.099)	4 (.250)	3 (.120)	13 (.106)	16 (.103)
20 to 29	19 (.178)	20 (.153)	3 (.188)	3 (.120)	22 (.179)	23 (.147)
10 to 19	27 (.252)	25 (.191)	2 (.125)	2 (.080)	29 (.236)	27 (.173)
0 to 9	31 (.290)	42 (.321)	0	1 (.040)	31 (.252)	43 (.276)
Total	107	131	16	25	123	156

Note: Percentages do not necessarily sum to 1.00 because of rounding error.

TABLE 9:5

Shortest Cabinet Per Parliament: Interwar–Postwar Contrasts

Cabinet Durability (months)	Multiparty Parliaments		Majority Party Parliaments		All	
	Interwar	Postwar	Interwar	Postwar	Interwar	Postwar
50 or more	11 (.172)	15 (.195)	5 (.357)	10 (.476)	16 (.205)	25 (.255)
40 to 49	8 (.125)	13 (.169)	2 (.143)	5 (.238)	10 (.128)	18 (.184)
30 to 39	8 (.125)	9 (.117)	2 (.143)	2 (.095)	10 (.128)	11 (.112)
20 to 29	10 (.156)	8 (.104)	3 (.214)	1 (.048)	13 (.167)	9 (.092)
10 to 19	9 (.141)	9 (.117)	2 (.143)	2 (.095)	11 (.141)	11 (.112)
0 to 9	18 (.281)	23 (.299)	0 (.000)	1 (.048)	18 (.231)	24 (.245)
Total	64	77	14	21	78	98

Note: Percentages do not necessarily sum to 1.00 because of rounding error.

change and domestic crisis? To the extent that the theory is applicable to each era, the higher degree of cleavage conflict during the interwar years suggests that the most relevant portion of the theory for that period should be the discussion of cabinet behavior under conditions of moderate to extremely high *a priori* constraints on bargaining; during the interwar years, minority cabinets should abound. By contrast, the lower degree of cleavage conflict during the postwar years indicates that the most relevant portion of the theory for those years should be the discussion of party behavior under low to moderate *a priori* bargaining constraints; oversized and minimum winning cabinets should predominate. Finally, the similarity in the general proportion of durable and transient cabinets in the two eras indicates that the theory must nevertheless account for fairly similar ranges in cabinet durability.

PARTY SYSTEMS AND CABINET COALITIONAL STATUS

Table 9:6 provides a frequency listing of cabinets at various ranges on the cabinet coalitional status index, indicating that expected differences do occur. For all cabinets in the interwar period, approximately 27 percent were oversized, 27 percent were minimum winning, and 46 percent were undersized. In the postwar years, 31 percent were oversized, 34 percent were minimum winning, and 35 percent were undersized. Clearly, minority cabinets predominated in the interwar years whereas the postwar years evidence a marked increase in the proportion of minimum winning and oversized cabinets. More striking is the contrast between eras in the frequency of highly deviant cabinets. Defining a highly deviant cabinet as one exceeding the absolute coalitional status score of .19, 64 percent of the highly deviant minority cabinets formed in the interwar

TABLE 9:6

A Frequency Distribution of Cabinet Coalitional Status Scores:
Interwar–Postwar Contrasts

Cabinet Coalitional Status	All Cabinets		Cabinets in Multiparty Parliaments	
	Interwar	Postwar	Interwar	Postwar
+.400 to highest	7 (.057)	9 (.058)	6 (.056)	7 (.053)
.200 to .399	9 (.073)	22 (.147)	9 (.084)	19 (.145)
.100 to .199	5 (.041)	8 (.051)	4 (.037)	6 (.046)
.001 to .009	12 (.098)	10 (.064)	10 (.093)	9 (.069)
.000 (mwc)	33 (.268)	53 (.340)	21 (.196)	36 (.275)
—.001 to —.099	13 (.106)	22 (.141)	13 (.121)	22 (.168)
—.100 to —.199	17 (.138)	17 (.109)	17 (.159)	17 (.130)
—.200 to .399	16 (.130)	12 (.077)	16 (.150)	12 (.092)
—.400 to lowest	11 (.089)	3 (.019)	11 (.103)	3 (.023)

Note: Percentages do not necessarily sum to 1.00 because of rounding error.

years whereas 65 percent of the highly deviant oversized cabinets formed in the postwar era. Finally, as Table 9:6 indicates, these general differences hold when behavior among multiparty parliaments in the two time periods is compared. It remains to be determined, however, whether differences in coalitional status are associated systematically with variation in party system characteristics within the two eras.

Table 9:7 presents the relationship between cabinet coalitional status, cleavage conflict, and party system fractionalization (x) instability. The cell entries are the average coalitional status scores for all cabinets in parliaments obtaining cleavage conflict scores in the range listed to the left and Psf x Psi scores in the range listed at the top of the table. In both the interwar and the postwar years, as an average, cabinets in each cleavage conflict range approximate minimum winning status under conditions of low fractionalization (x) instability while they deviate signifi-

TABLE 9:7

Coalitional Status, Cleavage Conflict,
and Fractionalization (x) Stability: Contrasts of Relationships
Between Interwar and Postwar Years

	(Interwar)			(Postwar)	
Cleavage Conflict	Interaction of Fractionalization and Instability (Psf x Psi)		Cleavage Conflict	Interaction of Fractionalization and Instability (Psf x Psi)	
	(low)	(high)		(low)	(high)
4	−.172 (9)	−.244 (21)	4	(0)	−.370 (5)
3	−.102 (7)	−.164 (30)	3	−.059 (31)	−.117 (12)
2	−.006 (11)	+.132 (27)	2	.001 (21)	+.166 (38)
1	+.059 (7)	+.290 (10)	1	+.046 (39)	+.150 (10)

Code: Cleavage Conflict   Fractionalization (x) Stability
          1 = lowest to 2.049   1 = .00 to .99 (low)
          2 = 2.050 to 2.349   2 = 1.00 to highest (high)
          3 = 2.350 to 2.649
          4 = 2.650 to highest

cantly from minimum winning status under conditions of high fractionalization (x) instability.

Table 9:8 presents the CPSI3 scores that result when the standardized cleavage conflict scores are multiplied with the Psf x Psi scores. In each era, and for multiparty parliaments as well as all parliaments, cabinets in parliaments receiving highly positive CPSI3 scores are of undersized (minority) status. Cabinets in parliaments receiving highly negative scores are of oversized status. Cabinets in the intermediate range approximate minimum winning status as an average. Thus in both the interwar years and the postwar years, conditions of low to moderate cleavage conflict together with high fractionalization (x) instability produce oversized cabinets. Conditions of moderate to high cleavage conflict together with high fractionalization (x) instability

TABLE 9:8

Average Coalitional Status Scores in Selected Ranges
on CPSI3 Index: Interwar–Postwar Contrasts

CPSI3	All Cabinets		Cabinets in Multiparty Parliaments	
	Interwar	Postwar	Interwar	Postwar
4.50 to highest	−.142 (7)	−.338 (4)	−.142 (7)	−.338 (4)
3.00 to 4.49	−.190 (13)	—	−.190 (13)	—
1.50 to 2.99	−.236 (16)	−.500 (1)	−.236 (16)	−.500 (1)
.50 to 1.49	−.186 (24)	−.120 (13)	−.199 (22)	−.120 (13)
.01 to .49	−.055 (9)	−.069 (37)	−.063 (7)	−.080 (33)
.00 to −.49	.023 (18)	.005 (28)	.027 (15)	.007 (19)
−.50 to −1.49	.071 (19)	.084 (46)	.063 (12)	.054 (39)
−1.50 to −2.99	.278 (9)	.249 (24)	.313 (8)	.262 (22)
−3.00 to lowest	.363 (7)	.161 (3)	.363 (7)	—

Note: The cell entries indicate the average coalitional status scores for cabinets.

produce undersized cabinets. Low to moderately high cleavage conflict conditions together with low fractionalization (x) instability are associated with cabinets that approach minimum winning status as an average. These conclusions, however, must be qualified.

While the general relationship between the party system characteristics and cabinet coalitional status does hold for each era, there is a significant difference between eras in the strength and patterning of the relationship. Table 9:9

TABLE 9:9

Regression Coefficients
Contrasting Interwar and Postwar Patterns:
Determinants of Coalitional Status

Relationship (Independent → Dependent)	Interwar r	Postwar r
DCC → CCS	−.566	−.412
CPSI3 → CCS	−.601	−.542
CPSI1, 2, 3 → CCS	.627	.562
CPSI1, 2, 3 (logged) → CCS	.679	.602

presents the appropriate regression coefficients. In the interwar years, cleavage conflict alone accounted for approximately 32 percent of the variance in cabinet coalitional status. The interaction of fractionalization and instability with cleavage conflict (CPSI3) increased the variance explained to 36 percent. Utilizing logarithmic transformation of all three CPSI scores in an additive model, the variance explained increases to 46 percent. By contrast, during the postwar years cleavage conflict accounted for only 17 percent of the variance in cabinet coalitional status; the interaction of fractionalization and instability with cleavage conflict (CPSI3) increases the variance explained to 20 percent and, utilizing logarithmic transformations of all three CPSI variables, to 36 percent. These results, based on all cabinets for peacetime parliaments, suggest three conclusions. First, cleavage conflict is a much more significant determinant of cabinet coalitional status in the interwar than postwar period. Second, when entered into a complex interaction term with cleavage conflict, party system fractionalization and instability increase the variance explained in each era but particularly the postwar period. Third, the logarithmic transformation of the CPSI scores produces a greater increase in explained variance in the interwar years, indicating that a curvilinear pattern is more pronounced for the interwar than postwar years.

These differences reflect the contrasts in bargaining conditions that characterize the two eras. In the theory presented in Chapter 2, a symmetrical relationship was posited between cabinet coalitional status and the interaction of *a priori* willingness to bargain with information certainty. High information certainty should produce minimum winning cabinets in a wide range of cleavage conflict conditions. By contrast, low information certainty should produce opposite tendencies: oversized cabinets in conditions of high *a priori* willingness to bargain; undersized cabinets in conditions of low *a priori* willingness to bargain. One modification to this symmetrical pattern was expressed, however. In conditions of extremely high bargaining constraints, undersized cabinets should form irrespective of the degree of information certainty: information certainty could influence the extent to which cabinets are undersized, but not the existence of undersized cabinets. In other words, beyond the threshold point where a majority set of parties are no longer willing to bargain, the influence of *a priori* willingness to bargain increases as a determinant of cabinet coalitional status whereas the influence of information certainty decreases. In the operational terms of this study, therefore, among parliaments experiencing extremely high levels of cleavage conflict, the degree of cleavage conflict characterizing the parliament should have greater influence on cabinet coalitional status than among parliaments experiencing low to moderately high degrees of cleavage conflict. By contrast, fractionalization and instability should have less influence on cabinet coalitional status among extremely conflictual parliaments than among less conflictual ones.

The special nature of cabinet formation and maintenance in conditions of high cleavage conflict is important because the interwar and postwar periods differ in the proportion of parliaments experiencing extremely high cleavage conflict. This difference can account for the variation between the two eras in the strength and pattern of the relationship between the party system characteristics and cabinet coalitional status. Treating 2.65 as an arbitrary threshold, 25 percent of the interwar parliaments received extremely high cleavage conflict scores whereas less than 2 percent of the postwar parliaments received similar scores (see Table 9:1). As a consequence, the interwar era contains that set of parliaments for which cleavage conflict should have the greatest influence on cabinet coalitional status whereas the postwar era does not; thus the greater influence of cleavage conflict on cabinet coalitional status during the interwar years. From the opposite perspective, virtually all of the postwar parliaments fall in the cleavage conflict range for which party system fractionalization and stability should be most significant; thus the greater interactive role of fractionalization and instability during the postwar years. Finally, since a significant proportion of the interwar parliaments fall in the highly polarized range whereas few of the postwar parliaments approach that range, the interaction of fractionalization (x) instability with high cleavage conflict augments the curvilinear relation between the CPSI scores and cabinet coalitional status among interwar parliaments to a much greater degree than in the postwar period. In the interwar years, high fractionalization and instability are augmenting a tendency toward undersized cabinets that is already present among parliaments experiencing extremely high cleavage conflict. In the postwar years, such parliaments are less prevalent. It is for this reason that the logarithmic transformation of the CPSI scores increases the variance explained for the interwar years more than for the postwar years.

CABINET COALITIONAL STATUS AND CABINET DURABILITY

The foregoing sections have established that differences do exist in the parliamentary party systems of the interwar and postwar parliaments. Nevertheless, the overall relationships between party system attributes and cabinet coalitional status do hold for each era; to the extent that contrasting patterns distinguish the two time periods, these patterns seem consistent with those that the theory would suggest for the varying cleavage conflict conditions that characterize each era. Nothing has been established, however, concerning cabinet durability during the two time periods. Is cabinet durability associated with cabinet coalitional status during each era? Are the associations strong? Are there differences between the interwar years and postwar years in the nature of the relationship?

Table 9:10 presents the average durability in months for cabinets at various levels in the cabinet coalitional status

TABLE 9:10

Average Cabinet Durability
In Selected Ranges on the Coalitional Status Index:
Interwar–Postwar Contrasts

Cabinet Coalitional Status	All Cabinets		Cabinets in Multiparty Parliaments	
	Interwar	Postwar	Interwar	Postwar
.400 to highest	8.0	9.9	7.7	6.0
.200 to .399	11.4	16.9	11.4	14.1
.100 to .199	35.6	17.5	34.8	13.0
.001 to .99	17.2	20.5	14.3	19.8
.000 (mwc)	49.1	62.9	52.4	53.6
—.001 to —.099	27.9	29.3	27.9	29.3
—.100 to —.199	21.2	13.5	21.2	13.5
—.200 to —.399	17.6	14.3	17.6	14.3
—.400 to lowest	13.4	9.7	13.4	9.7

Note: The cell entries indicate the average durability of cabinets at varying ranges in cabinet coalitional status.

index. First, and most importantly, the patterns indicate that cabinet durability in each era is related to cabinet coalitional status. In each period, minimum winning cabinets are by far the most durable, averaging 49 months in the interwar years and 63 months in the postwar years. As cabinets deviate from minimum winning status, cabinet durability decreases. During the interwar years, oversized cabinets last 16.5 months and undersized cabinets averaged 20.2 months; among the most deviant cabinets (those exceeding .19), oversized cabinets averaged 9.9 months and undersized cabinets averaged 15.9 months. During the postwar years, oversized cabinets averaged 16.4 months and undersized cabinets averaged 19.9 months. Among the highly deviant postwar cabinets, oversized cabinets averaged 14.9 months and undersized cabinets averaged 13.4 months.

Aside from the existence of the relationship in each era, the differences and similarities between eras are interesting. The main difference between the two periods is the greater durability of minimum winning cabinets for the postwar years. This difference occurs because single party majority cabinets were actually less durable than minimum winning coalitions during the interwar years: single party majority cabinets averaged forty-three months in the interwar years whereas minimum winning coalitions lasted approximately fifty-two months. The durability of minimum winning coalitions is relatively similar for interwar and postwar multiparty parliaments. During the postwar years, single party majority cabinets were considerably more durable than minimum winning coalitions (averaging eighty-five months as compared to fifty-three months).

Of the foregoing patterns, the greater transiency of interwar single party majority governments is the most interesting. This pattern may occur partly as a result of the greater crisis environment of the interwar years and the greater flexibility of minimum winning coalitions in surviving the electoral impact of the crises. In other words, it may be easier to build a minimum winning coalition that controls a fairly sizable bloc of parliamentary seats and that can thereby survive short-term electoral fluctuation than it is to sustain a single party majority government from election to election during an age of perpetual crisis. When two parties coalesce to govern, each controlling over 30 percent of the vote, for example, a sizable loss during parliamentary elections is required to defeat the coalition. By contrast a single party majority of 51 to 55 percent of the vote (the classic situation) is less flexible in meeting such short-term shifts. While a case-by-case study would be necessary to support the argument, and will not be attempted here, it is a plausible suggestion, implying that minimum winning coalitions—especially those involving fairly large parties—might be more appropriate to durable government during crisis situations than the classical single party majority cabinet in a competitive two or two and one-half party system.

Aside from the patterns distinguishing minimum winning cabinets in the two eras, deviant cabinets evidence a slight but fairly systematic pattern, falling faster during the postwar years than the interwar years. This pattern is particularly noticeable among oversized multiparty parliaments that deviate from minimum winning status by a score of at least .10 and among undersized cabinets that depart from minimum winning status by at least a score of −.10. Among oversized cabinets in multiparty parliaments, interwar cabinets lasted fifteen months in contrast to approximately twelve months' duration during the postwar years. Among undersized cabinets experiencing moderate to extreme deviancy, interwar cabinets lasted approximately eighteen months in contrast to thirteen and one-half months during the postwar years. No firm reason can be given for the interwar–postwar differences in the behavior of deviant cabinets, but it is interesting to speculate on the contrast. As emphasized earlier, interwar parliaments were less institutionalized than postwar parliaments. It is reasonable to expect that this factor may have contributed to the interwar–postwar differences. Because parties were relatively unexperienced in party negotiations and lacked norms fully supportive of parliamentary maneuvering, they may have felt more committed to the cabinets formed in the parliament: thus the tendency toward greater durability among deviant cabinets during the interwar years.

The foregoing discussion indicates that broad environmental and institutional differences between eras may have altered somewhat the form of the relationship between cabinet coalitional status and cabinet durability. Historical context does appear to exert an effect on the relationship between coalitional status and cabinet durability. An interesting consequence is that the strength of the relationship in each era is greater than for the entire time period. Cabinet coalitional status accounts for 31 percent of the variance (w^2) in cabinet durability for the interwar and postwar periods combined. When the two time periods are separated so that the difference in the form of the relationship can be considered, cabinet coalitional status accounts for 35 percent of the interwar variance and 37 percent of the postwar variance in cabinet durability.

PARTY SYSTEMS AND CABINET DURABILITY: INTERWAR–
POSTWAR CONTRASTS

A final consideration remains. To what extent do the party system characteristics account for cabinet durability? Table 9:11 presents the appropriate regression coefficients for all cabinets in the interwar and postwar years. This table indicates that significant relationships do exist in both eras, though the patterning and strength of the relationships differ. Among interwar parliaments, CPSI3 accounts for almost 16 percent of the variance in cabinet durability. The critical factor, however, is the curvilinear nature of the pattern: CPSI3 (logged) accounts for approximately 28 percent of the variance in cabinet durability. With the addition of CPSI1 (logged) and CPSI2 (logged), the party system characteristics account for approximately 29 percent of the variance in cabinet durability. By contrast, among postwar parliaments, CPSI3 accounts for approximately 9 percent of the variance in cabinet durability. CPSI3 (logged) accounts for approximately 17 percent of the variance; including the two other CPSI variables increases the variance explained to approximately 20 percent. These results indicate that the logarithmic transformation of the CPSI scores in the interwar years produces a greater increase in variance

TABLE 9:11

Regression Coefficients
Contrasting Interwar and Postwar Patterns:
Determinants of Cabinet Durability

Relationship (Independent → Dependent)	Interwar r	Postwar r
DCC → cabinet durability	−.146	−.116
CPSI1 → cabinet durability	−.300	−.214
CPSI2 → cabinet durability	−.274	−.222
CPSI3 → cabinet durability	−.384	−.300
CPSI1, 2, 3 → cabinet durability	.397	.311
CPSI1 (logged) → cabinet durability	−.451	−.231
CPSI2 (logged) → cabinet durability	−.404	−.245
CPSI3 (logged) → cabinet durability	−.527	−.415
CPSI1, 2, 3 (logged) → cabinet durability	.537	.448

explained (an increase of approximately 14 percent) than for the postwar years (an increase of approximately 10 percent). Once again, the large number of unstable, extremely polarized and hyperfractionalized parliaments during the interwar years create a significant curvilinear pattern. Since such parliaments are less evident in the postwar years, the curvilinear pattern is less evident and thus the logarithmic transformation is less significant (though by no means trivial).

In addition to these differences the strength of the relationship between party system characteristics and cabinet coalitional status is greater for the interwar years than for the postwar years. This result is consistent with those found earlier in this chapter. During both the interwar and postwar years, cabinet coalitional status accounted for roughly the same percentage of variance in cabinet durability, though the form of the relationship differed between the two periods. A significant difference obtained, however, in the strength of the relationship between the party system characteristics and cabinet coalitional status in the two time periods; the parliamentary party system is much more influential for the interwar years than for the postwar years. It is for this reason that a difference obtains in the strength of the relationship between party system characteristics and cabinet durability. The party system characteristics are more influential determinants of cabinet coalitional status during the interwar years than the postwar years. Since cabinet coalitional status explains roughly the same degree of variance in cabinet durability for both eras, the parliamentary party system accounts for more variance in cabinet durability during the interwar years than postwar years.

CONCLUSION

In the introduction to this chapter, several reasons were given for contrasting behavior in the interwar and postwar periods. First, it was noted that the predictions of the theory might hold for one period but not for another, forcing reexamination of the theory. In no instance have serious discrepancies occurred between predictions and findings. All expected patterns hold for each time period:

1. Party System Characteristics and Cabinet Coalitional Status

a) for the interwar years, the complex interaction of fractionalization, instability, and cleavage conflict account for more than 45 percent of the variance in coalitional status;

b) for the postwar years, the complex interaction of party system variables accounts for 36 percent of the variance in coalitional status.

2. Cabinet Coalitional Status and Cabinet Durability

a) for the interwar years, cabinet coalitional status accounts for approximately 35 percent of the variance in cabinet durability.

b) for the postwar years, cabinet coalitional status accounts for approximately 37 percent of the variance in cabinet durability.

3. Party System Characteristics and Cabinet Durability

a) for the interwar years, the interaction of fractionalization, instability, and cleavage conflict account for approximately 29 percent of the variance in cabinet durability;

b) for the postwar years, the party system variables account for approximately 20 percent of the variance in cabinet durability.

Second, the introduction suggested that the historical eras might differ in the bargaining conditions and, consequently, in the coalitional patterns predominating in the two time periods. Clear differences do emerge:

1. Parliaments experiencing moderate to high cleavage conflict predominated during the interwar years, with extremely polarized parliaments constituting 25 percent of the interwar parliaments; during this time period, undersized cabinets were the most frequent type of cabinet.

2. Parliaments experiencing low to moderate cleavage conflict predominated during the postwar years, with minimum winning and oversized cabinets characterizing the era.

3. The relationship between cleavage conflict and cabinet coalitional status was greater for the interwar than postwar years; the increase in explained variance owing to the interaction of cleavage conflict with fractionalization and instability was greater for the postwar years. Both of these patterns were attributed to the presence of extremely conflictual party systems during the interwar years.

Third, temporal contrasts were conducted in the expectation that such a procedure might uncover patterns peculiar to a particular time period, suggesting a unique influence of historical era on the process of cabinet formation and maintenance. Such a pattern was uncovered in contrasts between eras in the relationship between coalitional status and cabinet durability. While the strength of the relationship in each time period was roughly the same, the pattern of the relationship differed: minimum winning cabinets were more durable and deviant cabinets generally less durable for the postwar years than for the interwar years. These contrasting patterns were attributed—though only in a speculative fashion—to broad historical differences between the two eras, specifically the more institutionalized and less crisis-filled nature of the postwar parliaments.

Finally, interwar–postwar contrasts were conducted in order to determine if analytic continuities do exist in the cabinet processes characterizing these two eras. The party systems of interwar parliaments differ to such a degree from those of the postwar years that it is tempting to treat each period as a separate world, adhering to distinct and unrelated norms of behavior. The patterns uncovered in this study emphasize that the differences between the two eras do not necessitate different explanatory models. While this study leaves considerable room for additional analysis of unexplained variance within each era, the theory presented in this study applies fairly well to both eras. It is true that the party systems have changed considerably over the years, with a marked decrease in polarization evident during the postwar years. These changes indicate that analysis of interwar parliaments should emphasize party behavior under conditions of low *a priori* willingness to bargain whereas postwar analysis should emphasize party behavior under the opposite bargaining constraints. Throughout these two eras, nevertheless, parties' underlying quest for power has not altered. In each era, it is minimum winning cabinets that endure.

IV | Conclusion

10 | The Analysis of Parliamentary Coalitions: Problems and Prospects

The significance and underlying thesis of this study is summarized best perhaps by the British parliamentary analyst, W. L. Middleton, writing in 1932:

> No political system can evade the problem of authority. It must be a principle aim of any constitution, even of the most democratic, to produce Governments which shall govern, which shall possess real initiative and command. ... If a wide stretch of experience be reviewed it will be found that the power of the Executive ... has varied very greatly from one legislature to another. ... The explanation of these variations is not far to seek. ... A ministry exercises its power ... not directly, but through the majority to which it looks for support. If a Government has a confident and continuous command of its majority, it can be firm in its handling of the Chamber. It can be a Government which governs. If, on the contrary, it has only a loose hold over its majority, it is less able to impose respect for the proper attributes of the Executive. It is the variation in the efficiency of this machinery which accounts for the fluctuation of executive authority. Everything depends on the majority ... on the degree of confidence in the Ministry which it possesses. ...

And, as Middleton concludes, "where all majorities are coalitions, this means that everything depends on the nature of the coalition. The Executive is strongest when the Government is the trusted agent of a coalition of natural allies. . . ."[1] Though Middleton wrote a generation before the introduction of game-theoretic analysis into political science, his examination of parliamentary behavior, and the broader generalizations he drew from that analysis, illuminate immeasurably the calculations and maneuvers endemic to the quest for parliamentary power. In a very real sense, this study attempts to explicate, operationalize, and refine Middleton's insights by employing a modified version of contemporary game theory.

Durable cabinets can form and do form in multiparty systems. A critical element in the formation and maintenance of the cabinet is "the nature of the coalition": its coalitional status. If a cabinet achieves minimum winning status, it probably will endure. Among multiparty parliaments, minimum winning coalitions are most likely to form in conditions characterized by information certainty and by a moderate to highly generalized willingness of parties to bargain.

Transient cabinets arise in a multiparty setting if the cabinet deviates from minimum winning status. Deviant cabinets can be of two types: oversized cabinets (those greater than minimum winning) and undersized cabinets (those less than minimum winning). The formation of deviant cabinets is determined by the complex interaction of information certainty and *a priori* willingness to bargain. In parliaments characterized by high *a priori* willingness to bargain combined with low information certainty, oversized cabinets will form. In conditions characterized by low *a priori* willingness to bargain and low information certainty,

[1] W. L. Middleton, *The French Political System* (London: Ernest Benn, Ltd., 1932), pp. 151-154.

undersized cabinets will form. As argued in Chapter 3 information certainty and *a priori* willingness to bargain are influenced by the party system existing in parliament.

These conclusions have two very general implications. First, the conclusions raise serious questions about prevailing views on the relationship between party systems and democratic government. The concluding chapter will address these questions. Second, while the findings in this study are not overwhelming in their statistical power, they are systematic and significant, particularly when the wide range of countries and historical conditions is considered. By their very existence, therefore, these findings underscore the need for serious attention to the methodology employed in the analysis of coalitions: is there perhaps even more explanatory power in coalition theories than present methodology allows us to ascertain? The remainder of this chapter specifies more fully the methodological problems referred to, emphasizing problems of theory interpretation and research design as they apply to this study; technical problems of measurement were raised in Part II. Many of the methodological problems evident in this work are shared with a number of coalition analysts. It is my hope that clear, open recognition of the problems will engender greater concern with them, guide future coalitional analysts in the application of coalition theory to other political settings, and aid scholars in the evaluation and modification of this study.

THEORY-INTERPRETATION

The generalizations of formal theories, as analytic truths derived from a set of simple assumptions and specified parameters, do not provide explanations of real-world behavior. The theorems must be interpreted empirically before explanation can ensue. This procedure is often referred to as a "bridging process."[2] The problem inherent in this process —that of linking theoretical concepts to empirical or "experimental" observations—is stated clearly by Nagel:

> . . . though theoretical concepts may be articulated with a high degree of precision, rules of correspondence coordinate them with experimental ideas that are far less definite. The haziness that surrounds such correspondence rules is inevitable, since experimental ideas do not have the sharp contours that theoretical notions possess. This is the primary reason why it is not possible to formalize with much precision the rules (or habits) for establishing a correspondence between theoretical and experimental ideas.[3]

Nagel is noting here the difficulty of empirical interpretation in areas where experimental conditions may be approached and where theories are well developed. In the current study—based on a "quasi-deductive" theory and nonexperimental observations—empirical interpretation is even more difficult.

Specifying the Units of Action

A first problem in the interpretation of coalition theory is determining the relevant units of action: who are the actors in the coalitional game? This decision is critical because testing the predictions of coalition theory assumes that actors can be identified clearly: otherwise it is impossible to determine if the predictions have proved correct. If a researcher assumes that actors as individuals are the units

[2] For an excellent discussion of these problems in the context of public choice theories, see Oran R. Young, "Political Choice" (unpublished manuscript, University of Texas at Austin, 1974).

[3] Ernest Nagel, *The Structure of Science* (New York: Harcourt, Brace and World, Inc., 1961), p. 100.

of coalition, then in any political setting (such as a legislature) a minimum winning coalition would be 50 percent plus one of the individuals (legislators); departure from that number would contradict the theory's predictions (given a minimum winning prediction). Under such an assumption, few if any of the parliaments examined in this study would contain minimum winning cabinets. From a different perspective, however, departure from 50 percent plus one would be appropriate to minimum winning status. If the units of action are ideological factions, geographic delegations, or political parties, a minimum winning coalition could range from 50 percent plus one upwards. The critical factor in such situations would be the legislative weight (reliable voting strength) of the coalitional units.

In this study, political party has been employed as the unit of action. This assumption is largely valid for most parliaments; the literature on parliamentary behavior argues fairly clearly that party is the most important unit of coalition negotiation.[4] Nevertheless, interparty alliances (at the electoral or parliamentary level as in France)[5] and intra-

[4] The assumption is shared, for example, with Michael Leiserson, "Coalitions in Politics: A Theoretical and Empirical Study" (unpublished Ph.D. dissertation, Yale University, 1966); Eric Browne, "Testing Theories of Coalition Formation in the European Context," *Comparative Political Studies* 3 (January 1971); Eric Browne and Mark N. Franklin, "Aspects of Coalition Payoffs in European Parliamentary Democracies," *APSR* 68 (June 1973); Sven Groennings, "Patterns, Strategies and Payoffs in Norwegian Coalition Formation," in Sven Groennings, W. E. Kelly, and Michael Leiserson, eds., *The Study of Coalition Behavior* (New York: Holt, Rinehart and Winston, Inc., 1970); Abraham De Swaan, "An Empirical Model of Coalition Formation as an N-Person Game of Policy Distance Minimization," in Groennings, Kelly, and Leiserson, eds., *The Study of Coalition Behavior.*

[5] Middleton, *The French Political System*, pp. 53-133; Maurice Duverger, *Political Parties* (New York: John Wiley and Sons, 1963), pp. 330-351, 410-411.

party factions (as in the Italian Christian Democratic Party) may also influence coalition negotiations or coalition maintenance. In Italy, for example, it is often the unhappiness of a Christian Democratic faction with its ministerial payoffs within the DC, rather than the DC's unhappiness with its overall proportion of cabinet seats, that brings down a coalition government.[6]

Because of the foregoing problems, the choice of party as the unit of behavior in this study has both negative and positive consequences. From a positive standpoint, party is a fairly unambiguous behavioral unit that can be isolated across all countries without the imposition of a significant number of subjective judgments as to its identity and size. "Party" has a fairly clear substantive interpretation in the literature on comparative politics.[7] And the consistent use of party as the analytic unit of behavior allows this study to provide a baseline against which to compare future studies that depart from a consistent use of party. On the negative side, however, the use of party builds in biases in the analysis for those parliamentary settings in which factions or interparty alliances play a significant role. The extent and direction of the bias is difficult to estimate without

[6] See the discussion of Italian cabinet formation and maintenance in Giorgio Galli and Alfonso Prandi, *Patterns of Political Participation in Italy* (New Haven: Yale University Press, 1970). See also Raphael Zariski, "Intra-Party Conflict in a Dominant Party: The Experience of Italian Christian Democracy," *Journal of Politics* 27 (February 1965); Raphael Zariski, "The Italian Socialist Party: A Case Study in Factional Conflict," *APSR* 56 (June 1962), 372-390. For France see Duncan MacRae, Jr., "Intraparty Divisions and Cabinet Coalitions in the Fourth French Republic," *Comparative Studies in Society and History* 5 (January 1963), 164-211.

[7] Two illustrative discussions of the concept are Leon D. Epstein, *Political Parties in Western Democracies* (New York: Praeger Publishers, 1967), pp. 1-19; Frank Sorauf, *Party Politics in America* (Boston: Little, Brown and Co., 1968), pp. 1-25.

exhaustive case-by-case analysis of the parliaments in this study, a procedure beyond the author's current resources. It must be emphasized, furthermore, that even with intimate knowledge of a parliamentary setting, the determination of "actor" is not an easy or straightforward process.

Attention must be given to the conceptual meaning of actor before a case-by-case determination of actors can be made. At a definitional level, an actor is a unit of behavior concerned with obtaining specified payoffs in a particular situation: an actor has a preference ordering in regard to acceptable payoffs and is capable of maneuvering to obtain those payoffs. Political parties meet this definition in a general sense because they possess party platforms, caucusing procedures, caucus leaders, and so forth. To the degree that studies depart from party as the basic actor—arguing, for example, that ministerial preference orderings in a parliament are more clearly represented by intraparty factions or interparty alliances, then for each of these behavioral units, general support must be given that they meet the definition of an actor. Among the criteria that could be employed to determine the identity and composition of actors are: (1) commonality of goal-orientation; (2) commonality of preference ordering; (3) mechanisms for sharing or distributing payoffs; (4) mechanisms for interpersonal communication and planning.

Actor Motivation

Aside from advancement in problems with actor identification, a second area for analytic refinement and extension of the present study is to broaden the conception of actor motivations. This study does not exhaust all of the motivational elements that could be subsumed within the general framework outlined in Chapter 2. For example, policy payoffs are not included in the study. As the analysis is extended

in the future, this omission could have significant implica·
tions. Obtaining ministerial seats in the cabinet may be the
most direct manner by which parties in a parliamentary
coalition assure policy victories. Nevertheless, some coalitions may be sustained by parties that, though not in the
cabinet, deliver their votes on the promise of specific policy
behavior by the cabinet.

Judging from the comparative literature, supporting parties are not relevant to most parliamentary settings. There
appears to be a widespread norm that all parties in the supporting coalition are in the cabinet. This norm results in a
large part because parties desire specific ministerial positions: one aspect of policy payoff will normally be control
of vital ministries that regulate the policy areas of particular
concern to specific parties (the agriculture ministry for
Agrarian parties, and so forth). Nevertheless, the norm is
not applicable to all parliamentary settings. For cases where
supporting parties do play a formal role in coalition support,
a slightly different conception of coalitional status is required. For example, coalitional status could be calculated
with a party outside of the cabinet considered as a relevant
coalition partner if arrangements could be uncovered linking the party and its votes to the cabinet in return for policy
considerations. The systematic inclusion of such behavior
into the analysis of parliamentary coalitions could indicate
that a good deal of unexplained variance in this study resulted from the omission of these supporting parties. For
example, a fair number of durable undersized cabinets
exist in this study; it could be that these cabinets are formal-
ly supported by explicit extraministerial parties and that a
slightly expanded concept of minimum winning status
would be appropriate.[8]

[8] For example, consider D. A. Rustow's discussion of minority
parliamentarian in *The Politics of Compromise: A Study of Parties*

The Bargaining Conditions

Assuming that one can identify the actors in a coalitional game and specify the relevant behavorial motivations, a third problem is to specify the behavioral outcomes expected from the actors. Among other factors, this specification entails the consideration of the bargaining conditions that exist in parliament. By bargaining conditions I mean those features of the coalitional situation—independent of the structure of the game itself—that constrain actors' calculations. While many relevant bargaining conditions may exist, the two considered in this study are information certainty and *a priori* willingness to bargain.[9] It should be clear that even in regard to these two bargaining conditions, this study has not exhausted the consideration of empirical indicators. I argue that variations in specific party system characteristics should be interpreted as variation in information certainty and *a priori* willingness to bargain. My arguments are plausible; unfortunately, they are not definitive. A major area for continued refinement of this study is the examination of the actual linkage of fractionalization and stability with information certainty, and cleavage conflict with willingness to bargain. For example, a set of case studies might be useful, employing survey techniques to compare willingness to bargain and information certainty among parliamentarians in different party systems.[10]

---

and Cabinet Government in Sweden (Princeton: Princeton University Press, 1955).

[9] For a useful discussion of bargaining conditions in the U.S. Congress, see Barbara Hinckley, "Coalitions in Congress: Size and Ideological Distance," *Midwest Journal of Political Science* 16 (May 1972), 197-207.

[10] Within the past decade several attitudinal studies of parliamentarians have emerged, though not focused on coalitional behavior as such. See Robert D. Putnam, *The Beliefs of Politicians: Ideology, Conflict and Democracy in Britain and Italy* (New Haven: Yale

In addition, it must be emphasized that the foregoing party system variables do not exhaust the relevant indicators of information certainty and willingness to bargain. At a systemic level, further variables could be useful. Both the size of the parliament and the size of the nation-state might affect bargaining conditions.[11] As suggested in Chap-

---

University Press, 1973); Gordon J. DiRenzo, *Personality, Power and Politics* (Notre Dame, Ind.: Notre Dame University Press, 1967); Hans Daalder and Jerrold D. Rusk, "Perceptions of Party in the Dutch Parliament," in Samuel C. Patterson and John C. Wahlke, eds., *Comparative Legislative Behavior: Frontiers of Research* (New York: Wiley-Interscience, 1972); Allan Kornberg and Robert C. Frasure, "Policy Differences in British Parliamentary Parties," *APSR* 65 (September 1971).

[11] An interesting analysis of the impact of size on democratic politics is contained in Robert A. Dahl and Edward R. Tufte, *Size and Democracy* (Stanford: Stanford University Press, 1973).

An interesting proposal relating the size of the largest parliamentary party to coalition politics in multiparty systems is presented by David Nachmias. He argues that parliaments with a dominant (though nonmajority) party experience a peculiar form of coalition politics in which "coalitions larger than necessary to win are formed," and calls, therefore, "for the inclusion of an additional parameter in minimal range models." "This parameter can be identified as veto power—i.e., the extent to which a single party dominates the process of coalition formation." While I find this to be an interesting and creative idea, and one that should be examined more exhaustively, I am not persuaded by Nachmias' illustration of it with the Israeli example. I feel that the peculiar nature of Israeli coalition politics can be more persuasively explained by the peculiar international situation of Israel in the Middle East, producing domestic politics akin to that seen in many other Western nations during wartime: durable oversized parliamentary coalitions.

Additionally, I find the conceptual argument difficult. How does one define party dominance as an attribute independent of its perceived effect? If size is the sole criterion, then a number of examples of fairly large parties scattered throughout Western parliamentary politics would be considered dominant parties—yet they have been unable to force themselves into coalitions. Consider, for example, the Social Democrats in Norway during the 1960s, who controlled between 45 and 49 percent of the parliamentary seats yet were omitted

ter 9, the institutionalization of the parliament might influence information certainty. For example, Polsby has argued that the existence of universalistic-automatic criteria is one attribute of an institutionalized legislature.[12] It would seem a plausible argument that such a situation—with well-developed precedents, rules, norms, and impersonal codes—facilitates the ability of actors to communicate and interact in a patterned, open, stable manner conducive to information certainty. A third important systemic variable could be federalism. In nations with federal arrangements, provincial or state parliaments could provide an experimental setting in which party coalitions could be attempted between long-time adversaries, with the intermediate provincial experience making national-level coalitions more possible than they would be without the provincial experience.[13]

Finally, this study has focused exclusively on bargaining

---

from the coalitions that governed. Perhaps size together with strategic ideological position can be considered the definitional components of dominance. If so, Nachmias' concept of dominance possibly can be integrated with Axelrod's concept of minimal connected winning coalitions in such a manner as to successfully account for deviant cases scattered throughout the data in this study. Firm conclusions in that regard, however, must await future analysis. See David Nachmias, "Coalition Politics in Israel," *Comparative Political Studies* 7 (Oct. 1974), 316-333; Robert Axelrod, *Conflict of Interest* (Chicago: Markham Publishing Co., 1970).

[12] Nelson Polsby, "The Institutionalization of the House of Representatives," in Herbert Hirsch and M. Donald Hancock, eds., *Comparative Legislative Systems* (New York: The Free Press, 1971); see also the various essays in Allan Kornberg, ed., *Legislatures in Comparative Perspective* (New York: David McKay Co., Inc., 1973): of particular interest is the framework presented by Andrew J. Milnor and Mark N. Franklin, in "Patterns of Opposition Behavior in Modern Legislatures."

[13] On federalism see William S. Livingston, *Federalism and Constitutional Change* (Oxford: at the Clarendon Press, 1956); and *Federalism in the Commonwealth* (London: Cassell and Co., 1963).

conditions characterizing a parliament as the unit of analysis. Fractionalization, stability, and cleavage conflict, as employed in this study, are all constant for the life of a parliament. Yet information certainty and *a priori* willingness to bargain may vary significantly within the life of a parliament. Part of the variation could occur as a result of changes in party system fractionalization or cleavage conflict during the life of a parliament: parties may merge or split during a parliamentary session; national crises may polarize parties on a cleavage during the midst of a parliament. In addition, the bargaining conditions could vary within a parliament in response to the development or reduction of interpersonal animosities between party leaders; closeness of mandatory elections; success or failure of critical policies associated with specific parties; and so forth.

Determining the Operative Decision Rules

A final problem to be mentioned in theory-interpretation, though assuredly not the final problem that could be considered, is the determination of the operative decision rules: what parliamentary margin constitutes a "winning" margin.[14] In other words, assuming that there is a point in the parliamentary process at which actors can be said to win—that point being the installation of a cabinet that has a good probability of enduring—serious consideration must be paid to identifying the decision rules by which the parliamentary actors will determine that victory. Most analysts assume that a bare parliamentary majority (50 percent plus

[14] For two useful studies of the operative decision rules in congressional coalition politics see Barbara Hinckley, "Coalitions in Congress: Size in a Series of Games," *American Political Quarterly* (August 1973), pp. 339-359; David Koehler, "The Legislative Process and the Minimal Winning Coalition," in Richard Niemi and Herbert Weisberg, eds., *Probability Models of Collective Decision-Making* (Columbus, Ohio: Charles Merrill, 1972), pp. 149-164.

one) is the operative rule. This is the formal level required for the installation of a cabinet. But is the formal decision rule the actual decision rule? There are several reasons why the parties might not treat a bare nominal majority as the level of winning: (1) the ability of a cabinet to implement certain policies (such as constitutional revisions) might require extraordinary majorities; (2) a nominal majority surpassing 50 percent plus one might not be a long-term reliable majority; (3) a cabinet might require an oversized majority in order to remain viable in all policy areas. We could envision, for example, a cabinet of three parties (A with 20 percent of the seats, B with 31 percent of the seats, and C with 20 percent of the seats); on foreign policy A and B could form the parliamentary majority whereas B and C could form the domestic policy majority. This situation can be termed a "revolving" minimum winning cabinet and could follow the general behavioral patterns attributed to minimum winning cabinets in Chapter 2. The present study treats 50 percent plus one of the legislators in all lower houses of parliament as the operative level for a winning coalition. By applying this same decision rule across all parliaments, consistency is maintained and a baseline for comparison is established. Nevertheless, case analyses could modify the conclusions of this study by determining systematically that different decision rules are applicable in specific parliamentary settings.[15]

RESEARCH DESIGN

A second set of problems encountered in this study center on the research design. Within the social sciences, no single

[15] For a comprehensive listing of other factors to consider in coalitional analysis, see Groennings, "Notes toward Theories of Coalition Behavior in Multiparty Systems," in Groennings, Kelly, and Leiserson, *The Study of Coalition Behavior*.

research design will suffice normally as a comprehensive test of theoretical propositions. The difficulties facing social scientists range from data availability and reliability to serious disputes over the proper methodology to employ in the analysis of the data that we do have. Leaving aside the more philosophical problems, three limitations are particularly relevant to the present study.

Control of Background Variables

This study has tested hypotheses by examining covariation among specified variables across a set of "similar parliamentary systems." Similar systems analysis was employed in order to control—at least to a degree—the background factors that might otherwise critically distort the tests. Obviously, all such factors have not been controlled. War years have been omitted because, in the extreme crisis environment of such periods, parties may well forego the parliamentary game, seeking to save the game; in such periods, durable grand coalitions are not unknown. It is equally possible that peacetime parliaments may experience similar environmental pressures, producing behavior that is deviant in the analysis in this study.

One of the most deviant cases in this study, for example, is the 1928 "Weimar" Cabinet in Germany. Despite the highly conflictual ($DCC = 2.78$), unstable ($Psi = .35$), and fractionalized ($Psf = 8.28$) conditions in parliament ($CPSI3 = 4.55$), an oversized nineteen-month cabinet formed. A good argument can be made that this cabinet formed in an attempt to save the parliamentary game, though in violation of the behavioral patterns consistent with playing the game.[16] Because of inadequate data whereby to specify all parliaments that might entail similar con-

[16] Henry A. Turner, Jr., *Stresemann and the Politics of the Weimar Republic* (Princeton: Princeton University Press, 1963), p. 240.

ditions, the 1928 Weimar Cabinet has been included in all statistical analysis in this study. Nevertheless, it and other cabinets may well detract from the statistical explanatory power obtained in this study—but for reasons quite consistent with the theory. A systematic analysis of deviant cabinets must await the cumulation of a richer body of literature in regard to specific parliaments. In the meantime, background factors—that may depress the statistical explanatory power of this study—remain uncontrolled.

Within-Parliament Analysis

A second limitation in the research design of this study—and a limitation expressly acknowledged from the outset—is the lack of focus on within-parliament behavior. The theory in Chapter 2 describes a process of cabinet resolution for deviant cabinets. While this study has determined that deviant cabinets do in fact last for a shorter time than minimum winning cabinets, it has not examined the process of that resolution within parliament. It is the author's intention to devote future analysis to the patterns of within-parliament behavior. The current study provides a very basic foundation indicating the general power of the propositions when applied without regard to initial or subsequent cabinets: later work will examine the extent to which within-parliament behavior corresponds to the patterns suggested in the theory and the degree to which knowledge of a cabinet's temporal position in a parliamentary sequence increases the general statistical explanatory power attained by the theory.

As a suggestive indication of within-parliament behavior, however, Table 10:1 specifies the fate of initial cabinets for all peacetime parliaments (1918-1974) in which new cabinets formed. According to the process outlined in the theory, when a minimum winning cabinet forms as the

TABLE 10:1

The Fate of Initial Cabinets

Initial Deviant Cabinet	All Cabinets	Cabinets Deviant by .05 or more	Cabinets Deviant by .20 or more
Resolves toward *mwc*	29 (.165)	26	20
Increases departure from *mwc*	16 (.091)	14	5
Parliament dissolves early (before 36 months) and cabinet falls	36 (.205)	34	21
Cabinet lasts throughout parliament and for 36 months or more	17 (.097)	10	2
Initial Minimum Winning Cabinet			
Changes to another *mwc*	2 (.011)		
Departs from *mwc*	4 (.023)		
Parliament dissolves early (before 36 months) and cabinet falls	14 (.080)		
Cabinet lasts longer than 36 months	58 (.330)		
Total	176		

Note: Percentages do not necessarily sum to 1.00 because of rounding error.

initial cabinet in a parliament, it should endure. When the initial cabinet that forms is either oversized or undersized, parties should attempt to resolve the cabinet toward minimum winning status: cabinet resolution would ideally occur by the formation of a less deviant cabinet during the same parliament though early dissolution of parliament would also be a mechanism that might be employed. In Table 10:1, the behavior of deviant cabinets is divided into four categories: (1) resolving toward mwc; (2) increasing departure from mwc; (3) parliament dissolves early (before thirty-six months); (4) a cabinet lasts the life of a parliament (for a period of thirty-six months or more). The first and third categories are treated as consistent with the process of cabinet resolution; the second and fourth categories are treated as inconsistent. The behavior of initial minimum winning cabinets is divided into four categories: (1) changes to another minimum winning cabinet; (2) departure from minimum winning cabinet; (3) parliament dissolves early (before thirty-six months) and cabinet falls; (4) cabinet lasts more than thirty-six months. The first three categories are treated as inconsistent with the theory; the fourth category is treated as consistent with the theory. It should be noted that the threshold point for determining early parliamentary dissolution (earlier than thirty-six months) is an arbitrary decision; the legal limit on parliament varies considerably. In addition, the determination of early dissolution requires a resolution of a number of conceptual problems that will be addressed in later work. Another limitation with the presentation of the data in Table 10:1 is that it focuses solely on initial cabinets; the overall process of cabinet resolution may really approximate that pattern suggested in the theory despite the failure of the initial cabinet to resolve toward a less deviant cabinet (for example, the second cabinet may be followed by a much less deviant and more durable cabinet). For these reasons, Table 10:1 should be viewed as suggestive only, to be superseded by future work.

As a general pattern, Table 10:1 indicates that the process

of cabinet resolution and maintenance suggested in the theory does characterize initial cabinets within Western parliaments. Among all initial cabinets (including both deviant and minimum winning cabinets) approximately 70 percent conform to behavior consistent with the theory. Among initial deviant cabinets, the percentage approximates 66 percent whereas 74 percent of initial minimum winning cabinets conform to the appropriate pattern. The pattern for deviant cabinets is even more dramatic when those approximating minimum winning status are excluded. Among all initial cabinets deviating from minimum winning status by an absolute score of .05 or more, 71 percent conform to expected behavior. And among initial cabinets deviating from minimum winning status by an absolute score of .20 or more, 85 percent either resolved toward minimum winning status within the parliament's life or dissolved parliament early.

STATISTICAL ANALYSIS VS. CASE STUDIES

A final problem to be mentioned with regard to the research design in this study is its reliance on statistical analysis. Examples have been given that illustrate basic tendencies in the data, but systematic investigations of individual parliaments and cabinets have not been conducted. It is the author's view that the large-scale aggregate analysis employed in this study is a useful instrument for gauging the general validity of the propositions—assuming that the operational indicators are reasonably valid. On the other hand, statistical analysis will not suffice for political analysts to fully evaluate the utility of coalitional theories. In the foregoing section on theory interpretation I outlined a number of conceptual problems that could occur for specific parliaments. It is simply impossible to obtain sufficient information on all Western parliaments to ensure that the problems outlined earlier are resolved in aggregate analysis. Consequently, the findings of this study must be viewed as tentative and suggestive; a series of case studies by students of specific parliaments is highly desirable.[17]

CONCLUSION: A SYNTHESIS OF SCHOOLS

The discussion in the foregoing pages indicates that this study has encountered its share of methodological difficulties. The approaches taken to these methodological dilemmas, I believe, have been appropriate and justifiable within the resources currently available. The resolution of conceptual problems such as the identification of actors or the specification of minimum winning status has been consistent across all parliaments and in keeping with the balance of the comparative literature on Western party systems and parliaments. Aside from the omission of cabinets during war years and the omission of nonpartisan and provisional cabinets, all cabinets formed during the life of a parliament have been analyzed in this study, including some extremely deviant cabinets such as the 1928 Weimar Cabinet. Since insufficient information exists to characterize the "background" conditions of all parliaments, I have chosen to omit no deviant cabinets. To do otherwise would allow the possibility of unduly biasing the analysis in the direction predicted by the theory.

Nevertheless, the limitations specified in the foregoing pages must be treated quite seriously. While I believe that further resolution of the problems will strengthen rather

---

[17] An excellent exception to the generalization that case studies are lacking is Frederick C. Engelmann's study, "Haggling for the Equilibrium: The Renegotiation of the Austrian Coalition, 1959," *APSR* 56 (September 1962).

than weaken the explanatory power of the theory, this conclusion must await future studies. It should be evident, however, that the comparative examination of coalitional behavior is a fruitful area for analysis; there is a particular need for in-depth case studies of coalitional processes in individual parliaments throughout the historical time period covered in this study. Finally the methodological problems that remain in this study should not blind us to its contributions. Chapter 11 will focus on its substantive implications. In closing this chapter, I would like to stress an analytic advancement made in this study.

As mentioned in Chapter 1, this study is an extension and synthesis of two schools of comparative analysis. The first school I designate as the Lowell school. It has included a number of the outstanding scholars of comparative party systems. The school emphasizes the potentially critical influence that a parliament's party system can have on cabinet durability. In many ways, Lowell was a scholar generations ahead of his time in the breadth of his theoretical concerns and in his appreciation of comparative analysis; so powerful is his own work that it continues to mold our own conceptions of parliamentary politics today, almost eighty years since the publication of his seminal book. Unfortunately, the Lowell school has remained excessively inductive and descriptive. Its practitioners have failed to develop a coherent framework that could explain the linkage between party systems and cabinet durability.

The second school I designate as the Leiserson school. It has emphasized the potential applicability of coalitional theory to political and parliamentary settings. In applying this focus, however, two shortcomings have existed. The first limitation concerns the analytic question they have asked: how widespread are minimum winning coalitions (employing different definitions of this concept) in parliamentary settings? The utility of coalitional theory has been judged primarily on the basis of the answer to this question. This was an unfortunate mistake. In applying an analytic theory to a real-world setting, the first question must be this: can we interpret the elements of the theory so that it is applicable to the setting? Not least among the elements of a theory are its parametric assumptions. In coalitional theories two explicit or implicit assumptions are willingness to bargain and information certainty. As these factors vary, the *predictions* of the theory vary. In other words, coalitional theories do not only predict minimum winning coalitions. It is equally consistent (given certain conditions) for undersized or oversized coalitions to form. In applying coalition theory to a real-world setting, a critical consideration must be to determine the bargaining conditions that obtain in a specific setting. Only then can predictions of the theory be tested. Seen in this context, the critical analytic question is not how widespread one type of coalition is, but whether under the specified conditions the appropriate coalition forms. The failure to ask this question is a significant limitation of the Leiserson school. A second shortcoming of the school, related to the first one, is its failure to link the study of parliamentary coalitions to fundamental political questions. An analytic focus is useful primarily if it aids in the resolution of a critical paradigmatic puzzle or if it is relevant to a programmatic policy problem. The Leiserson school has not linked its study of coalitions to either type of perspective.

Thus we have the paradox. The Lowell school has focused on a significant problem (cabinet durability) and on observable empirical phenomena. But it has failed to generate a coherent theory explaining the covariation between its independent and dependent variables. By contrast, the Leiserson school has worked within a coherent and mathematically elegant theory. But this school has failed to link its analytic focus to a serious political problem—nor has the school coped with the problem of relating key elements of its theory (the bargaining conditions) to empirically observable referents.

It is in the context of this paradox that the analytic significance of this study can be grasped most clearly. The strategy has been to resolve the problems of each school by drawing on the strengths of the other, synthesizing them into a broader framework. According to this synthesis, party system characteristics do influence cabinet durability. The influence results from the coalitional status (and consequent durability) of cabinets that form under different party systems. The body of the study develops the linkage through a variety of theoretical and empirical analyses, drawing on an extensive body of cross-national data. Thus, even though there are shortcomings in the current study, I believe that the analysis presented here is significant. It presents a theoretical framework that clarifies some of the fundamental analytic problems in this area. It provides empirically supported generalizations from which future theoretical refinement and modification can ensue. It does focus on one of the key, recurring problems or puzzles of comparative politics: the requisites of durable government. And last but not least, it should aid in the revision of our preconceptions concerning party systems and democracy.

11 | Party Systems and Democracy

There can be little doubt that durable government is an important element in the success or failure of representative democracy. Under some conditions, the persistence of a specific set of officeholders may be detrimental to democracy. Few would argue that a governing group widely viewed as illegitimate, corrupt, or dictatorial should remain in office for the good of the democratic polity. As a general rule, however, democracy will not be served well by the rapid and persistent overthrow of its elected officials. Democratic governments should be responsive to the citizenry. One element of responsiveness is the ability to remove leaders from office and replace them with more acceptable ones. Yet responsiveness also entails the implementation of desired policy; persistent, rapid overthrow of governments can make impossible the authoritative, effective implementation of policy. If policy is to be enacted and enforced, whether that policy be radical or reactionary, the government must endure.

The durability of governments is a particular problem among parliamentary democracies. Since cabinets can be replaced by parliament virtually at will, the opportunity exists for a constant alteration in the cabinets that govern. With a consequent inability of cabinets to confront societal problems forcefully the entire fabric of the political community can unravel. The problem evident among parliamentary systems is summarized well by Bracher:

An especially weighty argument of the critics [of parliamentary government] is . . . the lack of stability of parliamentary governments. The twenty-one administrations of the fourteen years of the Weimar Republic were a frightening example. Even after World War II, the French Fourth Republic exhausted twenty-five administrations in the space of thirteen years. It is true that the rapid changes of cabinets were mitigated by the fact that there were only minor shifts in the personal component. But without a doubt, not only the total triumph of Hitler (and the ascent of broad circles in Germany) but also the more moderate victory of de Gaulle over parliamentary democracy are to be ascribed in no small way to discontent about the discontinuity of parliamentary state politics.[1]

Bracher's list of regimes weakened with the onslaught of transient cabinets might be enlarged to include the Third French Republic and Italy before the rise of Mussolini. Contemporary Italy is the nation most beset by the problem.[2]

[1] Karl Dietrich Bracher, "Problems of Parliamentary Democracy in Europe," in Herbert Hirsch and M. Donald Hancock, eds., *Comparative Legislative Systems* (New York: The Free Press, 1971), p. 354.

[2] For other relevant discussions on the nature of cabinet governments and their significance for the regime stability of parliamentary democracies, see W. L. Middleton, *The French Political System* (London: Ernest Benn, Ltd., 1932), especially pp. 151-154; W.G.S. Adams, "Has Parliamentary Government Failed?" in *The Modern State*, ed. by Mary Adams (London: George Allen and Unwin, Ltd., 1933); Karl Dietrich Bracher, *The German Dictatorship: The Origins, Structure and Effects of National Socialism*, trans. by Jean Steinberg (New York: Praeger Publishers, 1970); Gerhard Loewenberg, "The Influence of Parliamentary Behavior on Regime Stability," *Comparative Politics* 3 (January 1971), 177-179; Leon D. Epstein, *Political Parties in Western Democracies* (New York: Praeger Publishers, 1967); Ernest Fraenkel, "Historical Handicaps of German Parliamentarianism," in *The Road to Dictatorship*, trans. by Lawrence Wilson (Lon-

Transient cabinets are not limited in their effects solely to internal well-being of the polity. They also can have a significant detrimental effect on a nation's foreign policy, particularly if they create an international image of political irresponsibility. Consider for example the following editorial in the *New York Times* (January 13, 1922), reacting to the downfall of Briand's government:

> Premier Briand's abrupt resignation brings out, if it was not directly caused by, a French governmental defect. . . . It lies partly in the system of "groups" in the Chambre, making it necessary for the Ministry to be continually combining two or more of them, or balancing one against another. The result is that the Prime Minister always leads a threatened life. He maintains himself in power only by a continuous tour de force. A more skilled or less scrupulous logroller in the Chambre may any day upset him. . . .
>
> . . . Consider what has happened. Before going to Washington, he [Briand] had sought and obtained a vote of confidence. Then in December, after his conference in London with Lloyd George, he demanded a vote of con-

don: Oswald Wolff, 1964), pp. 27-37; Harry Eckstein, *Division and Cohesion in Democracy* (Princeton: Princeton University Press, 1966); Ferdinand A. Hermens, *Democracy or Anarchy?* (Notre Dame, Ind.: University of Notre Dame Press, 1941); William L. Shirer, *The Collapse of the Third Republic* (New York: Simon and Schuster, 1972); Richard K. Ullman and Sir Stephen King-Hall, *German Parliaments: A Study of the Development of Representative Institutions in Germany* (New York: Praeger Publishers, 1954), especially pp. 87-91; Phillip M. Williams, *Crisis and Compromise: Politics in the Fourth Republic* (Hamden, Conn.: The Shoe String Press, Inc., 1964); Giovanni Sartori, "European Political Parties: The Case of Polarized Pluralism," in *Political Parties and Political Development*, ed. by Joseph LaPalombara and Myron Weiner (Princeton: Princeton University Press, 1966).

fidence before leaving for Cannes. He got it from both houses of Parliament. But before the negotiation with which he had been entrusted had been completed, he was summoned back to Paris in consequence of what he bluntly called "underhand" work in the Chambre. . . .

The effect outside of France cannot fail to be unfortunate. . . . What standing will the French delegate now have at either conference? The feeling in England will be that a miserable intrigue of French politicians has interfered with plans of the utmost importance. . . . Whatever the true explanation of the overthrow of Premier Briand, the first effect of it will be highly damaging to French prestige abroad. It will be taken to mean that French politicians put their own selfish schemes above the representation of their country.

As indicated in Chapter 7, the Briand cabinet was the second oversized party coalition in the 1919 French Parliament, and it was overthrown by a third, less oversized cabinet. The fall of the Briand cabinet occurred in the midst of tedious international negotiations.

Because transient cabinets can have a detrimental effect on democratic government, political analysts have devoted considerable attention over the years to the conditions that give rise to cabinet durability. As a result of this analysis, the "myth of multipartism" has emerged—the view that multipartism is inconsistent with durable government. Two corollaries are "the myth of party coalitions" and the "myth of majority partism." The former view maintains that coalitions are necessarily transient; the latter view argues that majority partism is essential to cabinet durability. All three views are linked most closely with the work of Lowell.[3]

[3] A. Lawrence Lowell, *Governments and Parties in Continental Europe*, Vol. 1 (Cambridge: Harvard University Press, 1896); Lowell,

As Chapter 1 indicates, the myth of multipartism and its corollaries penetrate the literature on comparative party systems. Even when scholars have confronted evidence that should have questioned the validity of the perspectives, the myths have persisted. The perjorative view of multipartism among parliamentary analysts has permeated students of the American party system to such a degree that multipartism is dismissed outright as a viable conceptual possibility by American party reformers. Thus, in his analysis of four parties in America, Burns bemoans that "the consequence of the four-party system is that American political leaders, in order to govern, must manage multiparty coalitions just as heads of coalition parliamentary regimes in Europe have traditionally done." Burns rejects such coalition government because "it is notoriously unable to generate strong and steady political power."[4] Rather than supporting electoral and political reforms consistent with improving the governing potential of the four parties that he describes as products of the American political experience, Burns proposes to force "responsible two partism" in American politics.

SUMMARY OF THE FINDINGS

The findings of this study suggest that the time has come for party system analysts to reconsider the widespread preconceptions of multipartism. While cabinet durability is by no means the only dimension of effective, authoritative

---

The Governments of France, Italy and Germany (Cambridge: Harvard University Press, 1914).

[4] James Macgregor Burns, *The Deadlock of Democracy: Four Party Politics in America* (Englewood Cliffs, N.J.: Prentice-Hall, Inc., 1963), p. 260, 324.

government and not necessarily the most significant,[5] it is the indicator most scholars of parliamentary government have employed to measure strong and efficient government (Lowell) or intrasystem stability (Eckstein). Consequently, many of our preconceptions about the detrimental effects of multipartism derive from assumptions about the inherent transiency of governments in multiparty regimes. Yet it is really no truer to maintain that multiparty systems generate transient cabinets than it is to argue that party systems as a whole lead to transient government. The variation in cabinet durability among multiparty parliaments is virtually as great as is the variation among all parliaments including majority party systems. And while multiparty parliaments account for 75 percent of all peacetime parliaments held in the last fifty years, these multiparty parliaments account for 80 percent of all cabinets lasting for forty months or longer.

The foundation of durable government is simply a more complex and less clear-cut problem than suggested in simple dichotomy between multipartism and majority partism. A key to durable government is the coalitional status of the cabinet; minimum winning cabinets endure whereas cabinets that deviate from minimum winning status do not. A minimum winning cabinet refers to a ministry possessing a parliamentary majority but containing no party unnecessary to the winning margin. Minimum winning cabinets can form in both multiparty and majority party parliaments. In multiparty parliaments, minimum winning cabinets are party coalitions; in majority party parliaments, minimum winning cabinets are single party majority cabinets. Both types of minimum winning cabinets generally are durable.

[5] See for example the exchange of Leon Hurwitz with Michael Taylor and V. M. Herman, "Communications," APSR 65 (December 1971), 1148-1149.

Likewise, deviant cabinets can form both in multiparty and majority party parliaments. Two broad types of deviant cabinets exist: oversized cabinets (those majority cabinets that contain at least one extra party) and undersized or minority cabinets (those cabinets that lack sufficient ministerial parties to ensure majority status in parliament). Deviant cabinets among majority party parliaments are restricted historically to oversized cabinets. Both oversized and undersized cabinets have formed among multiparty parliaments. In both majority party and multiparty parliaments, deviant cabinets are nondurable.

The power of Lowell's thesis derives from the fact that majority party cabinets are a clearly distinguishable form of minimum winning government. Yet majority party governments are not the only type of minimum winning cabinet, nor the most prevalent. In addition, while it is true that minimum winning single party cabinets have outlasted minimum winning party coalitions, on the average, it is not true that minimum winning single party cabinets are always more durable than minimum winning coalitions. During the interwar years, minimum winning coalitions lasted longer than single party majority governments, on the average—a testament, possibly, to the greater flexibility of coalition government during an era of domestic unrest. And in those countries that have experienced both forms of minimum winning government, minimum winning coalitions lasted for approximately the same length of time as minimum winning single party governments. Clearly, neither the myth of party coalitions nor the myth of majority partism are sustained by the analysis of this study.

Among majority party parliaments as well as multiparty parliaments, cabinet coalitional status (and thus, indirectly, cabinet durability) is determined by the complex interaction of three party system variables: cleavage conflict, fractionalization, and stability. Cleavage conflict is important as a constraint on the *a priori* willingness of parties to bargain. In conditions of low cleavage conflict, parties should evidence a highly generalized *a priori* willingness to bargain; in such settings minimum winning and oversized cabinets exist. In conditions of high cleavage conflict, parties should evidence a less generalized *a priori* willingness to bargain. In such situations, minimum winning and minority cabinets exist.

Party system fractionalization and stability are important as influences on the certainty of information that exists in the parliamentary bargaining arena. Low fractionalization and high stability are conducive to information certainty. In such conditions, cabinets tend to approach minimum winning status. High fractionalization and instability are conducive to information uncertainty. Under these conditions, cabinets deviate from minimum winning status. If cleavage conflict is low, cabinets in fractionalized and unstable party systems are oversized; if cleavage conflict is high, cabinets in fractionalized and unstable party systems are minority governments. In either situation, deviant cabinets are nondurable. As to the relative significance of fractionalization and stability, the latter consistently accounts for more variance in dependent variables than fractionalization. More importantly, however, the most significant variable is the joint occurrence of fractionalization and instability. As a multiplicative interaction term, Psf (x) Psi accounts for more variation in the dependent variable than either fractionalization or instability examined separately or in an additive model.

As emphasized throughout this study, parliamentary life is much too complex to be described in simple typologies. For purposes of clarification and illustration, however, a four-part typology characterizes the overall findings of this study:

1. Unstable, depolarized, and hyperfractionalized parliaments experienced oversized cabinets. The classic multiparty examples of this situation occur in the French Third Republic and the early years of the French Fourth Republic. In such settings, information uncertainty so characterizes parliament that a number of transient cabinets form. Majority party examples include Great Britain (1931) and Italy (1948).

2. Unstable, polarized, and hyperfractionalized parliaments experience minority (undersized) cabinets. In such settings transient cabinets exist. The most extreme examples of this condition occur in Weimar Germany and in the 1956 parliament of the Fourth French Republic; in each of these cases, unstable, polarized hyperpluralism was followed by the fall of the republic. There are no majority party examples of this phenomenon.

3. Stable, depolarized, and low to moderately fractionalized parliaments generally experience durable minimum winning cabinets. Multiparty examples include Australia (1949) and West Germany (1972). Majority party examples include New Zealand and Great Britain during the 1950s and 1960s.

4. Stable, polarized, and low to moderately fractionalized parliaments generally experience durable minimum winning cabinets. Postwar Luxembourg provides a multiparty example of this situation. The primary exception to this rule occurs in highly polarized multiparty parliaments wherein parties are in such extreme conflict that no party will bargain with any other party. In such situations, transient minority cabinets will form.

These patterns hold for both the interwar and postwar years, with variation between eras occurring in the types of parliaments that exist. Unstable, polarized hyperpluralism is far more prevalent during the interwar years; consequently, transient minority cabinets are most prevalent during that era. Depolarized parliaments are more prevalent during the postwar years and, consequently, the proportion of oversized (particularly extremely oversized) cabinets is greater during the postwar era. Minimum winning cabinets are prevalent during both periods, though they are more predominant during the postwar years.

POLARIZATION, FRACTIONALIZATION, AND STABILITY:
NEW PERSPECTIVES

These findings have three important implications for our perceptions of the relationship of party systems and cabinet durability. First, party system polarization is not in and of itself a significant influence on cabinet durability. Because deviant cabinets are possible in both high and low levels of cleavage conflict (with undersized and oversized cabinets, respectively) there is only a slight relationship between cleavage conflict and cabinet durability. The relationship that does exist occurs because, in the most polarized multiparty parliaments, only minority cabinets form and they do tend to be transient. Short of extreme polarization, however, minimum winning cabinets as well as deviant cabinets exist. A polarized parliament is no guarantee of transient government; minimum winning cabinets may form. A depolarized parliament is no guarantee of durable government: oversized cabinets are possible. The ability of a nation to circumscribe conflict within fairly moderate and civil parameters does not guarantee durable government.

A second implication of these findings concerns party system fractionalization. The dichotomy between multiparty and majority party systems serves a real but limited purpose. Certainly, an important substantive change occurs when a nation moves from a parliament possessing a majority party to a parliament lacking one. In a highly polarized and/or unstable party system, this transition can virtually guarantee minority government. Likewise, the move from multipartism to majority partism, under the right conditions, can bring durable government to those polarized multiparty settings beset by minority government. On the other hand, the minimum winning party coalitions of moderate multipartism may allow a more flexible response to short-term electoral fluctuation than majority partism. Moves from multipartism to majority partism can bring about a transition from durable minimum winning coalition government to less durable, oversized governments, as happened in Germany from 1949 to 1953. And from a broad historical and comparative perspective, as Sartori emphasizes, the move from majority partism to moderate multipartism is far less important than the move from moderate multipartism to a hyperfractionalized regime. In a moderately defractionalized parliament, whether it be majority party or multiparty, minimum winning cabinets are quite possible in a stable party system experiencing low to moderately high polarization. It is the hyperfractionalized range wherein deviant cabinets form that are likely to experience persistent transiency. The critical factor for cabinet durability is not the existence of majority party or multiparty parliaments; rather it is the existence of low to moderate fractionalization rather than high fractionalization. A diversity of partisan views, none of which dominates political discourse, is not necessarily detrimental to durable government, so long as that diversity is maintained within moderate bounds.

Third, party system stability is a more important variable in Western parliamentary democracies than is often realized. Contemporary literature on European party systems stresses, quite rightly, that the structure of modern party systems is influenced by the cleavages that have emerged over the past several centuries. These cleavages have remained essentially frozen since the 1920s; no dramatic new cleavages have emerged though the salience of some has declined.[6] As a result, the identity of parties and the structure of most party systems have remained fairly constant during the past fifty years, particularly when compared to the changes that occurred during the preceding centuries. Nevertheless, the relative popularity of parties has varied during the past fifty years. Flash parties have emerged in some countries. And, because of the decline in salience of particular cleavages together with alterations in electoral laws, some parties have disappeared. Consequently, while party systems over the past fifty years may appear fairly stable from the long-term perspective, considerable short-term variation has occurred in the continuity of party systems between parliaments. This variation in the stability or continuity of parliamentary party systems has a significant influence on parliamentary government. In interaction with cleavage conflict, party system stability actually accounts for more variance in cabinet coalitional status and cabinet durability than does party system fractionalization. Significant short-term fluctuation in parties' strength may have little influence on the long-term structure of a nation's party system but considerable influence on the durability of a nation's cabinet governments.

[6] For this perspective see particularly Seymour M. Lipset and Stein Rokkan, "Cleavage Structures, Party Systems, and Voter Alignments," in Lipset and Rokkan, eds., *Party Systems and Voter Alignments* (New York: The Free Press, 1967).

CONCLUSION

This study has focused on one relatively narrow but significant puzzle: the durability of cabinets. Not all of the possible variables that might possibly influence cabinet durability have been incorporated into the analysis. Rather, the study has examined a longstanding thesis relating party systems and cabinet durability. The thesis has been challenged and in its place a revisionist interpretation has been offered. This interpretation, and the theory encompassing it, is not the "last word" on cabinet durability. Much variance remains unexplained, quite enough, in fact, to occupy the author and other analysts for some time. In addition, the theory developed in this study requires more elaboration and exploration. As Chapter 10 indicates, future modification of the analysis in this study may account for much of the unexplained variance in cabinet durability. This study is, therefore, a beginning and not an end.

Despite the initial and exploratory nature of this study, however, its findings do lead to one concluding perspective. Endless debates rage over the best procedures whereby to guarantee "responsible majority partism."[7] The myth of multipartism is so pervasive that political analysts seldom consider whether majority party government is really appropriate to a particular setting. Yet it is not multipartism

[7] The most famous of these debates centers on the effect of electoral laws. See George van den Bergh, *Unity in Diversity: A Systematic Critique of All Electoral Systems* (London: B. T. Batsford, 1956); A. Dami, "In Support of Proportional Representation," *International Social Science Bulletin* 3 (Summer 1951), 353-357; Maurice Duverger, *Political Parties* (New York: John Wiley and Sons, 1963); Ferdinand A. Hermens, *Democracy or Anarchy?* (Notre Dame, Ind.: University of Notre Dame Press, 1941); Enid Lakeman and James D. Lambert, *Voting in Democracies* (London: Faber and Faber, Ltd., 1955); Douglas W. Rae, *The Political Consequences of Electoral Laws* (New Haven: Yale University Press, 1967).

per se that gives rise to transient cabinets; they can exist in majority party systems as well. Majority partism will not stem the tide of national disintegration, as the experience of the First Austrian Republic demonstrates. And it should be little comfort that decades of majority party rule in Great Britain left a nation facing internal problems in the 1970s virtually as serious as those facing Italy, a nation beset by the more classic problem of cabinet transiency.

It is conceivable that too few parties are just as detrimental in particular settings as too many parties. Perhaps Lord Bryce was wrong when he wrote that since "there must be parties, the fewer and stronger they are, the better."[8] If a party system fails to provide broad representation of citizens' views, society may disintegrate because of (rather than despite) the existence of majority party rule. Could it not be that democracy will be better served by moderate forms of multipartism combined with a political structure allowing and encouraging coalition government than by a system forcing public opinion into two molds, effectively disenfranchising and alienating permanent minorities?[9]

This question is directed not only to students of parliamentary government but to students of American presidential-congressional politics as well. Because political scientists have lacked broadly comparative studies of multiparty politics, American scholars envision the behavior of the French Fourth Republic and Weimar Germany as prototypical multiparty regimes. As a result of these examples, multipartism is so abhorrent that attention is seldom directed to its potential advantages and to the alterations that

[8] James Bryce, *Modern Democracies*, Vol. 1 (New York: The Macmillan Co., 1921), pp. 121-122.

[9] For a balanced discussion of this question, see A. J. Milnor, *Elections and Political Stability* (Boston: Little, Brown and Co., 1969).

might make the overt politics of party coalitions possible. Throughout discussions of party system reform, American political analysts such as Burns bemoan the lack of "responsible," cohesive parties in America; at the same time, they dismiss the possibility of multipartism by referring to the European experience rather than seriously contemplating its advantages as well as disadvantages and the changes that might make it compatible with and desirable for presidential-congressional government.

Hopefully, the findings of this study will help remove the blinders from scholars concerned with parliamentary politics in Europe and the British Commonwealth as well as scholars concerned with American politics. Even when we focus on that conservative indicator—cabinet durability—multiparty systems are not nearly as homogeneous in their behavior nor as negative in their consequence as many scholars would suggest. Party coalitions can and do endure. Government durability should no longer serve as the rationale for eliminating from consideration the possibility of multiparty politics.[10] Preoccupation with the myth of multipartism has diverted attention among party analysts from the more fundamental questions: are cohesive, "responsible" parties desirable mechanisms of democratic government; if so, what types of party systems will aid authoritative, effective government within a parliamentary or presidential-congressional system *and* allow broadly responsive representation of a nation's citizenry? Political choice among several minority parties need not undermine political stability; quite the contrary, a party system reflecting a mod-

[10] For a broadly focused discussion of majority partism and multipartism see the three essays by Robert Dahl, "Patterns of Opposition," "Some Explanations," and "Epilogue," in Robert A. Dahl, ed., *Political Oppositions in Western Democracy* (New Haven: Yale University Press, 1966).

erately diverse range of views conceivably could integrate the citizenry through open recognition of and competition between competing minority perspectives, activating the instinct for community by the development of widespread appreciation of and commitment to democratic processes. A wider range of party system structures may be appropriate to the democratic polity than analysts have recognized. As party coalitions are not necessarily antagonistic to cabinet durability, multiparty politics may not be necessarily antithetical to responsive, authoritative government.

Appendix A

Part II specifies a variety of alternate operational definitions that could be employed to test the hypotheses presented in Part I. No attempt has been made to replicate every regression coefficient reported in Part III using these alternate operational procedures. The following selected regression coefficients are for the entire population of partisan cabinets for peacetime parliaments, 1918-1974, indicating that the general patterns reported in this study are sustained by the alternate operational definitions.

| | Dependent Variable | | |
Independent Variable	CCS1	CCS2	CCS3
CPSI1 W (Wildgen)	−.550	−.509	−.537
CPSI1 R (Rae)	−.535	−.507	−.521
CPSI2 Based on			
PsiA	−.555	−.518	−.541
PsiB	−.567	−.535	−.559
PsiC	−.580	−.550	−.578
PsiD	−.582	−.554	−.567
PsiE	−.561	−.527	−.545
CPSI3 W (logged)			
Based on			
PsiA	−.611	−.608	−.619
PsiB	−.613	−.594	−.600
PsiC	−.610	−.592	−.601
PsiD	−.632	−.601	−.622
PsiE	−.620	−.613	−.618
CPSI3 R (logged)			
Based on			
PsiA	−.552	−.513	−.542
PsiB	−.582	−.562	−.569
PsiC	−.584	−.565	−.573
PsiD	−.601	−.589	−.594
PsiE	−.574	−.553	−.561
	Cabinet Durability (logged)		
CCS1	.507		
CCS2	.491		
CCS3	.478		

Note: CCS1, CCS2, and CCS3 correspond to the three measures of cabinet coalitional status presented in Chapter 6. CPSI1 W and CPSI1 R present the CPSI1 scores discussed in Chapter 7 employing the Wildgen fractionalization measure (CPSI W) and the Rae measure (CPSI R).

The five variations on the CPSI2 index are based on the five alternate measures of Party System Stability presented in Chapter 4. The ten variations on the CPSI3 index combine the two fractionalization indices and the five stability indices.

Appendix B: The Location of Parliamentary Parties on Salient Cleavage Dimensions

This appendix presents the positions given parliamentary parties in each country on the cleavage dimensions deemed salient for each parliament. These evaluations were made by the author on the basis of the relevant literature in political science and history; the Selected Bibliography indicates the basic works examined in making the judgments. Columns 1, 2, and 3 indicate party positions on economic conflict, clericalism, and regime support, respectively. Column 4 indicates the party positions on cleavage peculiar to a specific country; these cleavages are listed in Table 5:1.

All countries except France have two models—the interwar and postwar positions. In specific countries slight changes were made in party positions on these models from parliament to parliament; the concluding notes specify these changes. For France, extensive party change occurred from parliament to parliament and, consequently, each French parliament has its own specific model. No alterations were made for any country during the life of a particular parliament. In some cases minor parties are omitted because sufficient information could not be obtained to allow a reliable judgment as to their cleavage positions.

Cleavage Positions
1 = economic conflict
2 = clericalism
3 = regime support
4 = miscellaneous country-specific cleavages

Country (era)	Parties	Cleavage Positions			
		1	2	3	4
Australia					
(interwar)	Ctry	1			
	Lib	2			
	Lab	−3			
(postwar)	Ctry	0			
	Lib	2			
	Lab	−3			
Austria					
(interwar)	Hmt	4	−3		6
	CS	3	3		1
	PGN	1	−2		3
	SD	−3	−3		1
(postwar)	AP	2	2		
	PGN	1	−3		
	SD	−3	−2		
	Comm	−5	−2		
Belgium					
(interwar)	Lib	2	−2		
	FN	−1	1		
	Cath	0	3		
	Soc	−3	−1		
	Comm	−5	−5		
(postwar)	Lib	2	−2		
	Cath	1	2		
	FSF	0	2		
	WF	0	2		
	FN	−1	1		
	W Lab	−1	2		
	Soc	−3	−1		
	Comm	−6	−5		
Canada					
(interwar)	Lib-Con	3			3
	UF	0			−3
	L-Lib	−1			−2
	Prog	−3			−3
	CCF	−4			−4
	Lab	−4			−3
	Soc Cred	−4			−4

Country (era)	Parties	Cleavage Positions			
		1	2	3	4
(postwar)	Cons	2			−2
	Lib	−2			3
	Soc Cred	3			−3
	N Dem	−4			0
Denmark					
(interwar)	Ind	4			
	Cons	3			
	Lib	1			
	S Tax	0			
	Rad Lib	−1			
	SD	−4			
	Comm	−5			
(postwar)	Cons	3			
	Lib	1			
	Jus	0			
	Rad Lib	−1			
	SD	−3			
	Soc	−4			
	Comm	−6			
Finland					
(interwar)	PP	4			−5
	N Coal	3			−3
	Swed P	2			3
	Agr U	1			−4
	NPP	−1			−3
	SD	−4			0
	S Lab	−5			0
(postwar)	N Coal	2			−2
	Swed P	2			3
	Agr U	1			−3
	Lib	−1			−2
	SD	−3			0
	LW Soc	−4			0
	Comm	−5			0
France					
(interwar)	L Rep	2	0	−1	
1919	Rad	1	−2	−3	
	Soc Rad	−1	−2	−3	
	Rep Soc	−2	−2	−3	

Country (era)	Parties	Cleavage Positions			
		1	2	3	4
France (cont.)	U Soc	−4	−3	3	
	Prog	3	1	1	
	Act Lib	0	3	0	
	Cons	4	4	3	
1924	Rad-Rad Soc	−1	−2	−3	
	Rep Soc	−2	−2	−2	
	L Rep	0	−1	−1	
	Soc	−4	−3	3	
	Comm	−5	−4	4	
	Ind	4	4	4	
	URD	3	2	1	
	L Rep	0	−1	−1	
	GRD	1	0	0	
	Demo	1	3	−1	
1928	URD	2	2	1	
	L Rep	0	−1	−1	
	Rad Rep	0	−1	0	
	Soc Rad	−1	−2	−3	
	Rep Soc	−2	−2	−2	
	Soc	−3	−3	2	
	Comm	−5	−4	5	
	Cons	4	4	5	
1932	Comm	−5	−4	6	
	Soc Comm	−4	−4	5	
	Soc	−3	−3	2	
	ISRS	−2	−2	−2	
	Soc Rad	−1	−2	−3	
	Ind Rad	0	0	1	
	L Rep	0	0	−1	
	Pop Demo	1	3	0	
	Ind Rep	0	0	1	
	URD	2	2	2	
	Cons	4	4	6	
1936	Comm	−5	−4	5	
	Soc	−3	−3	1	
	Rep Soc	−2	−2	−2	
	Ind Soc	−2	−2	−2	
	Soc Rad	−1	−2	−3	
	Ind Rad	1	0	1	
	L Rep	1	0	−1	
	Pop Demo	0	3	0	

Country (era)	Parties	Cleavage Positions			
		1	2	3	4
	URD	2	2	3	
	Cons	4	4	5	
(postwar)	Comm	−4	−4	2	
1945, 1946I,	MRP	−2	2	−2	
1946II	Soc	−3	−3	−3	
	Rad Soc	0	−1	0	
	UDSR	0	−1	−1	
	Rep Lib	2	1	0	
	Ind Rep	1	1	−1	
	Gaul	−1	0	3	
	PST	3	1	0	
1951	Comm	−5	−4	5	
	Soc	−3	−3	−1	
	MRP	−2	2	−2	
	Rad	0	−1	0	
	UDSR	0	−1	−1	
	Cons	2	1	0	
	Gaul	−1	0	2	
1956	Comm	−5	−4	5	
	Soc	−3	−3	−1	
	Rad	1	−1	0	
	UDSR	0	−1	−1	
	MRP	−2	2	−2	
	Cons	3	1	0	
	Gaul	−1	0	2	
	Pouj	3	0	4	
Germany					
(interwar)	DNV	3	2	5	
	DV	2	1	3	
	Z	0	3	−3	
	DD	1	−1	−1	
	SD	−3	−2	−3	
	BZ	2	4	1	
	Comm	−5	−4	6	
	Ind Soc	−3	−2	1	
	Nz	0	−3	6	
(postwar)	Comm	−6	−4		
	SD	−3	−2		
	CDU/CSU	0	2		
	FD	2	−2		

Country (era)	Parties	Cleavage Positions			
		1	*2*	*3*	*4*
Germany (*cont.*)	BP/BHE	2	3		
	DP	2	1		
	Z	1	3		
Great Britain					
(interwar)	Cons	3			
	Lib	−1			
	Lab	−3			
	Comm	−5			
(postwar)	Cons	2			
	Lib	−1			
	Lab	−3			
	Comm	−5			
Iceland					
(interwar)	Ind	3			
	FR	0			
	Prog	−1			
	SD	−3			
	Comm	−5			
(postwar)	Ind	2			
	Prog	0			
	SD	−3			
	Comm	−5			
Ireland					
(postwar)	FG	3			−3
	FF	0			2
	Agr	−1			−1
	CNP	−1			3
	Lab	−3			−1
Italy					
(postwar)	Comm	−5	−2	1	
	Soc	−3	−3	0	
	Rep	−1	−3	−2	
	DC	−1	1	−3	
	Lib	1	0	−3	
	NF	3	4	3	
	Mon	2	4	0	
	SD	−2	−1	−2	

Country (era)	Parties	Cleavage Positions			
		1	2	3	4
Luxembourg					
(interwar)	Lib	2	0		
	CD	1	2		
	Rad Soc	−2	−2		
	Soc	−3	−3		
	Comm	−6	−6		
(postwar)	Demo	2	0		
	CS	0	2		
	Soc	−3	−3		
	Comm	−6	−6		
The Netherlands					
(interwar)	N Soc	5	−2		
	Pol Ref	4	3		
	Cath St	1	2		
	AR	1	2		
	CHU	1	2		
	Lib F	3	−1		
	SD	−3	−2		
	Comm	−5	−4		
(postwar)	PPF	3	−1		
	Cath P	0	2		
	AR	0	2		
	CHU	0	2		
	Lab	−3	−2		
	Pol Ref	3	3		
	P Soc	−4	−3		
	Demo '66	−4	−3		
	Demo Soc '70	−2	−3		
	Pol Rad	−4	−3		
	Comm	−5	−3		
	Agr	3	0		
New Zealand					
(interwar)	Ref	3			
	Lib	0			
	Lab	−3			
(postwar)	Ref	2			
	Lab	−3			

Country (era)	Parties	Cleavage Positions			
		1	2	3	4
Norway					
(interwar)	Cons	4			3
	Lib Ven	2			2
	AGR	1			−1
	CP	0			3
	Lib	0			−3
	Wk	−2			−1
	SD	−4			−1
	Lab	−5			−1
	Comm	−7			−1
(postwar)	Cons	3			0
	Agr	1			0
	CP	0			3
	Lib	0			−3
	Lab	−3			0
	Soc	−4			0
Sweden					
(interwar)	Cons	3			3
	Agr	2			2
	Prog	0			−1
	Lib	0			1
	SD	−3			−3
	Soc	−4			−4
	Comm	−5			−6
(postwar)	Cons	2			
	Lib	0			
	Agr (Cen)	−1			
	SD	−3			
	Comm	−5			

Notes: The following changes were made in the cleavage positions of specific parties.

Australia: During the postwar years, the Country Party moves to 0 in 1949.

Austria: During the interwar years, Social Democrats move from −3 to −4 on the economic cleavage in 1927; in 1930 on the clericalism cleavage, the Social Democrats move to −4, Pan German Nationalists move to −3, and Christian Socialists move to 4.

Canada: During postwar years, the Conservative Party is placed at +3 on economic cleavage for 1945 and 1949. Thereafter it moves to +2. NDP is at −2 on regionalism cleavage for 1945 and 1949, then moves to 0 and in 1958 to +1.

Denmark: During 1920 Social Democrats move to −3; in 1953 the Conservatives move to +2 and in 1957 the Social Democrats move to −2.

Finland: In 1930, the National Coalition moves to +2 on economic cleavage; in 1929, the Socialist Labour Party and the Social Democrats move to −1; in 1945, the Communists are at −4 on economic cleavage; in 1948 they move to −5; in 1966 they move to −4.

Germany: In 1924, DNVP moves to +3 and DVP moves to +2 on regime support cleavage; 1928, DVP moves to +1 on regime support cleavage; 1930, DVP and DNVP move to +3 and +4 on regime support cleavage.

Great Britain: In 1924 the Conservatives move to +2 on the economic cleavage.

Italy: In 1953, Neofascists move to +5 on economic cleavage; 1948, Communists move to +3 and in 1953 to +4 on regime support cleavage; 1958, Neofascists move to +4 on regime support cleavage and Socialists move to +1.

Luxembourg: In 1945, Communists are at −5 on both cleavages; they move to −6 in 1948.

Norway: In 1930, Labour moves to −4 on economic cleavage; in 1936, Labour moves to −3.

Sweden: In 1932, Agrarians move to +1 on economic cleavage and in 1936 Agrarians move to 0 while Liberals move to +1; in 1932 Communists move to −5 on foreign policy dimension while Agrarians move to +1.

Selected Bibliography

GENERAL WORKS

Cross-National Perspectives on Politics and Parliamentary Government

Adams, Mary, ed. *The Modern State*. London: George Allen and Unwin, Ltd., 1933.

Bagehot, Walter. *The English Constitution*. New York: D. Appleton, 1877.

Beyme, Klaus von. *Die Parlamentarischer Regierungssysteme In Europa*. Munich: R. Piper and Co., 1970.

Birch, A. H. *Representation and Responsible Government*. London: George Allen and Unwin, Ltd., 1964.

Blondel, Jean. *An Introduction to Comparative Government*. New York: Praeger Publishers, 1969.

————. "Party Systems and Patterns of Government in Western Democracies." *Canadian Journal of Political Science* (June 1968).

Bracher, Karl Dietrich. "Problems of Parliamentary Democracy in Europe." In *Comparative Legislative Systems*. Edited by Herbert Hirsch and M. Donald Hancock. New York: The Free Press, 1971.

Bryce, James. *Modern Democracies*. Vols. i and ii. New York: The Macmillan Company, 1921.

Cnudde, Charles F. and Dean E. Neubauer, eds. *Empirical Democratic Theory*. Chicago: Markham, 1969.

Daalder, Hans. "Cabinets and Party Systems in Ten Smaller European Democracies." Report to the Round Table Conference on European Comparative Politics, Turin, Italy, September 10-14, 1969.

Dahl, Robert. *Polyarchy.* New Haven: Yale University Press, 1971.

Dahl, Robert and Edward R. Tufte. *Size and Democracy.* Stanford: Stanford University Press, 1973.

Duverger, Maurice. *Political Parties.* London: Methuen and Co., Ltd., 1951.

Eckstein, Harry. "A Theory of Stable Democracy." In *Division and Cohesion in Democracy.* Princeton: Princeton University Press, 1966. Appendix B.

Flanigan, William H. and Edwin Fogelman. "Patterns of Democratic Development." In *Macro-Quantitative Analysis.* Edited by John V. Gillespie and Betty A. Nesvold. Beverly Hills, Calif.: Sage Publications, 1971.

Friedrich, Carl J. *Constitutional Government and Democracy.* Boston: Ginn and Co., 1950.

Gurr, Ted Robert. *Why Men Rebel.* Princeton: Princeton University Press, 1970.

Hermens, Ferdinand A. *Democracy or Anarchy?* Notre Dame, Ind.: Notre Dame University Press, 1941.

Huntington, Samuel P. *Political Order in Changing Societies.* New Haven: Yale University Press, 1968.

Laski, Harold J. *Parliamentary Government in England.* New York: The Viking Press, 1938.

Lijphart, Arend. "Typologies of Democratic Systems." *Comparative Political Studies* 1 (April 1968), 3-44.

Livingston, William S. *Federalism and Constitutional Change.* Oxford: at the Clarendon Press, 1956.

————. *Federalism in the Commonwealth.* London: Cassell and Co., 1963.

Loewenstein, Karl. *Political Power and the Governmental Process.* Chicago: The University of Chicago Press, 1957.

Lowell, A. Lawrence. *Governments and Parties in Continental Europe.* Vols. i and ii. Cambridge: Harvard University Press, 1896.

Milnor, A. J. *Elections and Political Stability.* Boston: Little, Brown and Co., 1969.

Mosca, Gaetano. *The Ruling Class.* Edited and revised with an introduction by Arthur Livingston. New York: McGraw-Hill Book Co., 1939.

Putnam, Robert D. *The Beliefs of Politicians.* New Haven: Yale University Press, 1973.

Rae, Douglas. *The Political Consequences of Electoral Laws.* New Haven: Yale University Press, 1967.

Sartori, Giovanni. *Democratic Theory.* New York: Praeger Publishers, 1965.

————. "European Political Parties: The Case of Polarized Pluralism." In *Political Parties and Political Development.* Edited by Joseph LaPalombara and Myron Weiner. Princeton: Princeton University Press, 1966.

Sinclair, John E. "Legislators and Lobbyists in Canada and the United States: The Impact of Institution on Individual Behavior." Unpublished Ph.D. dissertation, State University of New York, 1973.

Taylor, Michael and V. M. Herman. "Party Systems and Governmental Stability." *APSR* 65 (March 1971).

Tingston, Herbert. *Political Behavior.* Totowa: Bedminister, 1963.

Parties, Parliaments and Cleavage Systems

Alford, Robert. *Party and Society.* Chicago: Rand McNally, 1963.

Allardt, Erik and Stein Rokkan, eds. *Mass Politics: Studies in Political Sociology.* New York: The Free Press, 1970.

Ameller, Michael. *Parliaments.* London: Cassell and Co., Ltd., 1966.

Blondel, Jean. *Comparative Legislatures.* Englewood Cliffs, N.J.: Prentice-Hall, 1973.

Campion, C.M.F. and D.W.S. Liddendale. *European Parliamentary Procedure: A Comparative Handbook.* London: George Allen and Unwin, Ltd., 1953.

Codacci-Pisanelli, Giuseppe. *Parliaments: A Comparative Study on the Structure and Functioning of Representative Institutions in Forty-One Countries.* New York: Praeger Publishers, 1961.

Dahrendorf, Rolf. *Class and Class Conflict in Industrial Society.* Stanford: Stanford University Press, 1959.

Dogan, Mattei and Richard Rose. *European Politics: A Reader.* Boston: Little, Brown and Co., 1971.

Epstein, Leon D. *Political Parties in Western Democracies.* New York: Praeger Publishers, 1967.

Hirsch, Herbert and M. Donald Hancock, eds. *Comparative Legislative Systems: A Reader in Theory and Research.* New York: The Free Press, 1971.

Janda, Kenneth. *A Conceptual Framework for the Comparative Analysis of Political Parties.* Edited by Harry Eckstein and Ted Robert Gurr. A Sage Professional Paper, Comparative Politics Series #01-002, Vol. 1.

King, Anthony. "Political Parties in Western Democracies: Some Skeptical Reflections." *Polity* 10 (Winter 1969).

Kirchheimer, Otto. "Majorities and Minorities in Western European Governments." *Western Political Quarterly* 10 (June 1957), 318-339.

————. "The Waning of Opposition in Parliamentary Regimes." *Social Research* 24 (1957), 127-156.

Kornberg, Allan and Lloyd D. Musolf. *Legislatures in Developmental Perspective.* Durham, N.C.: Duke University Press, 1970.

Kornberg, Allan. *Legislatures in Comparative Perspective.* New York: David McKay Co., Inc., 1973.

LaPalombara, Joseph. "Political Party Systems and Crisis Government: French and Italian Contrasts." *Midwest Journal of Political Science* 2 (May 1958), 117-142.

———— and Myron Weiner, eds. *Political Parties and Political Development.* Princeton: Princeton University Press, 1966.

Lipset, Seymour M. and Stein Rokkan. "Cleavage Structures, Party Systems, and Voter Alignments: An Introduction." In *Party Systems and Voter Alignments: Cross-National Perspectives.* Edited by Seymour M. Lipset and Stein Rokkan. New York: The Free Press, 1967.

Loewenberg, Gerhard, ed. *Modern Parliaments: Change or Decline.* Chicago: Aldine, 1971.

————. "The Influence of Parliamentary Behavior on Regime Stability." *Comparative Politics* 3, No. 2 (January 1971), 177-179.

Meynard, Jean. "Introduction: General Study of Parliamentarians." *International Social Science Journal* 13 (1961), 5131.

Michels, Robert. *Political Parties: A Sociological Study of the Oligarchical Tendencies of Modern Democracy.* New York: The Free Press, 1962.

Patterson, Samuel C. and John C. Wahlke, eds. *Comparative Legislative Behavior: Frontiers of Research.* New York: Wiley-Interscience, 1972.

Rokkan, Stein. *Citizens, Elections, Parties.* New York: David McKay Co., Inc. 1970,

Rose, Richard and Derek Unwin. "Social Cohesion, Political Parties and Strains on Regimes." *Comparative Political Studies* 2 (1969), 7-67.

Seitz, Steven Thomas. "Ideology and Public Policy: A Reconsideration of Mass Belief Systems and the Formation of Public Policy." Unpublished Ph.D. dissertation, University of Minnesota, 1972.

Shively, W. Phillips. "Party Identification, Party Choice, and Voting Stability." *APSR* 66 (December 1972).

Sjöblom, Gunnar. *Party Strategies in a Multiparty System* Berlingska Boktryckeriet, Sweden: Lund, 1968.

Sorauf, Frank. *Party and Representation.* New York: Atherton Press, 1963.

Thomas, John C. "The Decline of Ideology in the West: A Longitudinal Study of the Changing Orientations of Political Parties in Twelve Nations." Unpublished Ph.D. dissertation, Northwestern University, 1974.

Wheare, K. C. *Legislatures.* London: Oxford University Press, 1963.

General Models of Politics

Aranson, Peter, Melvin Hinch, and Peter Ordeshook. "Election Goals and Strategies: Equivalent and Non-equivalent Candidate Objectives." *APSR* 68 (March 1974), 135-152.

Arrow, Kenneth J. *Social Choice and Individual Values*. New York: John Wiley and Sons, 1951.

Barry, Brian M. *Sociologists, Economists, and Democracy*. London: The Macmillan Co., 1970.

Buchanan, James M. "An Individualistic Theory of Political Process." In *Varieties of Political Theory*. Edited by David Easton. Englewood Cliffs, N.J.: Prentice-Hall, Inc., 1966.

Buchanan, James M. and Gordon Tullock. *The Calculus of Consent*. Ann Arbor: The University of Michigan Press, 1967.

Converse, Philip E. "The Problem of Party Distance in Models of Voting Change." In *The Electoral Process*. Edited by M. Kent Jennings and S. Hamon Zeigler. Englewood Cliffs, N.J.: Prentice-Hall, Inc., 1966, pp. 175-207.

Downs, Anthony. *An Economic Theory of Democracy*. New York: Harper and Row, 1957.

Ferejohn, John A. and Morris P. Fiorina. "The Paradox of Not Voting: A Decision Theoretic Analysis." *APSR* 68 (June 1974).

Frolich, Norman, Joe A. Oppenheimer, and Oran R. Young. *Political Leadership and Collective Goods*. Princeton: Princeton University Press, 1971.

Harsanyi, John C. "Rationalist-Choice Models of Political Behavior vs. Functionalist and Conformist Theories." *World Politics* (July 1969), pp. 513-538.

Kaplan, Morton A. *System and Process in International Politics*. New York: John Wiley, 1957.

Luce, R. Duncan and Howard Raiffa. *Games and Decisions*. New York: John Wiley, 1957.

March, James G. "Party Legislative Representation as a Function of Election Results." *Public Opinion Quarterly* 21 (Winter 1957-1958), 521-542.

Mitchell, William C. "The Shape of Political Theory to Come: From Political Sociology to Political Economy." *American Behavioral Scientist* 11 (November-December 1967).

Olson, Mancur, Jr. *The Logic of Collective Action*. New York: Schocken Books, 1960.

Rapoport, Anatol. *Fights, Games, and Debates.* Ann Arbor: The University of Michigan Press, 1961.

Riker, William H. and Peter Ordeshook. *An Introduction to Positive Political Theory.* Englewood Cliffs, N.J.: Prentice-Hall, 1973.

Schelling, Thomas C. *The Strategy of Conflict.* London. Oxford University Press, 1960.

Simon, Herbert A. *Models of Man.* New York: John Wiley and Sons, Inc., 1957.

Stokes, Donald E. "Spatial Models of Party Competition." *APSR* 57 (June 1963), 368-377.

Thorson, Stuart J. "The Role of Mathematics in Political Theory Construction," Unpublished Ph.D. dissertation, University of Minnesota, 1972.

Tullock, Gordon. *Toward a Mathematics of Politics.* Ann Arbor: The University of Michigan Press, 1967.

Young, Oran R. "Political Choice." University of Texas at Austin, 1974. (Typewritten.)

———. *Systems of Political Science.* Englewood Cliffs, N.J.: Prentice-Hall, 1968.

Studies of Coalition Processes

Axelrod, Robert. *Conflict of Interest.* Chicago: Markham, 1970.

Brams, Steven and J. E. Garrigo-Pices. "Deadlock and Bandwagons in Coalition Formation." Paper presented at the 1973 Annual Meeting of the APSA, New Orleans, La., September 1973.

Browne, Eric. "Testing Theories of Coalition Formation in the European Context." *Comparative Political Studies* 3 (January 1971).

——— and Mark N. Franklin. "Aspects of Coalition Payoffs in European Parliamentary Democracies." *APSR* 68 (June 1973).

Butterworth, R. L. "A Research Note on the Size of Winning Coalitions." *APSR* 65 (September 1971), 741-745.

Caplow, Theodore. "A Theory of Coalitions in the Triad." *American Sociological Review* 21 (August 1956), 489-493.

———. "Further Developments of a Theory of Coalitions in the

Triad." *American Journal of Sociology* 64 (March 1959), 488-493.

Damgaard, Erik. "The Parliamentary Basis of Danish Governments: The Patterns of Coalition Formation." *Scandinavian Political Parties* 4 (1969), 30-57.

Frolich, Norman. "The Instability of Minimum Winning Coalitions." Paper presented at the 1974 Annual Meeting of the Public Choice Society, New Haven, Spring 1974. In *APSR* 66 (September 1975), 943-946.

Gamson, William. "Coalition Formation at Presidential Nominating Conventions." *American Journal of Sociology* 68 (September 1962), 157-171.

————. "An Experimental Test of a Theory of Coalition Formation." *American Sociological Review* 26 (August 1961), 564-573.

————. "A Theory of Coalition Formation." *American Sociological Review* 26 (June 1961), 373-382.

Groennings, Sven, E. W. Kelly, and Michael Leiserson, eds. *The Study of Coalition Behavior.* New York: Holt, Rinehart and Winston, Inc., 1970.

Particularly the essays by Merkl, Rosenthal, Groennings, Leiserson, Kelly, and De Swaan.

Hinckley, Barbara. "Coalitions in Congress: Size in a Series of Games." *American Political Quarterly* (August 1973), 339-359.

————. "Coalitions in Congress: Size and Ideological Distance." *Midwest Journal of Political Science* 16 (May 1972), 197-207.

Koehler, David. "The Legislative Process and the Minimal Winning Coalition." *Probability Models of Collective Decision-making.* Edited by Richard Niemi and Herbert Weisberg. Columbus, Ohio: Charles Merrill, 1972, 149-164.

Leiserson, Michael Avery. "Coalitions in Politics: A Theoretical and Empirical Study." Unpublished Ph.D. dissertation, Yale University, 1966.

————. "Factions and Coalitions in One-Party Japan: An Interpretation Based on the Theory of Games." *APSR* 62 (September 1968), 772-776, 784-786.

Neumann, John von and Oskar Morgenstern. *The Theory of Games and Economic Behavior*. Princeton: Princeton University Press, 1944.

Riker, William H. *The Theory of Political Coalitions*. New Haven: Yale University Press, 1962.

Rohde, David. "A Theory of the Formation of Opinion Coalitions in the U.S. Supreme Court." *Probability Models of Collective Decision-making*. Edited by Richard G. Niemi and Herbert F. Weisberg. Columbus, Ohio: Charles Merrill, 1972.

Shepsle, Kenneth A. "On the Size of Winning Coalitions." *APSR* 68 (June 1974).

Uslaner, Eric M. "Conditions for Party Responsibility." Unpublished Ph.D. dissertation, University of Indiana, 1973.

Measurement and Methodology

Bill, James A. and Robert L. Hardgrave, Jr. *Comparative Politics: The Quest for Theory*. Columbus, Ohio: Charles E. Merrill Co., 1973.

Blalock, Herbert M. and Ann B. Blalock, eds. *Methodology in Social Research*. New York: McGraw-Hill, 1968.

Brodbeck, May, ed. *Readings in the Philosophy of the Social Sciences*. New York: The Macmillan Co., 1968.

Coleman, Stephen. "Measurement and Analysis of Political Systems." Unpublished Ph.D. dissertation, University of Minnesota, 1972.

Dogan, Mattei and Stein Rokkan, eds. *Quantitative Ecological Analysis in the Social Sciences*. Cambridge: The M.I.T. Press, 1969.

Dray, William. *Laws and Explanation in History*. London: Oxford University Press, 1957.

Feigl, Gerbert and Grover Maxwell, eds. *Scientific Explanation, Space, and Time*. Vol. 3: *Minnesota Studies in the Philosophy of Science*. Minneapolis: University of Minnesota Press, 1962.

Galtung, John. *Theory and Methods of Social Research*. New York: Columbia University Press, 1967.

Gillespie, John V. and Betty A. Nesvold, eds. *Macro-Quantitative Analysis*. Beverly Hills, Calif.: Sage Publications, 1971.

Hays, William L. *Statistics*. New York: Holt, Rinehart and Winston, Inc., 1963.

Holt, Robert T. and John E. Turner. *The Methodology of Comparative Research*. New York: The Free Press, 1970.

Janda, Kenneth. *Comparative Political Parties: A Cross-National Handbook*. New York: The Free Press, 1976, forthcoming.

Kaplan, Abraham. *The Conduct of Inquiry: Methodology for Behavioral Science*. San Francisco: Chandler Publishing Co., 1964.

Keesing's Contemporary Archives, Vol. 7-24. London: Keesing's Publications, 1945-1974.

Kemeny, John G. *A Philosopher Looks at Science*. Toronto: D. Van Nostrand Co., Inc., 1959.

Kuhn, Thomas S. *The Structure of Scientific Revolutions*. Chicago: The University of Chicago Press, 1962.

Merritt, Richart L. and Stein Rokkan. *Comparing Nations: The Uses of Quantitative Data in Cross-national Research*. New Haven: Yale University Press, 1966.

Nagel, Ernest. *The Structure of Science*. New York: Harcourt, Brace, and World, Inc., 1961.

Polya, George. *Mathematic and Plausible Reasoning*. Vol. 1, 2. Princeton: Princeton University Press, 1954.

Przeworski, Adam and John Sprague. "Concepts in Search of Explicit Formulation: A Study in Measurement." *Midwest Journal of Political Science* 40 (May 1971).

Przeworski, Adam and Henry Teune. *The Logic of Comparative Social Inquiry*. New York: Wiley-Interscience, 1970.

Rae, Douglas W. and Michael Taylor. *The Analysis of Political Cleavages*. New Haven: Yale University Press, 1970.

Rokkan, Stein and Jean Meyriat. *International Guide to Electoral Statistics*. The Hague: Mouton, 1969.

Sartori, Giovanni. "Concept Misformation in Comparative Politics." *APSR* 64 (December 1970).

Shannon, Claude E. and Warren Weaver. *The Mathematical*

Theory of Communication. Urbana: University of Illinois Press, 1959.

Shiveley, W. Phillips. *The Craft of Political Research*. Englewood Cliffs, N.J.: Prentice-Hall, Inc., 1973.

Sternberger, Dolf and Dieter Nohlen. *Die Wahl Der Parlamente*. Berlin: Walter De Gruyter and Co., 1969.

Teggart, Frederick J. *Theory and Processes of History*. Berkeley: University of California Press, 1962.

Theil, Henri. *Economics and Information Theory*. Amsterdam: North Holland Publishing Co., 1967.

Weber, Max. *The Methodology of the Social Sciences*. Translated and edited by Edward A. Shils and Henry A. Finch. Glencoe, Ill.. Free Press, 1949.

Wildgen, John K. "The Measurement of Hyperfractionalization." *Comparative Political Studies* 4 (July 1971).

PARTIES AND PARLIAMENTS OF SPECIFIC COUNTRIES

General Collections

Almond, Gabriel. "The Christian Parties of Western Europe." *World Politics* 1 (1948), 30-58.

Brady, Alexander. *Democracy in the Dominions*. Toronto: University of Toronto Press, 1947.

Dahl, Robert A., ed. *Political Oppositions in Western Democracies*. New Haven: Yale University Press, 1966.

Essays on Austria, Belgium, France, Germany, Great Britain, Italy, Netherlands, Norway, and Sweden.

Einaudi, Mario and François Goguel. *Christian Democracy in Italy and France*. Notre Dame, Ind.: University of Notre Dame Press, 1952.

Elder, Neil. "Parliamentary Government in Scandinavia." *Parliamentary Affairs* (Summer 1960), 363-373.

Fogarty, Michael P. *Christian Democracy in Western Europe, 1820-1953*. Notre Dame, Ind.: University of Notre Dame Press, 1957.

Henig, Stanley and John Pinder, eds. *European Political Parties*. London: George Allen and Unwin, Ltd., 1969.

Essays on Austria, Belgium, France, Germany, Ireland, Italy, Netherlands, Scandinavia, Switzerland, United Kingdom.

Lipset, Seymour M. and Stein Rokkan, eds. *Party Systems and Voter Alignments: Cross-national Perspectives*. New York: The Free Press, 1967.

Essays on Anglo-American systems, Finland, France, Great Britain, Italy, New Zealand, and Norway.

Neumann, Robert G. *European and Comparative Government*. New York: McGraw-Hill Book Co., Inc., 1955.

Neumann, Sigmund, ed. *Modern Political Parties: Approaches to Comparative Politics*. Chicago: University of Chicago Press, 1955.

Ogg, Frederic Austin. *European Governments and Politics*. New York: The Macmillan Co., 1943.

Rogger, Hans and Eugen Weber. *The European Right: A Historical Profile*. Berkeley: University of California Press, 1965.

Shotwell, James T., ed. *Governments of Continental Europe*. New York: The Macmillan Co., 1940.

Australia

Crisp, Leslie F. *The Parliamentary Government of the Commonwealth of Australia*. London: Longmans, Green and Co., 1961.

Ellis, Ulrich R. *A History of the Australia Country Party*. Parkville: Melbourne University Press, 1963.

Davies, Alan F. *Australian Democracy*. London: Longmans, Green and Co., 1958.

Davis, S. R., W. McMahon, A. A. Calwell, and L. C. Webb. *The Australian Party System*. Sydney: Angus and Robertson Ltd., 1954.

Duncan, W.G.K., ed. *Trends in Australia Politics*. Sydney: Angus and Robertson, Ltd., 1935.

Encel, S. *Cabinet Government in Australia*. Parkville N. 2, Victoria: Melbourne University Press, 1962.

Hughes, Colin A. and B. D. Graham. *A Handbook of Australian Government and Politics 1890-1964.* Canberra: Australia National University Press, 1968.

Japp, James. *Australian Party Politics.* New York: Cambridge University Press, 1964.

Miller, J.D.B. *Australian Government and Politics.* London: Gerald Duckworth, 1964.

Overacker, Louise. *The Australian Party System.* New Haven: Yale University Press, 1952.

Austria

Bader, William B. *Austria Between East and West 1945-1955.* Stanford, Calif.: Stanford University Press, 1966.

Engelmann, F. C. "Haggling for the Equilibrium: The Renegotiation of the Austrian Coalition, 1959." *APSR* 56 (September 1962).

Gulick, Charles A. *Austria from Hapsburg to Hitler.* Berkeley: University of California Press, 1948.

Powell, G. Bingham, Jr. *Social Fragmentation and Political Hostility: An Austrian Case Study.* Stanford, Calif.: Stanford University Press, 1970.

Proudfoot, Mary Macdonald. *The Republic of Austria 1918-1938: A Study in the Failure of Democratic Government.* London: Oxford University Press, 1946.

Secher, Herbert P. "Coalition Government: The Case of the Second Austrian Republic." *APSR* 52 (September 1958).

Shell, Kurt L. *The Transformation of Austrian Socialism.* New York: State University of New York, 1962.

Steiner, Kurt. *Politics in Austria.* Boston: Little, Brown and Co., 1972.

The Benelux Countries

Bone, Robert C. "The Dynamics of Dutch Politics." *Journal of Politics* 24, No. 1 (February 1962), 23-49.

Cooper-Prichard, A. H. *History of the Grand Duchy of Luxembourg.* Printed and published by P. Linden, 1950.

Daadler, Hans. "Parties and Politics in the Netherlands." *Political Studies* 3, No. 1 (February 1955), 1-16.

Eyck, F. Gunther. *The Benelux Countries*. Princeton: D. Van Nostrand Co., Inc., 1959.

Friedman, David. "Political Parties." *The Netherlands*. Edited by Bartholomew Landheer. Berkeley: University of California Press, 1943.

Lijphart, Arend. *The Politics of Accommodation: Pluralism and Democracy in the Netherlands*. Berkeley: University of California Press, 1968.

Omond, G.W.T. *The Kingdom of Belgium and the Grand Duchy of Luxembourg*. Boston: Houghton Mifflin Co., 1923.

Putnam, Ruth. "The Luxembourg Chamber of Deputies." *APSR* 14 (August 1920), 607-634.

Raalte, Ernest Van. *The Parliament of the Kingdom of the Netherlands*. London: Hansard Society, 1959.

Senelle, Robert. *The Political, Economic, and Social Structure of Belgium*. Brussels: Ministry of Foreign Trade, 1970.

Taylor-Whitehead, W. J. *Luxembourg*. London: Fletcher and Son, Ltd., 1951.

Canada

Clokie, Hugh McDonald. *Canadian Government and Politics*. The Macmillan Co., 1946.

Dawson, Robert Macgregor and W. F. Dawson. *Democratic Government in Canada*. Revised by Norman Ward. Toronto: University of Toronto Press, 1971.

Kornberg, Allan. *Canadian Legislative Behavior: A Study of the Twenty-fifth Parliament*. New York: Holt, Rinehart and Winston, 1967.

McHenry, D. E. *The Third Force in Canada: The Cooperative Commonwealth Federation, 1932-1948*. Berkeley: University of California Press, 1950.

Mallory, James R. *The Structure of Canadian Government*. New York: St. Martin's Press, 1971.

Morton, W. L. *The Progressive Party in Canada*. Toronto: University of Toronto Press, 1950.

Pickersgill, J. W. *The Liberal Party*. Toronto: McClellan and Stewart, 1962.

Thorburn, Hugh G., ed. *Party Politics in Canada*. Toronto: Prentice-Hall, Inc., 1963.

Ward, Norman. *The Canadian House of Commons: Representation*. Toronto: University of Toronto Press, 1963.

Williams, John R. *The Conservative Party of Canada*. Durham, N.C.: Duke University Press, 1956.

France

Barron, Richard. *Parties and Politics in Modern France*. Washington, D.C.: Public Affairs Press, 1959.

Brogan, D. W. *France Under the Fourth Republic 1870-1939*. New York: Harper and Brothers Publishers, n.d.

Buell, Raymond Leslie. *Contemporary French Politics*. New York: D. Appleton and Co., 1920.

Campbell, Peter. *French Electoral Systems and Elections Since 1789*. Hamden, Conn.: Anchor Books, 1958.

Derfler, Leslie. *The Third French Republic, 1870-1940*. Toronto: D. Van Nostrand Co., Inc., 1966.

Duverger, Maurice. *The French Political System*. Chicago: The University of Chicago Press, 1958.

Earle, Edward Mead, ed. *Modern France: Problems of the Third and Fourth Republics*. Princeton: Princeton University Press, 1951.

Goguel-Nyegaard, François. *France Under the Fourth Republic*. Ithaca, N.Y.: Cornell University Press, 1952.

Gooch, R. K. "France and the Low Countries." Governments of Continental Europe. Edited by James T. Shotwell.

Greene, Nathanael. *Crisis and Decline: The French Socialist Party in the Popular Front Era*. Ithaca, N.Y.: Cornell University Press, 1968.

Lamour, Peter J. *The French Radical Party in the 1930's*. Stanford, Calif.: Stanford University Press, 1964.

Leites, Nathan. *On the Game of Politics in France*. Stanford: Stanford University Press, 1959.

MacRae, Duncan, Jr. "Intraparty Divisions and Cabinet Coalitions in the Fourth French Republic." *Comparative Studies in Society and History* 5 (January 1963), 164-211.

————. *Parliament, Parties and Society in France.* New York: St. Martin's Press, Inc., 1967.

Marcus, John T. *French Socialism in the Crisis Years, 1933-1936.* New York: Praeger Publishers, 1958.

Mendès-France, Pierre. *A Modern French Republic.* Translated by Anne Carter. New York: Hill and Wang, 1962.

Middleton, W. L. *The French Political System.* London: Ernest Benn Ltd., 1932.

Osgood, Samuel M. *French Royalism Under the Third and Fourth Republics.* The Hague: Martinus Nijhoff, 1960.

Sharp, Walter Rice. *The Government of the French Republic.* New York: D. Van Nostrand Co., Inc., 1938.

Shirer, William L. *The Collapse of the Third Republic.* New York: Simon and Schuster, 1972.

Soltav, Roger H. *French Parties and Politics 1871-1921: with a New Supplementary Chapter Dealing with 1922-1930.* London: Oxford University Press, 1930.

Tarr, Francis de. *The French Radical Party: From Herriot to Mendès-France.* London: Oxford University Press, 1961.

Williams, Philip M. *Crisis and Compromise: Politics in the Fourth Republic.* Hamden, Conn.: The Shoe String Press, Inc., 1964.

————. *French Politicians and Elections, 1951-1969.* Cambridge: The University Press, 1970.

Germany

Almond, Gabriel A. "German Political Parties." *Germany and the Future of Europe.* Edited by Hans J. Morgenthau. Chicago: University of Chicago Press, 1951.

Bölling, Klaus. *Republic in Suspense: Politics, Parties, and Personalities in Postwar Germany.* Translated by Jean Steinberg. New York: Praeger Publishers, 1964.

Bracher, Karl Dietrich. *The German Dictatorship: The Origins, Structure, and Effects of National Socialism*. Translated by Jean Steinberg. New York: Praeger Publishers, 1970.

Chalmers, Douglas A. *The Social Democratic Party of Germany*. New Haven: Yale University Press, 1964.

Dahrendorf, Rolf. *Society and Democracy in Germany*. Garden City, N.Y.: Doubleday and Co., 1969.

Fraenkel, Ernest. "Historical Handicaps of German Parliamentarianism." *The Road to Dictatorship*. Translated by Lawrence Wilson. London: Oswald Wolff, 1964, 27-37.

Grazia, Juan J. Linz Storch de. "The Social Bases of West German Politics." Unpublished Ph.D. dissertation, Columbia University, 1959.

Heidenheimer, Arnold J. *The Governments of Germany*. New York: Crowell-Collier, 1961.

Heneman, Harlow James. *The Growth of Executive Power in Germany: A Study of the German Presidency*. Minneapolis: The Voyageur Press, 1934.

Jäckh, Ernst. *The New Germany*. London: Humphrey Milford, 1927.

Kitzenger, Uwe W. *German Electoral Politics*. London: Oxford University Press, 1960.

Kosok, Paul. *Modern Germany: A Study of Conflicting Loyalties*. Chicago: The University of Chicago Press, 1933.

Loewenberg, Gerhard. *Parliament in the German Political System*. Ithaca, N.Y.: Cornell University Press, 1966.

Loewenstein, Karl. "The Parliamentary System under the Weimar Constitution of Political Parties." *Governments of Continental Europe*. Edited by James T. Shotwell.

Passant, E. J. *A Short History of Germany, 1815-1945*. Cambridge: The University Press, 1960.

Pinney, Edward L. *Federalism, Bureaucracy, and Party Politics in Western Germany: The Role of the Bundesrat*. Chapel Hill: The University of North Carolina Press, 1963.

Pollock, James K., Jr. "The German Party System." *APSR* 23 (November 1929), 859-891.

Ullmann, Richard and Sir Stephen King-Hall. *German Parliaments: A Study of the Development of Weimar Representative Institutions in Germany.* New York: Praeger Publishers, 1954.

Great Britain and Ireland

Ayearst, Morley. *The Republic of Ireland: Its Government and Politics.* New York: New York University Press, 1970.

Beer, Samuel H. *British Politics in the Collectivist Age.* New York: Random House, 1965.

Butler, D. E. *The Electoral System in Britain Since 1918.* Oxford: The Clarendon Press, 1963.

Butt, R. *The Power of Parliament.* London: Constable, 1967.

Campion, Lord. "Developments in the Parliamentary System Since 1918." In *British Government Since 1918.* Edited by Sir John Anderson. London: George Allen and Unwin, 1950.

Chester, D. N. "Development of the Cabinet 1914-1949." In *British Government Since 1918.* Edited by Sir John Anderson. London: George Allen and Unwin, 1950.

Christoph, James B. "Consensus and Cleavage in British Political Ideology." *APSR* 59 (1965).

Chubb, Basil. *A Source Book on Irish Government.* Dublin: Institute of Public Administration, 1964.

Crick, Bernard. *The Reform of Parliament.* Garden City, N.Y.: Doubleday and Co., 1965.

Holt, Robert T. and John E. Turner. *Political Parties in Action: The Battle of Barons Court.* New York: The Free Press, 1968.

Jennings, Sir Ivor. *Parliament.* Cambridge: The University Press, 1969.

————. *Party Politics.* Cambridge: The University Press, 1962.

Lyman, Richard W. *The First Labour Government 1924.* London: Chapman and Hall, 1957.

McCracken, J. L. *Representative Government in Ireland.* London: Oxford University Press, 1958.

McElevee, William. *Britain's Locust Years, 1918-1940.* London: Faber and Faber, Ltd., 1962.

McHenry, Dean E. *The Labour Party in Transition*. London: George Routledge and Sons, Ltd., 1938.

McKenzie, Robert T. *British Political Parties*. London: William Heinemann, 1963.

Morrison, Herbert. *Government and Parliament: A View from the Inside*. London: Oxford University Press, 1959.

Ranney, Austin. *Pathways to Parliament*. Madison: University of Wisconsin Press, 1965.

Richards, Peter G. *Honourable Members: A Study of the British Backbenchers*. London: Faber and Faber, Ltd., 1959.

Shinwell, Emmanuel. *The Labour Story*. London: Macdonald, 1963.

Wilson, Trevor. *The Downfall of the Liberal Party*. Ithaca, N.Y.: Cornell University Press, 1966.

Italy

Adams, John C. and P. Barille. *The Government of Republican Italy*. Boston: Houghton-Mifflin, 1961.

DiRenzo, Gordon J. *Personality, Power and Politics*. Notre Dame, Ind.: Notre Dame University Press, 1967.

Galli, Giorgio and Alfonso Prandi. *Patterns of Political Participation in Italy*. New Haven: Yale University Press, 1970.

Germino, Dante and Stefano Passigli. *The Government and Politics of Contemporary Italy*. New York: Harper and Row, 1968.

Hughes, Serge. *The Fall and Rise of Modern Italy*. New York: The Macmillan Co., 1967.

LaPalombara, Joseph. "Italy: Fragmentation, Isolation and Alienation." *Political Culture and Political Development*. Edited by Lucian Pye and Sidney Verba. Princeton: Princeton University Press, 1967.

Sartori, Giovanni. "European Political Parties: The Case of Polarized Pluralism." In *Political Parties and Political Development*. Edited by Joseph LaPalombara and Myron Weiner. Princeton: Princeton University Press, 1966.

————. "Parliamentarians in Italy." *International Social Science Journal* 13 (1961).

Zariski, Raphael. "Intro-Party Conflict in a Dominant Party: The Experience of Italian Christian Democracy." *Journal of Politics* 27 (1965), 3-34.

————. "The Italian Socialist Party: A Case Study in Factional Conflict." *APSR* 56 (1962), 372-390.

————. "Party Factions and Comparative Politics." *Midwest Journal of Political Science* 4, 27-51.

————. *Italy: The Politics of Uneven Development.* Hinsdale, Ill.: Dryden Press, 1972.

New Zealand

Brown, Bruce M. *The Rise of New Zealand Labour.* Wellington: Milburn, 1962.

Chapman, R. M., W. K. Jackson, and A. V. Mitchell. *New Zealand Politics in Action.* London: Oxford University Press, 1962.

Lipson, Leslie. *The Politics of Equality: New Zealand: Adventures in Democracy.* Chicago: University of Chicago Press, 1948.

Milne, R. S. *Political Parties in New Zealand.* Oxford: The Clarendon Press, 1966.

Mitchell, Austin V. *Government by Party: Parliament and Politics in New Zealand.* Christchurch: Whitcombe and Tombs, Ltd., 1966.

Webb, Leicester. *Government in New Zealand.* Wellington: Department of Internal Affairs, 1940.

The Scandinavian Countries

Andren, Nils. *Government and Politics in the Nordic Countries.* Stockholm: Almquist and Wiksell, 1964.

Arneson, Ben A. *The Democratic Monarchies of Scandinavia.* New York: D. Van Nostrand Co., Inc., 1939.

Eckstein, Harry. *Division and Cohesion in Democracy: A Study of Norway.* Princeton: Princeton University Press, 1966.

Enckell, Arvid. *Democratic Finland.* London: Herbert Joseph, Ltd., n.d.

Griffiths, John C. *Modern Iceland.* London: Pall Mall Press, 1969.

Groennings, Sven. "Patterns, Strategies and Payoffs in Norwegian Coalition Formation." In *The Study of Coalition Behavior.* Edited by Sven Groennings, E. W. Kelly, and Michael Leiserson. New York: Holt, Rinehart and Winston, 1970.

Hastad, Elis. *The Parliament of Sweden.* London: The Chriswick Press, 1957.

Hancock, M. Donald. *Sweden: The Politics of Postindustrial Change.* Hinsdale: The Dryden Press, 1972.

Jones, W. Glyn. *Denmark.* New York: Praeger Publishers, 1970.

Miller, Kenneth E. *Government and Politics in Denmark.* Boston: Houghton-Mifflin Co., 1968.

Nordal, Johannes and Valdimar Kristinson. *Iceland: Handbook of the Central Bank of Iceland.* Reykjavik: Isa folda printsmioja, 1966.

Novsianen, Jaakko. *The Finnish Political System.* Translated by John H. Hodgson. Cambridge: Harvard University Press, 1971.

Pedersen, Morgens N. "Consensus and Conflict in the Danish Folketing, 1945-1965." *Scandinavian Political Studies* 2 (1967), 143.

Rokkan, Stein and Henry Valen. "Regional Contrasts in Norwegian Politics." *Mass Politics.* Edited by Allardt and Rokkan.

Rustow, D. A. *The Politics of Compromise: A Study of Parties and Cabinet Government in Sweden.* Princeton: Princeton University Press, 1955.

―――. "Scandinavia." *Modern Political Parties.* Edited by Neumann. Chicago: University of Chicago Press, 1955.

Spencer, Richard C. "Party Government and the Swedish Riksday." *APSR* 39 (June 1945), 437-458.

Stehovever, Jan. "Longterm Ecological Analysis of Electoral Statistics in Denmark." *Scandinavian Political Studies* 2 (1967), 944.

Storing, James A. "Unique Features of the Norwegian Storting." *Western Political Quarterly* 16 (March 1963), 161.

Thorsteinsson, Thorstein, ed. *Iceland 1936*. Reykjavik-Rikisprintsmidjar: Antenberg, 1936.

Toivola, Vrho, ed. *Introduction to Finland, 1960*. Helsinki: Werner Söderström Osakeyhtio, 1960.

Torgersen, Ulf. "The Trend Toward Political Consensus: The Case of Norway." In *Mass Politics*. Edited by Erik Allardt and Stein Rokkan. New York: The Free Press, 1970.

Törnudd, Klaus. *The Electoral System of Finland*. London: Hugh Evelyn Ltd., 1968.

Valen, Henry and Daniel Katz. *Political Parties in Norway: A Community Study*. London: Tavistock Publications, 1964.

Valros, Fredrik. *Finland 1946-1952*. Helsinki, 1953.

Wuorinen, John H. *Nationalism in Modern Finland*. New York: Columbia University Press, 1931.

Index

Library of Congress Cataloging in Publication Data

Dodd, Lawrence C   1946-
  Coalitions in parliamentary government.

  Bibliography: p.
  1. Cabinet system.   2. Coalition governments.
1. Title.
JF331.D6   321.8′043   75-2986
ISBN 0-691-07564-6

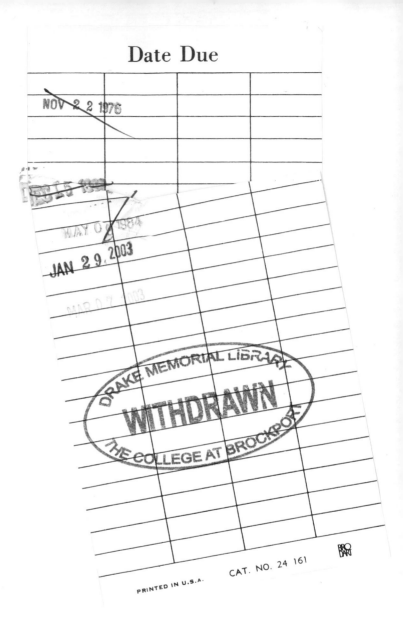